Earl Stanhope

History of England

comprising the reign of Queen Anne until the Peace of Utrecht

Earl Stanhope

History of England

comprising the reign of Queen Anne until the Peace of Utrecht

ISBN/EAN: 9783742844309

Manufactured in Europe, USA, Canada, Australia, Japa

Cover: Foto ©ninafisch / pixelio.de

Manufactured and distributed by brebook publishing software
(www.brebook.com)

Earl Stanhope

History of England

HISTORY

OF

ENGLAND

COMPRISING

THE REIGN OF QUEEN ANNE

UNTIL THE PEACE OF UTRECHT

BY

EARL STANHOPE.

1701—1713.

COPYRIGHT EDITION.

IN TWO VOLUMES. — VOL. II.

LEIPZIG

BERNHARD TAUCHNITZ

1870.

The Right of Translation is reserved.

CONTENTS

OF VOLUME II.

CHAPTER IX.

CHAPTER X.

CHAPTER XI.

CHAPTER XII.

CHAPTER XIII.

CHAPTER XIV.

CHAPTER XVI.

THE AGE OF ANNE.

HISTORY OF ENGLAND.

CHAPTER IX.

O_F the military operations which marked the year CHAP.
IX.
1707. 1707, those in Spain should be first related, as much the earliest in date and as having considerable influence upon the rest.

In the last days of 1706, Peterborough had landed again at Barcelona bringing with him a large sum of money which he had raised in Italy. He travelled along the coast by easy journeys to Valencia, where Charles was then residing. All his letters show him in high spirits and volatile as ever. Thus he wrote to Stanhope early on the 10th of January, the day he intended to arrive: "I shall not be able to come to Valencia till the evening, and so must put off the dinner to the more agreeable meal a supper, when Colonel Breton and myself intend to mortify you with the account of our happy days in Italy. Of the nights we will say nothing."

Arriving at Valencia Peterborough could not fail to be warmly greeted by the Marquis of La Casta, the Count of Villa Franquesa, and those other gentlemen to whom he had so generously sent supplies for their equipage in the last campaign. With the King there was a total change. The Earl discreetly assigned 13,000 pistoles of the money brought from Genoa to His Majesty's own special use; and His Majesty at once laid aside his former bitterness against the English chief; showing him henceforth every token of the highest regard. "My Lord," so Stanhope reports to Sir Charles Hedges, "has expressed himself dissatisfied with me for having writ formerly to the Secretary that there was a misunderstanding betwixt the King and his Lordship. I have always thought it my duty to represent matters here as I apprehended them to be. Whether I was then mistaken or not in the account I gave will probably have been seen by the letters the King and his Lordship writ to England. As I thought it my duty to give an account when it seemed to me there was a difference between them, so I think my-self obliged to do the same when there is a seeming good understanding, without entering into the motives that occasioned either their difference or their recon-ciliation."

Peterborough had returned to Spain much in the character as he conceived of a volunteer, not having the seniority to command nor yet the temper to be commanded. He took part however in several Councils of War to determine the operations for the next campaign; one especially five days after his arrival and another on the 4th of February. At Charles's desire all the officers present gave their opinions in writing. That of Peterborough was entirely for the defensive at this time. He urged the importance of maintaining the provinces of the Crown of Aragon and the risks that would attend a new invasion of Castille. Stanhope on the other hand observed that they might soon ex-pect considerable reinforcements. When last year the

Ministers in England finally relinquished their scheme
of a descent upon the coast of France, they determined
that the body of troops appointed for that service
should be transferred to Spain. Earl Rivers, the
General in command of those troops, and Sir Cloudes-
ey Shovel, the Admiral of the Fleet which conveyed
them, had written to announce their arrival at Lisbon,
and might in another fortnight anchor in Alicant Bay.
Such forces, said Stanhope, have not been sent over
by the Queen to pine away as garrisons. When
joined to those already in Valencia—English and
Dutch, Portuguese and Catalans—they would be more
than a match for Berwick. Why then not march forward and give battle?

Notwithstanding the weight which Peterborough
might justly claim from his former and great successes,
it was Stanhope's plan which found most favor with
the other chiefs assembled, especially Galway and Das
Minas. An offensive system for the next campaign was
therefore resolved upon. Peterborough still remon-
strated. But his career in Spain, or indeed in any
military sphere, was now drawing to a close. His ec-
centric course, so wholly self-relying, so independent of
orders from home, had given great offence, and brought
him several reprimands from the Ministers in England,
more especially on the ground of confused accounts,
and of constant bickerings with the King of Spain.

Then the Earl was apprised how at the beginning
of December the Seals had been taken from Sir Charles
Hedges and granted to Lord Sunderland. He immediately wrote to the new Secretary a long letter to
vindicate his conduct on all points, and urging also
numerous complaints of his own. "But my Lord," he

CHAP.
IX.
——
1707.

said, "I will esteem nothing hardship from the Queen, but count all that has passed happy opportunities of showing my greatest zeal for her service. I think there is a little gallantry in the case, and that I receive mortifications as lovers do which only increase the passion. . . My Lord, I most heartily congratulate your coming into public business in the office you are in. It is my misfortune it was not sooner, for I am sure not only of your justice but favor, and very confident you will approve of these endeavours of mine."[1]

This confidence as it proved was entirely erroneous. The new Secretary of State carried with him into office, what indeed had brought him there, the strongest party attachments. Like the other Whig chiefs of that day he warmly supported Galway, whom they looked upon as one of themselves, while with his rival they had little or no connection. Urging Peterborough's real failings, and not duly mindful of his as real services, Sunderland had been little more than a month in possession of the Seals ere he prevailed upon the Queen to sanction his recall. Not only this, but in writing the despatch to the English chief, Sunderland announced the recall in the sharpest and bitterest terms. "Her Majesty having been informed by letters from Genoa, that your Lordship has taken up great sums of money there at a most extravagant price, has commanded me to acquaint you that she has ordered the Bills for the said money not to be accepted, the same having been drawn without any authority or permission from Her Majesty, and at

---

[1] To the Earl of Sunderland, Valencia, Feb. 27, 1707. This letter, which I derive from Coxe's transcripts, takes up no less than sixteen closely written folio pages. On the same day the same indefatigable penman wrote a second supplementary letter to Sunderland and another also of great length to Marlborough.

such a price which if answered must affect all the re- CHAP. IX
mittances that shall be necessary to be made for the
public service the whole year. . . I am commanded at 1707.
the same time to take notice to your Lordship of the
extraordinary manner in which you left Spain, where
you had so great a trust committed to you by Her
Majesty's Commissions, to go to negotiate matters with
other Princes without any orders from the Queen for
so doing or any credentials to those Princes. Upon
all these accounts, I am commanded by Her Majesty
to let your Lordship know, that it is her pleasure that
you return forthwith to England, to acquaint Her Majesty with the reasons and grounds of your proceedings."

This despatch bears the date of January 14 Old
Style, and did not come to Peterborough's hands till
March New Style. It affected his interests in more
than one respect. The Bills from Genoa having been
protested by the Government, Peterborough had to
defray from his private fortune the difference between
the prices of accommodation and the prices current,
which upon the entire sum amounted to several thousand pounds. But the Earl ever generous, nay even
lavish of his money, felt far more keenly the imputation on his public character. "Sir," he wrote to
Stanhope, "you would little expect, I believe, that all
objections are now reduced to my having taken up
without order and with such loss such considerable
sums at Genoa. Surely if ever extraordinary measures
were to be taken it was when an army was in such
extraordinary necessity; and four or five thousand
pounds more or less ought not to be brought in balance
with the loss or safety of an army. Any other answer

but this I think superfluous. But, Sir, had not the necessity of the English army required it, I could as you know have disposed the whole sum without loss to England. The Portuguese were wise enough to desire the money at the price; and no other nation but would have thanked me for my zeal. I am confident you will inform the Court of the necessity and of the service, which however I only desire they will forgive."[2]

Even before he received the letter of recall, Peterborough had determined to quit Spain, where he held no command, and go back to the Duke of Savoy. He embarked from Valencia, and after touching at Barcelona steered for the coast of Italy. With him were three English men-of-war; one of them, the Resolution, commanded by his second son, a gallant sea-officer, Captain Henry Mordaunt. In their way they fell in with a French squadron of greatly superior force, and the Resolution was especially hard-pressed. Mordaunt however maintained the conflict for several hours with great bravery; until at last finding his ship much shattered he ran her on shore. The Earl, who had gone on board the Enterprise frigate, received a contusion in a subsequent attack, but found the enemy desist, and on the 1st of April got safe into Leghorn.

Peterborough showed himself far less incensed than might have been expected at the terms of his dismissal. He did not break off his correspondence with the Ministry in England. On the contrary he wrote several letters both to Sunderland and Marlborough, assuring them that he should be able when they met to explain every point in his conduct to their entire satisfaction.

---

[2] Letter dated Barcelona, March 25, 1707 (MS.).

Meanwhile he seemed in no hurry to go home. His
restless spirit impelled him to divers negotiations and
cabals with the Courts both of Turin and Vienna, which
having no direct authority from his own could attain
no practical result.

On the 7th of February the English fleet, with the
troops under Lord Rivers's orders, had arrived at Alicant.
According to Stanhope's plan the military operations
should have been at once begun. But instead of these
there arose a controversy between Lords Rivers and
Galway as to the chief command; a controversy which
continued for three weeks, and which was terminated
only by the moderation and good temper of Lord Rivers,
who leaving the troops behind him re-embarked for
England. Then at least the campaign should have
commenced. Then however a still more serious difficulty was interposed by Charles. He was jealous that
he could not at his pleasure direct the movements
of the troops; and he gave his principal confidence at
his time to Count Noyelles, who was jealous also
on his own account. Under the influence of this
intriguing officer Charles suddenly declared himself
resolved to quit the army and go back to Barcelona,
on the plea that an attack was threatened from the side
of Roussillon. All remonstrances against this scheme
from the other chiefs at Valencia proved of no avail;
and Charles set out upon his journey on the 7th of
March. His absence as an adviser from the scene
of operations might perhaps have been borne with
equanimity; but it was no light matter that he took
with him or there detained Dutch and Catalan troops
to the number of several thousand men. Stanhope as
English Envoy to his Court was also bound to attend

him; and thus to his own great chagrin, found himself debarred from taking part as he had expected in the army's advance upon Castille.

The evils of disputed or divided command had for a long time past been urged by Stanhope on the Ministers in England; and he had advised that Prince Eugene might if possible be sent to Spain as almost the only man to whose authority all the nations and all the chiefs concerned would willingly bow. But the Court of Vienna could by no means spare Eugene from its own more immediate objects; and thus the main army of the Allies in Spain in this year as in the last was after many jars left to the joint and incapable direction of the Earl of Galway and the Marquis Das Minas.

The time which the Allies had lost was not lost by King Louis. He saw the importance of pressing the war in Spain, and with that view resolved to make a sacrifice elsewhere. By his orders there was signed at Milan a Convention with Prince Eugene, according to which the French garrisons were to relinquish the fortresses which they still retained in Northern Italy, and to march back without molestation to their frontiers. [3] In this manner some eighteen or twenty thousand good French troops became disposable for active service, and part of them were at once sent across the Pyrenees. Louis had also resolved to signalise his Spanish army by placing at its head a Prince of the Blood. Thus while he left the Duke of Berwick as second in command he named as chief his nephew the Duke of

---

[3] See this Convention (which, says Sismondi, *avait la forme d'une capitulation*) in Lamberty, vol. IV. p. 391.

Orleans, who was burning to retrieve his disaster at Turin.

Early in April after long delays Galway and Das Minas began their forward movement. Having first destroyed some of the enemy's outlying magazines they invested the castle of Villena, but speedily changing their purpose raised the siege and pressed onward to give battle. They came in sight of Berwick's army on the morning of the 25th, and found that he had taken post on an open plain, with the small town of Almanza behind him. By that time, Berwick had already received great part of his expected reinforcements, although the Duke of Orleans, who had made a circuit through Madrid to pay his respects to the King and Queen, had not yet arrived.

Destitute of exact intelligence as much as of military skill, the Allied Generals were not apprised of Berwick's accession of troops and consequent superiority of numbers. That superiority was above all in horse, which, in a bare and open country, could act with especial advantage. On the whole the Bourbon army was of five-and-twenty thousand men, while that of the Allies much thinned by recent sickness fell short of eighteen. It could not fail to be noticed that both the pretenders to the Crown, the one but twenty-four, the other but twenty-two years of age, had quitted their armies only a few weeks or months before, and were moping in their palaces, instead of leading the battle in which their fate would be decided. "What fools we are to fight for such louts!"—this as rumour says was once the exclamation of Peterborough.[4]

4 Voltaire, Siècle de Louis XIV., vol. I. p. 342, ed. 1752. See also Sismondi, vol. XXVII. p. 25.

The Allied chiefs, discerning when too late their great inferiority in cavalry, endeavoured to atone for it in their order of battle, alternating squadrons of horse with battalions of infantry, upon their wings. Galway who had taken his post at the left wing began the onset that same day the 25th of April, towards three in the afternoon. He fought as always with great bravery but was ere long disabled by a sabre-cut above the eyes, while his troops were thrown into confusion by a charge of the enemy's cavalry. A similar fate befel the right wing of the Allies under its Portuguese chief the Count of Atalaya. Das Minas himself commanded in the centre and for a time seemed to prevail; he broke the first line of the French and Spaniards; he caused the second to waver; he enabled two English battalions to pierce through. Already had they reached the very walls of Almanza when, as Berwick relates it, the fortune of the day in that quarter was turned by a Spanish chief Don Joseph Amezaga; the same who three years later was slain by Stanhope in single combat. Amezaga drawing together two squadrons of the Spanish regiment called Ordenes Viejos came to the rescue of his countrymen, and with their aid overthrew the two English battalions.[5] Das Minas was soon afterwards severely wounded and compelled to quit the van; and the rout of the Allies in all their three divisions was entire. Only their cavalry, about 3,500 in number, could escape; the infantry found themselves hemmed in on a bare plain with no hedge or ditch to shelter them, and were for the most part either made prisoners or cut down. Two of the chiefs, Count Dohna and Major-General Shrimpton, with about thirteen battalions

5 Memoires de Berwick, vol. i. p. 253.

ıade their way in a body to the neighbouring hills; CHAP. IX.
1707.
ut next day failing in provisions and surrounded by
ıe enemy's horse they were compelled to surrender.
)n the whole this fatal battle of Almanza cost the
.llies the whole of their baggage and artillery, twenty-
)ur pieces in number, with one hundred and twenty
anners; with at least 4,000 slain and 8,000 prisoners.
'he loss of the Bourbon army in killed and wounded
·as estimated at 2,000.

On the day after the battle the Duke of Orleans
rrived in Berwick's camp, scarce able to conceal his
eep mortification that his ill-timed politeness at Madrid
ad lost him the glory of command in so great a
.ctory. However he at once applied himself with
erwick to improve the auspicious occasion, and seeing
o foes left before them they led their army by Buñol
ıll on the city of Valencia.

It is the quality of great chiefs to maintain an ever-
uoyant hopeful spirit and to plan some new encounter
ıı the very morrow of defeat. Galway did not belong
ı that class. Brave as he had been in the battle, he
as so wholly cast down in mind by its result as to
espair not only of the campaign but even of the war.
'ere are his own words to Marlborough, written only
ıo days afterwards: "I cannot, my Lord, but look
)on the affairs of Spain as lost by this bad disaster;
ır foot which was our main strength being gone; and
.e horse we have left chiefly Portuguese which is not
)od at all. . . All the Generals here are of opinion
.at we cannot continue in this kingdom; so I have
esired Sir George Byng to take on board again the
·cruits he had just landed at Alicant; and to call at
enia or Valencia for our sick, wounded, and baggage;

and have sent all to Tortosa, where we shall march
with the remnant of our horse." [6]   It soon appeared
however that the case of the Allies in Spain was by no
means so desperate as Galway at first conceived it,
and that although much must be relinquished something
might be still retained.

The battle of Almanza as the first gleam of returning fortune was hailed with great delight, not only by
the subjects of Louis in his own dominions, but by
all his partisans in Europe.   It might also even
among his enemies afford matter of triumph to the
detractors of Lord Galway.   We find Lord Peterborough discuss it with no generous spirit in a letter
to one of his friends in England; a letter of which
the rough draft in his own handwriting has been
preserved among the papers of his Secretary, Mr. Arent
Furly.   Here follows one passage: "No Irishman
could have proved a bolder hero against common sense
than our French General who, contrary to the sentiments of the whole nation concerned, the protestations
of so many Generals, and the repeated instances of a
King, pursues the rashest measures in the world and
meets a suitable fate. . . Too dearly have so many
brave men paid for these partialities at home."   And
in a subsequent letter to Stanhope Peterborough adds
no less bitterly: "I thank all those that have assisted
in sending me to London.   Pray present my service to
the Marquise de La Casta, and tell her I hope she
finds herself better in her new friendships than the
King has done in his new Generals."

Marching onwards from their field of victory D'Orleans and Berwick encountered no resistance and found

[6] Galway to Marlborough, letter dated Alegre, April 27, 1707.

e city of Valencia open its gates at their approach.
'ith equal ease they reduced the remainder of the pro-
nce except only the two seaports of Denia and Alicant
id the inland town of Xativa. Of the last Berwick
oceeded to make the siege. It was taken by assault,
teen days from the first investment, and was treated
· Berwick with most merciless severity, razing to the
ound as he did the greater part of the houses, and
.nging or sending into banishment the greater part of
ə men.

During that time the Duke of Orleans had separated
ım his colleague, to invade the kingdom of Aragon.
ə entered Zaragoza in triumph and reduced all
agon with ease. In the autumn, again combining
th Berwick, they undertook the siege of Lerida. It
.s a fortress strong alike by nature and by art; and
ey had beside them Galway and Stanhope who had
:en the field with the Allied cavalry now increased
5,000 men. Still that force was far too small to
ike a blow at the besiegers, and the garrison was
luced to capitulate, obtaining however advantageous
ms. Then the two Dukes returned to France, and
arles found himself enabled, in spite of his great
erse, to maintain himself as before in the principality
Catalonia.

Even before the battle of Almanza, Marlborough
l found the leading statesmen at the Hague much
lined to treat with France. Thus he writes: "In
ɔ conversations I have had with M. de Buys he has
ɛn very plain in telling me that he should think it a
y good peace, if we could persuade the Duke of
jou to be contented with Naples and Sicily. I am
ɪid there are a great many more in Holland of his

CHAP.
IX.
1707.

mind, but as we are very sure I think of making this campaign there may be many alterations before winter." [7]

In the campaign which was thus before him, the Duke had no longer to dread the impracticable temper and the wayward humour of Prince Louis of Baden. His Highness had died in his palace of Rastadt in the first days of this year. His pompous monument some thirty feet high, set off by a no less pompous inscription and by abundance of tawdry gilding, may still be seen in the parish church of Baden. [8]

Unhappily however, on the death of Prince Louis, the choice of his successor as General of the Empire gave little promise of better concert. The Margrave of Bareith, who was named to this important post, was a martinet trained in the same school as the Margrave of Baden, but with far less of knowledge and experience and full as much of pride. Such was the distrust which he inspired that several of the petty states of Germany withdrew or withheld their contingents.

At this moment however there was a still more pressing danger. Charles the Twelfth of Sweden had completed his conquest of Poland, had entered Saxony, and had fixed his head-quarters at Alt Ranstadt near Leipsick. It was called the camp of the three Kings, since there appeared in it at one time not only Charles himself but Stanislas, whom he had placed on the

---

[7] Marlborough to Godolphin, April 20, 1707.
[8] Here are some lines of the inscription as I copied them :—

Infidelium debellator, Imperii protector,
Atlas Germaniæ, hostium terror,
Quoad vixit semper vicit, nunquam victus
Nisi a communi fato
Quod nec magno heroi pepercit.

irone of Poland, and Augustus whom he had dis- CHAP.
laced from it, leaving to the latter merely the Elec- IX.
irate of Saxony and the empty Royal title. Already 1707.
i the heart of Germany and at the head of some
0,000 well-appointed and victorious troops, Charles,
he so chose it, might take part with decisive effect
i the side of France. Nor were the most eager soli-
tations wanting to engage him. Louis had by a
icret envoy represented to him the ancient glories of
ustavus Adolphus, and the close friendship which in
ose days subsisted between France and Sweden. He
id urged him to stand forward as the mediator of
iace, and promised to accept whatever terms he might
ipose.

King Charles upon his own part, had a long list of
ievances against the Emperor; as the closing of Pro-
stant Churches in Silesia; the insult offered to one of
s envoys by Count Zobor a nobleman of Hungary; and
e killing of two of his officers in a brawl at Breslau.
e had therefore some wish, unless his claims were
anted, to make the Emperor feel the force of his re-
ntment. But that wish was balanced by the impa-
ince to march once more against his first enemy the
iar, and to wage a war in Muscovy as glorious even
ough as toilsome as his war in Poland, when, as his
ime Minister boasted to the Prussian General
rumbkow, they would march eighty leagues without
isaddling the horses, and feeding them on the thatch
the houses."[9]

The mind of the young hero being still in this
ivering state, it was felt by both the Cabinets of
indon and of Vienna as of the utmost importance to

[9] Report from Grumbkow to Marlborough, January 11, 1707.

endeavour, by some skilful negotiator, to counteract the overtures of France, and to decide His Majesty's thoughts on the general politics of Europe. All looked to the victor of Blenheim as beyond any comparison the fittest for the office; nor did the Duke, engrossed though he was with other cares, decline that distant journey; but he found the idea of it produce much tremor in the Dutch. Having at last satisfied their leading statesmen with the promise of a prompt return, he set out from the Hague on the 20th of April taking Hanover in his route, and there passing some hours to pay his respects to the Elector.

Already had Marlborough by letter consulted His Electoral Highness upon a delicate point in the negotiation which was now before him. He was by no means inclined to rest solely on his own diplomatic skill. He had obtained the sanction of the Queen to grant, if need should be, secret gratuities from the English treasury to some of the Swedes in office. The Elector advised that Marlborough should offer a pension of 2,000*l.* a year to the Prime Minister Count Piper, and another of 1,000*l.* a year to Olaf Hermelin Councillor of State; and he added, with a just appreciation of the characters with whom they had to deal, that the first year should be paid them in advance. [1] Marlborough determined to abide by this prudent counsel.

Rapidly pursuing his journey Marlborough reached the camp of Alt Ranstadt; and next morning was received in due form by the King. "Sir," said the Duke, "I present to your Majesty a letter from the

---

[1] The Elector's reply to Marlborough dated April 8, 1707, is printed in Macpherson's State Papers, vol. II. p. 90.

Queen my mistress coming from her heart and written CHAP.
with her own hand. Had not her sex prevented it she   IX.
would have crossed the sea to see a Prince admired by   1707.
the whole universe. I am in this particular more
happy than the Queen; and I wish I could serve some
campaigns under so great a General as your Majesty
that I might learn what I yet want to know in the art
of war." [2]

Gross as was this flattery it was not too gross for
Charles. He expressed his pleasure at seeing in his
camp a chief so renowned and so discerning; and in
the conversations which ensued he was gradually won
over to the English interests. His resentment against
the Court of Vienna was partly soothed by the persuasive powers of Marlborough; and partly satisfied by the
concessions which the Duke was empowered to announce. As regards the nice point of the secret pen-
sions Olaf Hermelin at once accepted the offer that
was made him. Count Piper on the contrary expressed
some scruples, but these being referred to the Countess
his wife they were quickly overruled.

Such was the promising train of negotiations which
in only a few days' sojourn Marlborough was able to
lay. It is true that after his departure some further
difficulties and jealousies arose; but these also were
composed by Marlborough through the aid of private
letters to both parties, so that at last there was con-

---

[2] Coxe's Marlborough, vol. III. p. 169. While the Great Duke was thus
dulatory to the King he took a high tone with the Ministers. Finding in his
first visit to Count Piper that due etiquette was not shown him he marked his
displeasure in a manner no doubt very striking and effectual, but not quite
decorous to relate. See however a note to Smollett's History, book I. ch. IX.
sect. 22. The tale is fully told by M. Adlerfeld (who was himself present) in
his Histoire Militaire de Charles XII., vol. III. p. 151, ed. 1740.

cluded a treaty between the Emperor and the King of Sweden, deciding in an amicable manner the divers points at issue. Then the King put an end to the fears which his presence had inspired. He raised his camp in Saxony and marched back across the Oder and Vistula to commence in an evil hour for himself his campaigns against the Czar. Marlborough on his part had returned to Holland, making on his way short visits to the Courts both of Berlin and Hanover, but using such despatch that he reached the Hague on the 8th of May, only eighteen days since he had left it.

From the Hague Marlborough repaired to Brussels, and from Brussels to Anderlecht, where he took the command of his army. It amounted to 97 battalions and 164 squadrons. The enemy as he learnt had 102 of the former and 168 of the latter, and were encamped in the neighbourhood of Mons, under the Elector of Bavaria and the Duke of Vendome. "They have more battalions than we but ours are largest; and on the whole I believe our army is stronger than theirs;"— so says Marlborough in one of his letters at this time. But he found his friends grievously depressed by two pieces of ill news. One was from Spain of the battle of Almanza; another scarcely less adverse from 'the lines of Stollhofen.

These lines which the Margrave of Baden had so long defended were now held by the Margrave of Bareith, with even less capacity and with diminished numbers. Marshal Villars, who commanded the French army in Alsace, was not slow to discern and to profit by this favourable opportunity. By way of feint he announced a great ball at Strasburg on the 20th of May; he gave his last orders to his officers in the

ntervals between the dances; and at five in the morn-
ng on quitting the festivity, he commenced his march.
3y way of diversion, he had already despatched the
Count de Broglie with a body of troops on the left
)ank to seize the small islands in the Rhine; and the
uttack, which was made on the morning of the 22nd
rom various sides, was attended with success on every
)oint. The Margrave taken by surprise was utterly
outed. He fled in disarray while Villars seized the
ents and magazines, and demolished the dykes and
luices which strengthened the works.

Not satisfied with this first success, Villars continued
o press on the fugitive Margrave, and overspread the
)pen country of Wurtemberg and Franconia, levying
icavy contributions far and wide. One of his parties
:ven skirted the plain of Hochstädt, almost within sight
)f Blenheim. Through the whole of Southern Germany
here now arose a loud cry against their unfortunate
:ommander; but the slow and ceremonious forms of
he Empire were found to place considerable difficulties
n the way of his removal. The Margrave moreover
tood on his defence, pleading that not he but his
rmy was to blame.

This question like almost every other in the war—
uch is the penalty of superior genius—came to be re-
:rred to Marlborough, and cost him a long course of
rduous solicitation. He earnestly pressed the Court
f Vienna that the Margrave should be set aside with
ll civility but with no delay, and that in his place
hould be appointed the Elector of Hanover, whom he
rged on political even more than on military grounds.
'oth the Emperor and the Elector hesitated; the one
s to the offer, the other as to the acceptance. But

Marlborough with his usual skill and patience overcame
every obstacle, though not till after some weeks delay.
The new chief could not take the field till past the
middle of September when it was too late for any opera-
tion of importance; and Villars shortly afterwards in
pursuance of orders from Versailles led back his army
to the left bank of the Rhine.

Another object, unconnected with his own military
sphere, which Marlborough had zealously pressed, was
the invasion of Provence. He desired to see Toulon
besieged by an army under Prince Eugene in concert
with the troops of the Duke of Savoy and with the
fleet of Sir Cloudesley Shovel. The taking of this
fortress, which was understood to be in no good condition for defence, would cripple the best fleet of the
French, would lose them their main depository of naval
magazines, and might perhaps by that single stroke ter-
minate the war. The Emperor however showed himself but lukewarm and half-hearted to this enterprise.
He regarded it as planned especially for the advantage
of the two Maritime Powers, and would have preferred
to employ his own forces on his own more immediate
objects. Still however the great ascendency of Marlborough prevailed in the end with the Court of Vienna.
Prince Eugene was directed to lead an Austrian army
to besiege Toulon, while the aid of the Duke of Savoy
was purchased by the grant of considerable subsidies.

But on one point Joseph was found inflexible. Notwithstanding the earnest remonstrances addressed to
him, urging that all the forces disposable in Lombardy
should be concentrated for the single and paramount
object of Toulon, he was determined to send a detachment of his army to the conquest of Naples. Early in

the summer therefore, one of his Generals, Count Daun, began his march towards the Abruzzi mountains at the head of less than 9,000 men. Small as was this body of troops it proved more than sufficient for its purpose. No resistance, or next to none, was encountered by Daun. The city of Naples opened its gates to him on the 8th of July with every token of joy; the people issuing forth to greet him with boughs of olive in their hands, and on their hats; also breaking into fragments and casting into the sea a bronze statue of Philip the Fifth.[3] The Duke of Escalona (Marquis of Villena in Spain) who was Philip's Viceroy, retired to the stronghold of Gaeta, the usual resource of fugitives from Naples; this however was ere long besieged and taken by assault; and the whole of the kingdom submitted quietly to its new dominion. At nearly the same period and with as little of resistance, did the island of Majorca and the district of Orbitello in Tuscany renounce their allegiance to King Philip and proclaim King Charles.

Louis the Fourteenth was deeply impressed with the vital importance of Toulon; and no sooner thought it threatened than he sent thither the Maréchal de Tessé, directing also to that quarter the best troops that he could spare. As regards the defences of the place Tessé made at first most discouraging reports. "Toulon" he wrote to the King "is not a fortress but rather a garden. . . What should be the Glacis is overspread with large country-houses, with orchards, and with convents. All these are being demolished, but it a work of time. We have however 4,000 peasantry

---

[3] Complete History of Europe, 1707, p. 271. Muratori, Annali d'Italia,

and the sailors from your Majesty's fleet, who are labouring night and day."[4]

This energy of preparation on the part of France
was much assisted by the wavering and lingering course
of the Allies. It was not till the 26th of July that
Prince Eugene and the Duke of Savoy came in sight
of Toulon. By that time the town had been put into
a state of defence and connected by regular lines with
an entrenched camp which Tessé had formed upon the
neighbouring hills. The Allied army, wasted by sickness and thinned by desertion, could scarcely number
more than 25,000 effective men; and the loss of the
9,000 detached to Naples was now severely felt. Moreover much jealousy prevailed between the two cousins
who commanded, each desiring to cast the brunt of the
war on the forces of the other.

At the outset Eugene had some successes. He
carried the heights of St. Catherine, and by the aid of
the English Admiral disembarked several heavy cannon
from the ships which he turned against the town. But
only a few days later Tessé brought up some considerable reinforcements and was enabled to retake the
St. Catherine heights. Larger succours to the French
were announced, to be commanded by the Duke of
Burgundy the heir apparent of the Crown, and a separate corps under Count Medavi was already hovering
on the flank of the Allies. Besides the danger of being
thus cut off from Piedmont, they were streightened by
a growing scarcity of provisions; and finally hopeless
of success they resolved to raise the siege. This they
did accordingly in the night of the 20th of August,
wending back by slow marches to the Var; and from

4 Mémoires militaires de la Succession d'Espagne, vol. VII. p. 109.

thence as they had come, across the Col de Tende. Tessé was severely censured for having failed to harass and assail his foes in their difficult retreat. Complaints against him from some of his own officers came up to Versailles; and never again did Louis entrust to him the command of any army. Eugene on the other hand, finding himself not pursued, was able to retrieve his share of the campaign by an important service at its close; he reduced from Turin the town of Susa commanding the passage of the Alps.

There remains to tell the campaign of Marlborough in Flanders, which from his just renown and his superior numbers might well have been expected to atone for the mischances of the rest. Strange to say it proved the most inactive and unimportant of all. The English chief desired to tempt the French to a battle upon advantageous terms; but the French were determined not to venture unless the advantage were upon their side. It was found moreover that the Dutch Deputies had returned to their former system of caution and cavil, scared as they were by the late disasters at Almanza and Stollhofen. The Duke took up a strong position at Meldert between the two Gheets and the Dyle, and there he was encamped for many weeks. The French were in his front in an equally strong position at Gembloux.

In August however Marlborough received intelligence that Vendome had detached thirteen battalions and twelve squadrons to the relief of Provence; and upon this the Dutch desisted from opposing any movement in advance. The Duke promptly passed the Dyle and marched first upon Genappe and then upon Nivelles, hoping to bring Vendome to a general engagement. But Vendome, who had better reasons than ever to remain on the defensive, steadily fell back as Marlborough marched forward; and there was yet another check to Marlborough in most heavy summer rains.

It was at this period that the erratic Peterborough arrived at the English headquarters. Since he left Italy he had visited both the Court of Vienna and the camp of Alt Ranstadt; teeming with projects of all kinds both to Imperialists and Swedes. His letter to General Stanhope from Alt Ranstadt was in his usual lively vein. "I write to you from the country of wonders and uncertainty—from a place famous for the presence of three Kings, that of Sweden, Augustus, and Stanislaus. . . . The King of Sweden gives more fears by his silence than ever any other monarch gave by his threats. It is undecided whether he is very wise or foolhardy; all we know is he has fifty thousand men mad enough to obey with pleasure all he can command."

Leaving Alt Ranstadt after no very satisfactory reception from King Charles, Peterborough had next proceeded to the camp of Marlborough, armed with large piles of state papers and most exuberant narratives of his conduct in Spain. Thus does Marlborough on the 15th of August describe it to the Duchess: "Since my last we have had one continued rain, so that neither the enemy nor we can stir out of our camps. I have at this time my winter clothes and a fire in my chamber; but what is worse the ill weather hinders me from going abroad, so that Lord Peterborough has the opportunity of very long conversations. What is said one day the next destroys, so that I have desired him to put his thoughts in writing." At last

fter a stay of ten days the Earl—greatly to the Duke's
:lief—set out for England to lay his case before the
ther Ministers. As Marlborough puts it to Godolphin,
he is very capable of pushing his animosities so far
; to hurt himself, and give a good deal of trouble to
:hers."

Meanwhile on the cessation of the rains Marl-
)rough resumed his advance and led his troops
:ross the Scheldt, but found the French still retire
:fore him until at last they took up their position in
)me new and strong lines, protected by the cannon
' Lille. Then Marlborough having lost all hope of
iy achievement brought the campaign to a close.
e repaired in the first place to the Hague; and thence
Frankfort, where he conferred with the Elector of
anover and Count Wratislaw the Emperor's Minister;
id he returned to England in the first week of No-
mber Old Style.

On reviewing the military transactions of 1707 in
rious parts of Europe, the balance of advantages
ll be seen, for the first time during several years, to
cline clearly and decidedly towards the scale of
ance. The Allies it is true had reduced the king-
)m of Naples, but the long misgovernment of that
untry by the imbecile Court of Madrid had rendered
both an easy prey and an unprofitable conquest.
lere had been a disastrous battle in Spain, there had
en none at all in Flanders. One Imperial army had
en forced in the lines of Stollhofen; another com-
lled to raise with heavy losses the siege of Toulon.
) wonder if considerable dissatisfaction was expressed,
)ecially in England and Holland, which paid by far
: largest share of the expense. Those countrymen

of Marlborough above all who dissented from his politics and opposed his party were eager to fasten upon him a personal imputation. They alleged that he was prompted to resist moderate terms of peace and to carry on indecisive campaigns solely by the sordid desire to retain as long as possible his enormous emoluments as commander-in-chief of two armies, the English and the Dutch.

It is painful to deal with such a charge as applied to such a man. It is painful to think that his passion for money could even for a moment give it any colour. But happily on a closer view it will be found to admit of decisive disproof. We may appeal for its refutation to his numerous letters addressed to the Duchess, as still preserved at Blenheim and as published in great part by Archdeacon Coxe—letters written in the closest confidence and unreserve, and most assuredly without the slightest notion that they could ever even at this distance of time meet any other eyes. Now these letters all through the years 1706 and 1707 show him yearning for repose—eager to relinquish his high posts at the first moment that he could with honor and duty. "Ease and the pleasure of being with you are what I most earnestly desire"—this with every variety of phrase is his constant aspiration. Nay in one passage of the year 1706 he alleges as a further motive the first touch which he began to feel of the infirmities of age. "Not that I take anything ill but that the weight is too great for me, and I find a decay in my memory." To the inroads of time upon him he indeed often refers, most commonly on public, sometimes also on family grounds. And thus on the 6th of June in the following year: "This day makes your humble servant fifty-seven. On all accounts I could wish myself younger, but for none so much as that I might have it more in my power to make myself agreeable to you whom I love with all my soul."[5]

The close of this campaign was followed by a worse disaster probably than any that its progress displayed. Sir Cloudesley Shovel and his fleet were returning from the siege of Toulon. They had reached the Scilly Isles in dark and tempestuous weather. There in the evening of the 22nd of October the Admiral's great ship the Association struck the Gilstone rock. So quickly did she go to pieces that as an eye-witness relates "in two minutes there was nothing more of him or of his ship seen;" and of the nine hundred persons then on board not a single one escaped. Lord Dursley in the St. George ran as great a peril and was saved by a most narrow turn; he struck the same ridge of rocks as Sir Cloudesley at almost the same moment; but the very wave which he saw drive in the Admiral's lights floated his own ship into deep water. But two other line-of-battle ships which followed, the Eagle and the Romney, were like the Association ingulfed. The fireships Phœnix and Firebrand ran ashore.

Of the crews and passengers of these three ships that perished, the Association, the Eagle, and the Romney, only one man was saved. He had been cast upon a reef called the Hellwethers, and some days elapsed in those stormy seas before a boat could put out for his rescue. It was noticed that the chaplain

---

5 See Coxe's Marlborough, vol. III. p. 96, 231, and 391. It is remarkable that although Coxe has inserted this letter fixing the Duke's birthday on the Duke's own authority as June 6 (New Style), he states it in his first page as June 24 (Old Style). The baptism was certainly upon the 23th.

of the Association had been summoned to go and had gone on board another ship in the course of the same day to administer the Holy Communion to a dying man, and it was solely to this accident that his own preservation was due.

The ships that were spared from this terrible disaster cast anchor at the Scillys, where they remained some days; all the survivors in a state of grief and consternation more easily imagined than described. As it chanced the purser of the Arundel being on shore discovered in the hands of some fishermen a large emerald ring which he knew to have been worn by Sir Cloudesley Shovel. This led to a stern inquiry and a prompt confession. It then appeared that the Admiral's body had been washed to land on the day after the wreck, beneath a Dolmen of the Druids at Porth Hellick, or the Bay of Willows, shown to the present day in St. Mary's Isle as the scene of this event. There it was found by the islanders who stripped and plundered it, and then to conceal their plunder buried it deep in the sand. They were commanded to show the spot and to disinter the body, which when again brought to light seemed but little decomposed either by the waves that had tossed it or the sand in which it had lain. It was now inclosed in a coffin and conveyed to London, where it was distinguished by a public funeral and subsequently also by a stately monument in Westminster Abbey.[6]

Sir Cloudesley Shovel at the time of his decease might be regarded as at the head of his profession.

---

[6] Compare two passages in Campbell's Lives of the Admirals, vol. IV. p. 32 and 323. Complete History of Europe, 1707, p. 343; and the Handbook for Devon and Cornwall, p. 347.

Born of humble parents in Suffolk and bred apprentice CHAP.
to a shoemaker he was led by natural impulse to the IX.
Navy, which he entered with no higher rank than that 1707.
of cabin-boy. But his merit quickly raised him from
step to step until high in command; and in the many
services upon which he was employed he was eminent
alike for his conduct and his courage. Other exploits
still might have been expected from that gallant man,
who, at the dire event of the Gilstone, was not yet
forty-seven years of age.

During the whole of this year, the Queen's personal
favor was as keenly contested as her superiority in
arms. There was rapidly rising on the ruins of the
Duchess of Marlborough's influence a young lady who,
according to the fashion of that time, was surnamed
not Miss but Mrs. Abigail Hill. Abigail was the
Duchess's cousin, daughter of a decayed City merchant,
and one of four brothers and sisters. The Duchess
in her account of these transactions boasts of the
kindness with which she provided for them all. Thus
one: "Her brother, whom the bottle-men afterwards
called honest Jack Hill, was a tall boy whom I clothed
(for he was all in rags) and put to school at St. Alban's."
But perhaps it may be thought that as regards the
interest of the military service her vindication recoils
against herself or at least against the Duke; for Her
Grace proceeds to say, "I afterwards got my Lord
Marlborough to make him Groom of the Bedchamber
to the Duke of Gloucester. And though my Lord
says said that Jack Hill was good for nothing, yet
to oblige me he made him his Aide-de-camp and
afterwards gave him a regiment."[7]

<hr>

[7] Conduct of the Duchess of Marlborough, p 218, ed. 1742.

The three remaining Hills were in like manner established by the Duchess at the public charge. Abigail was made a Bedchamber Woman to the Queen; her sister a laundress to the Duke of Gloucester; and her second brother obtained a place in the Customs. The Bedchamber Woman after a few years attracted the Queen's notice. Her placid temper and ingratiating manners might no doubt be favourably contrasted with the fretful and arrogant pretensions of her great protectress; and thus by degrees was Her Grace supplanted in Her Majesty's confidence and favor.

The Duchess states that for a long time she remained wholly unconscious of a rival. Her eyes were first opened in the summer of 1707, when she learnt that her cousin Hill had become the wife of Mr. Samuel Masham one of the Prince's gentlemen. On further inquiry it came out that, although the Duchess had not been apprised, the Queen herself was present at the marriage, which took place privately in the apartments of Dr. Arbuthnot, one of the physicians of the Household. Her Majesty on that occasion called for "a round sum" out of the Privy Purse, which was supposed to be her present to the rising favourite.

This incident brought some others to the Duchess's mind. "I remembered," she says, "that a long while before this being with the Queen, to whom I had gone very privately by a secret passage, on a sudden this woman, not knowing I was there, came in with the boldest and gayest air imaginable, but upon sight of me stopped, and immediately changing her manner and making a most solemn courtesy asked: 'Did your Majesty ring?'"

The Duchess thus roused to suspicion sharply

axed Abigail with deceit and ingratitude, and ad- CHAP.
IX.
1707.
lressed her Royal Mistress in strains of resentful ex-
)ostulation. By these as might be expected the breach
/as only widened. The Queen, without making any
hange in the offices held by the Duchess, accorded
) her less and less of her company and confidence,
nd in reply to her numerous letters at a rather later
eriod, directly charged her (to use Her Majesty's
wn words) with "inveteracy against poor Masham,"
nd with "having nothing so much at heart as the
iin of your cousin."

It was no mere question of Court honors or of
:minine wrangles. Besides being cousin to the Jen-
·ngs, Mrs. Masham had another cousinhood in a dif-
rent direction, but as near to Harley. With that
atesman, still a Minister, she was in constant and
miliar communication. The belief was strong that
natever influence she might gain over her Royal
istress would be exerted in pursuance of his counsels,
.d in promotion of his power. It was on Church
atters above all that Godolphin and the Marlboroughs,
ike and Duchess, mistrusted the insinuations of Har-
/. "For my part," says Her Grace, "the word Church
d never any charm for me in the mouths of those
10 made the most noise with it." But even in the
lmiest days of her Court favor she could not on
s one point overrule the Queen. Her Majesty on
s point regarded some of her Ministers as wholly
itudinarian, and rather inclined to the Tories, "whom,"
itinues the Duchess, "she usually called by the agree-
c name of the Church party."[8] It is certainly true
t Anne had no penetrating genius of her own to

---

[8] Conduct of the Duchess of Marlborough, p. 134.

guide her. She may well have been mistaken in any
particular cases. But she deserves this praise, that she
conscientiously felt, which some of her advisers did
not, the solemn responsibility of ecclesiastical appointments, and was unwilling to make them on mere party
or political grounds such as Godolphin urged.

Acting on these views, the Queen during many
weeks resisted or evaded a pressing recommendation
of Marlborough to name Dr. Potter Regius Professor
of Divinity in the University of Oxford. There was no
doubt as to Dr. Potter's character and learning, but
the Queen was not fully satisfied of his Church principles, and would greatly have preferred Dr. Smalridge.
"The consequence is," Marlborough wrote at last,
"that if Dr. Potter has not the Professor's place I will
never more meddle with anything that may concern
Oxford."[9] It was owing perhaps to this portentous
threat that Anne finally yielded.

At nearly the same time there arose another and
more important occasion. Two Sees, Exeter and
Chester, had to be filled, from the decease of Bishop
Trelawney and Bishop Stratford. The Queen, ap-
prehending some proposal which she would find dis-
tasteful, resolved to anticipate it by a decision of her
own. Without consulting any of her Ministers she
offered the vacant dignities to Dr. Blackall and Sir
William Dawes. It is not denied that these Divines
were, as Burnet says, "men of value and worth," but
it is alleged and with truth that they held High Church
and Tory opinions.

Godolphin and the Marlboroughs were, and with
good reason, much offended. They addressed some

<hr>

[9] To the Duchess, June 23, 1707.

'arm remonstrances to the Queen, who however could
ot recede from the promises already made. They
ıought that Her Majesty had acted at the secret in-
.igation of Harley, and Godolphin writing to the
.tter taxed him with this in angry terms. But as
ɡainst this we have not only Harley's solemn denial
ut the Queen's own Royal words. Thus did she ex-
ress herself to Marlborough who was still abroad: "I
elieve you have been told as I have that these two
ersons were recommended to me by Mr. Harley, which
 so far from being true that he knew nothing of it
ll it was the talk of the town. I do assure you these
.en were my own choice. They are certainly very
: for the station I design them; and indeed I think
yself obliged to fill the Bishops' Bench, with those
ιat will be a credit to it and to the Church, and not
ways to take the recommendations of 29 (the Whig
ınto)."

The persons to whom in this cypher the Queen
ferred, that is the heads of the Whig party then in
liance with the Ministers, showed themselves far more
censed on this occasion than even the Ministers
emselves. They declared that they must withdraw
eir support from the Government, unless on Church
ɪpointments the Queen were effectually coerced. It
ıs in vain that at a meeting of their principal men
 the House of Commons, the Dukes of Somerset and
evonshire appeared in the name of the Queen to
y, that although she had engaged herself so far in
lation to those two Bishoprics, and was bound to
lfil her promises, yet for the future she was resolved
 give the gentlemen present full satisfaction. They
ɛre only half appeased, when, a third Bishopric be-

coming opportunely vacant, the Queen seized the opportunity of preferring Dr. Trimnell, a Divine of thorough Whig principles and a former tutor of Lord Sunderland. Their chiefs still violently urged that Harley was at the bottom of some dark intrigue which he carried on with the aid of Abigail, and they insisted that this favourite of a favourite should no longer be permitted to hold the Secretary's Seals.

Finding that they could not immediately prevail in this favourite object, the Whig chiefs directed their wrath against Godolphin and Marlborough who, they said, were but half-hearted in the cause. They threatened to strike a blow more especially at the Duke, through the sides of his brother George. This brother, a sailor in profession and an Admiral in rank, was a leading member of Prince George's Council, and as such took a principal part in the direction of sea-affairs. Now as it chanced there were at this time some naval miscarriages to be complained of from the failure of cruisers and convoys in divers places and the consequent loss of several merchant-ships. But above all there was the loss of several men-of-war. Five line of battle ships had been ordered to the coast of Portugal as a convoy to a great fleet of merchantmen. Against these the French had combined a squadron from Dunkirk and another from Brest under Du Gué Trouin and the Chevalier de Forbin, two of their best commanders, and making fourteen sail in all. The Admiralty, it was alleged, had received but had neglected a warning of this intended junction. Off the Lizard then the English ships found themselves assailed by well-nigh threefold numbers, and in spite of their gallant defence were overpowered. Three of them were taken, and one blown up, so that only one escaped. But they had fought so long that the merchantmen were enabled meanwhile to make press of sail and to reach Lisbon in safety, without being pursued.

To arraign Admiral Churchill as the main cause of these mischances—to attack him on that account in Parliament, was naturally very tempting to the friends of Somers. For Churchill was still as Marlborough was once a zealous Tory; and he had been always what Marlborough was never, indiscreet and hot-headed, loving to revile the Whigs even when he could not counteract them. Nay it was commonly alleged that in his politics he was not only Tory but had a Jacobite leaning, and that for the succession to the throne he looked to St. Germain's.

Marlborough who was still upon the Continent did his best by letter to appease the Whigs. But he found all that he could urge very coldly received. Sunderland his own son-in-law answered him in reproachful terms. Halifax vouchsafed no reply at all to his pro-estations. Then brooding over "the contempt of Lord Halifax," for so he called it, the Duke's spirit rose, and he writes as follows to the Duchess: "England will take care of itself and not be ruined because a few men are not pleased. . . By my letter to the Queen you will see that I have endeavoured to do the Whigs the best office I can; but I shall think it a very return if they fall upon my brother George." Still Marlborough was cautious. Why should any brother bring him into trouble? And thus he adds: "I do with all my heart wish he would be so wise as to quit his place."

In the midst of these cabals the Parliament—the first Parliament of Great Britain—met on the 23rd of October. As usual the first week was occupied in forms. Mr. John Smith of Andover was for the second time elected Speaker; and the Scottish Peers and Members chosen according to the Articles of Union were in due form admitted. Then after another week's adjournment the Queen on the 6th of November delivered her opening Speech. In its terms as Godolphin had prepared them it endeavoured to smooth away some of the mischances of the war. Thus of one: "Although the attempt upon Toulon had not wholly its desired effect, it has nevertheless been attended with many great and obvious advantages to the common cause this year." Certainly it was wise to adhere to such general terms, since the "obvious advantages" of relinquishing an enterprise with heavy loss are by no means clear to view.

The House of Commons however, without any great notice of past deficiencies, voted the Supplies required for the due prosecution of the war, with such alacrity and promptitude that the Queen was enabled so early as the 18th of December to express her acknowledgments on that account. There were Estimates for 40,000 seamen, at 2,080,000*l.*; "the ordinary of the navy," 120,000*l.*; 50,000 landsmen in Flanders and 10,000 additional, 1,071,000*l.*; the proportion of the Palatines, of the Saxons and of the Hanoverians together, 86,000*l.*; guards and garrisons and 5,000 men on the fleet, 511,000*l.*; and the forces in Spain and Portugal, 586,000*l.* Besides these there stood as "Subsidies to the Allies" 494,000*l.*, with half-a-million for what were termed "the Duke of Savoy's augmenta-

tions" and a further grant of 100,000*l.* to the same
Prince as the Duke's "special service in 1707." Altogether the sums required and granted for naval and
military services came close upon 6,000,000*l.* It was
an amount which seemed altogether stupendous to the
financiers of Queen Anne's reign. "Six millions of
supplies and almost fifty millions of debt!" cried Swift
towards the end of the year; "the High Allies have
been the ruin of us!"

It soon appeared that the great alacrity in voting
the supplies was only intended to give a keener edge
to the reproaches on the ill conduct of the war. See,
it might be said, how ready we are in Parliament, and
how unready you are in office! It was found that the
leaders of the Whigs had contrived a temporary league
or combination for that object with the High Tory
chiefs. As usual in that age, the House of Peers was
considered the more important scene. No sooner had
it met than Lord Wharton started up as spokesman of
the Whigs to inveigh against the Government for the
decay of trade—as though trade could be expected to
flourish in the midst of a general war. He was supported by Lord Somers, who expatiated on the ill
condition and late mismanagement of the Navy.
Rochester and Buckingham for once appeared on the
same side. Thus, when the Earl of Stamford moved
in customary form, an Address of Thanks to the Queen
in return for her gracious Speech, he was answered,
that they ought in the first place to consider the state
of the Nation. So strong was the new confederacy,
or so timid the Prime Minister, that the Address of
Thanks was allowed to drop, and a day appointed
when the state of the nation might be further discussed.

The day appointed was the 19th of November, the House going into Committee with Lord Herbert of Cherbury in the Chair.[1] Then again Lord Wharton took the lead, presenting in the first place a petition from two hundred London merchants who complained of their great losses "by the ill-timing of convoys and want of cruisers." He descanted on these topics, and a keen debate ensued in which Admiral Churchill was not forgotten. Marlborough did not address the House in his brother's defence, but was observed as soon as the discussion was over to take Lord Wharton aside and expostulate warmly with him. The Queen also was present "incognito;" which was the phrase then used whenever Her Majesty came to hear a discussion without Royal state or attendance. Prince George was at this time gradually sinking under two mortal maladies, an asthma and a dropsy, and it must have been deeply painful to the Queen to witness the unsparing attacks on the department over which in name at least he continued to preside.

To bring this debate to a practical issue, it was moved by another Whig chief Lord Halifax, that a Committee should be appointed to receive proposals for the encouragement of trade and privateers in the West Indies. This motion implied that the Board of Admiralty would not of itself take the right and necessary measures, and might therefore be considered as indirectly a vote of censure. Nevertheless the Lord Treasurer, fearing to see it carried by the strength of the new Whig-Tory alliance, rose in a spirit of rather too tame submission, and declared himself

---

[1] Lords' Journals, Nov. 19, 1707. This entry fixes the date, which is inaccurately given in the Parliamentary History.

willing to second it. The Committee was accordingly
named.

Lord Peterborough's case was another subject of
attack. When the Earl had returned to England he
found both the Secretaries of State, though for different reasons, almost equally indisposed against him.
Harley, a man of slow routine, stood aghast not only
at Peterborough's faults but even at his merits. Sunderland, a most ardent Whig, was resolved on party
grounds to maintain Lord Galway under all vicissitudes
of fortune. After some delay, which his enemies inter-
preted as disrespect, Peterborough had applied to see
the Queen, but was answered by Sunderland that Her
Majesty must decline to receive him until after he had
explained to her satisfaction certain points that were
said to his charge. Thus repulsed by the Ministers
the Earl with his usual impetuosity threw himself into
the arms of the Tories. He employed his physician
Dr. Freind to compile a book in his praise; and he
urged his new friends to bring on his case in Parliament.

The main debate upon it took place in the Peers
on the 19th of December, the House going once more
into Committee on the State of the Nation, with Lord
Herbert in the Chair, and the Queen again present
'incognito." Then Rochester stood forth as the
champion of his brother Earl. First he recapitulated
the great services which Peterborough had performed.
'It has been the constant practice" he added "that
when a person of rank who has been employed abroad
in an eminent post returns home, he has either thanks
given him or else is called to an account. The same
ought to be done now."—Halifax supported Rochester
but in guarded terms, and only so far as his party ties

to Lord Galway would allow.   Like Rochester, he ex-
tolled Lord Peterborough's valor and skill; observing
however that a Vote of Thanks to him should be postponed until the whole course of his conduct had been
examined, according to his own request. Peterborough
himself spoke with great zeal for the public cause.
"We ought" he cried "to give the Queen nineteen
shillings in the pound rather than make peace till King
Charles is seated on his throne."   And he added that
if it were thought needful he was ready to return to
the scene of action and to serve even under the Earl
of Galway.   But this moderation came too late.   Even
one tithe of it if shown in Spain might have sufficed to
retain him with the troops and to raise him in effect to
the first rank among them. Now on the contrary he had
shut himself out from all prospect of further command.

But the debate of the 19th of December did not
treat of personal matters only.   The entire conduct of
the war was discussed.   "I remember" said Rochester
"the saying of a great General the old Duke of
Schomberg, that the attacking France in the Netherlands is like taking a bull by the horns.   My opinion
is therefore that we should stand on the defensive in
Flanders and send from thence 15 or 20,000 men
into Catalonia."   Nottingham who spoke next expressed
his entire concurrence in these views.

When Nottingham sat down, Marlborough immediately rose to show the dangers of what he might
truly call "such an undigested counsel," and the necessity of augmenting rather than diminishing our forces
in the Netherlands. The reasons he gave were mainly
two.   First that most of the enemies' strong places in
Flanders might be kept by one battalion in each,

whilst the great towns in Brabant which we had con- CHAP.
quered, as Ghent and Bruges, required twenty times IX.
that number of men for their preservation. Secondly, 1707.
that if our army in the Netherlands were weakened and
the French should in consequence, as they probably
might, gain very considerable advantages, the discon-
tented party in Holland would not fail to cry aloud
for peace. It was one of the very few occasions on
which we find Marlborough stirred to a burst of passion; "strange" said Rochester when replying "in that
Noble Peer who has ever been conspicuous for his
calmness and moderation." And Rochester added,
"There is, I again maintain it, an absolute necessity
for us English to succour King Charles, and the more
so since the Noble Earl (of Peterborough) has this day
reported to us the opinion of Prince Eugene; that the
German soldiers had rather be decimated than sent
into Spain."

Marlborough was allowed a rejoinder. "Although"
he said "it is improper to disclose secret projects in so
large an assembly, yet to gratify your Lordships I can
assure you that measures have been already concerted
with the Emperor for the forming of an army of
40,000 men under the Duke of Savoy, and for sending
powerful succours to King Charles; and it is to be
hoped that Prince Eugene may be prevailed upon to
go and command in Spain, in which case the Germans
would gladly follow him."

With this speech ended the debate. It had not
been possible for Somers and the Whigs to support the
views of Rochester as to the war in Flanders, pledged
as they had always been to the system of King William. Somers however applied himself to frame a

Resolution on which both Whigs and Tories could unite. Accordingly before Lord Herbert left the Chair the following words were moved by the Whig leader: "It is the opinion of this Committee that no peace can be honourable or safe for Her Majesty or her Allies, if Spain and the Spanish West Indies be suffered to continue in the power of the House of Bourbon." This Resolution was agreed to without a dissentient voice. Then, the House still in Committee, Wharton and Halifax acting in concert with Somers made two further motions which were combined in one Address. It prayed Her Majesty to continue to make the most pressing instances that the Emperor might send powerful succours to Spain with expedition and under the command of Prince Eugene, and might further reinforce both the army of the Duke of Savoy and his own upon the Rhine. This Address was unanimously carried, as was also in the whole House the Address of Thanks so long delayed for Her Majesty's Speech at the commencement of the Session.

The passing of these two Resolutions in Committee was the last act of the short-lived alliance at this time between the Whigs and Tories out of place. That alliance had already produced all the effect that Somers and his friends intended or desired. It had thoroughly terrified Godolphin. He had bent before it as the reed before the tempest, and he hoped by further submissions to dissolve it. He made at this juncture pressing overtures of reconciliation to the Whig chiefs. They were assured that Godolphin and Marlborough would henceforth make common cause with them, and carry through all their objects, however great might be the repugnance of the Queen.

On these conditions—on the prospect of seeing at CHAP.
an early period his party restored to power—Somers $\frac{\text{IX.}}{}$
was well content to relinquish all connection with the $1707.$
Tories. He signalised this change of course by a
step of singular skill and boldness, though not perhaps
altogether just to his late allies. At the close of the
debate on the 19th the Lords had appointed a Select
Committee to embody in the usual form for presenta-
tion to the Queen the Resolutions just reported from
the Committee of the House. It was supposed that
the business was merely verbal, and the Committee of
but little importance, nor was any umbrage taken when
its members were named almost wholly from the
Whigs. Scarce any Tory name but Rochester's appeared upon it.

The Committee having met next day as ordered
'at the Prince's lodgings near the House of Peers,"
Lord Somers was called to the Chair, and proceeded
at once to make a most important motion. It will be
remembered that the Resolutions as carried in the
House stated an opinion, that no peace would be safe
or honourable which left in the power of the House of
Bourbon Spain or the Spanish West Indies. That was
an opinion from which in all probability not even a
single member of either House of Parliament would
have dissented. But Somers now proposed to alter
these words into "Spain, the West Indies, or any part
of the Spanish monarchy." This made it a wholly
different question. This brought it into opposition
with the views more or less avowed at that period of
many eminent men both in England and in Holland.
This implied that not even Naples, nor Sicily, nor
Sardinia should be left to Philip on his consenting to

relinquish the throne of Spain. It was a proposal which neither Louis nor his grandson would accept unless in the most dire extremity, and it therefore seemed to involve a further vast effusion of blood and treasure, and a continuance of the war during several more campaigns.

The altered Resolution, with a new and according Preamble, was readily passed by the Select Committee, and was reported by Somers to the House at the earliest possible moment; the first business upon Monday the 22nd of December. Then Somers moved and the Lords ordered that a Message should be sent to the Commons desiring their concurrence in the proposed Address. So far as we can gather from the scanty records of this singular transaction it seems to have taken the Tories in both Houses by surprise. They had no time for concert or deliberation, and they may have feared to incur the popular disfavor by resisting the extension of the national claims. Certain it is that they remained entirely passive. Before the Peers rose that same day the Address was returned from the Commons as concurred in by that House, nor did any one of their Lordships raise his voice against it. It went up therefore to the Queen as the joint Address of the two Houses; and the Queen in her answer as framed by Godolphin and Marlborough declared herself fully of the opinion it expressed.

Thus did Somers prevail. By these means was he able to carry both the Houses very much further than very many of the principal men in either desired or designed, and to pledge the Parliament, so far as it could be pledged, to an indefinite prolongation of the war.

CHAPTER X.

ON the 1st of May, as already stated, the Act of Union came into practical effect. The earliest proceedings under it were such as still further to increase the disfavor with which it was viewed north of Tweed. New Commissioners of Customs and Excise had been named, consisting in great part of Englishmen. With them came a crowd of subordinate officers trained in the English methods and imposing them abruptly on the Scottish people, so that even where the new taxes were not burdensome they were at least vexatious. To enforce and carry through the collection of revenue the Scottish Privy Council appointed by a new Commission Scottish Justices of Peace, but the powers of these, being limited of course by the laws of their own country, were found to be feudal rather than fiscal and of slight avail for the purposes desired. In these departments and in others also the evils were strongly felt of several still subsisting distinctions. What might be well for Scotland was not well for North Britain.

It would indeed have been strange if the Court of St. Germain's had been slow to discern or willing to let pass the growing discontents in its ancient kingdom. Projects for an expedition to Scotland, combined with a popular rising, were submitted to the Court of Versailles. As a preliminary step Colonel Hooke, a Jacobite exile in the French service, was secretly sent over from the Continent to obtain authentic information and negotiate with the friends of the cause. In March, 1707, Hooke landed on the coast of Aberdeenshire, and went first for some days to Slains Castle, the seat of the Earl of Errol. Thence he proceeded in turn to divers other houses. The report which he presented to the French government on his return in the following July, as also the memorials which he brought from Scotland, were published half a century afterwards.[1]

Colonel Hooke, it appears, found not a few of the Peers and landed gentlemen willing to transmit to him professions of hearty zeal, and promises of future aid. But most of these carefully avoided any positive engagement or even any personal interview. The Duke of Hamilton, on whom he mainly relied, sent to him several times his favourite priest and secretary Mr. Hall, but declared himself too ill to see him, having lately had, he said, twenty-nine attacks of fever. The Duke of Athol in like manner took to his bed when he heard of Hooke's approach. The Earl of Breadalbane, now well nigh fourscore years of age, sent as many assurances to James as he ever had to William, and showed the utmost curiosity as to the intentions of his neighbours, but meanwhile would put his name to no document. Far different was the course of Lord Kinnaird. He signed the Memorial which was presented to him on the same day, and he refused to see the names of those who had signed before him, saying that what he did was from a principle of duty, and that he wanted no authority nor example to decide him.

The capacity of Hooke himself was scarcely equal to

---

[1] Secret History of Colonel Hooke's Negotiations in Scotland, London, 1760. This narrative should be compared with corresponding entries in the Lockhart Papers.

the delicate and difficult task which was assigned him. While he thus negotiated with the Lowland noblemen he seems to have neglected the Highland chiefs, although far the more important when a rising was in view. On the whole however he brought back to the Court of Versailles assurances from a certain number of great men in Scotland, that if their young King as they called him came over they would immediately take up arms with 30,000 vassals, followers and friends. But, to secure the young King and themselves while this army was forming, they required that Louis should send with him a French force of 10,000, or at the very least 5,000 men.

Louis on his part was well inclined to the enterprise, but postponed it for further consideration until the ensuing year. Meanwhile as we have seen the Parliament met. One paragraph in the Queen's Speech referred to Scotland, and invited the consideration of further measures to complete the Union. These were afterwards explained to be to abolish the separate Privy Council for Scotland, and to assimilate to the English practice the powers of the Justices of the Peace. A Bill to enact these changes—in its title "for rendering the Union of the two kingdoms more entire and complete"—was accordingly introduced in the Commons.

It is scarcely to be doubted that in the main this new legislation was greatly for the good of Scotland. The Privy Council in that country was altogether different from the Privy Council in England. It was armed with arbitrary powers and functions; and had been the willing instrument of the worst tyranny in the days of Charles the Second. Nevertheless the reform was most ill-

timed. It seemed in the fullest manner to confirm the
previous apprehensions that, when once the two Parliaments were united, the English members would avail
themselves of their far superior numbers to force down
an entire uniformity of system upon the Scottish people
—to deprive them it was said of their liberties and
laws.

With this exasperation of the general feeling the
benefits of the particular measure were of course wholly
disregarded. In the House of Commons the members
from Scotland, all or nearly all, opposed it. There however it was with little difficulty passed. But in the
Lords it was most fiercely fought. The representative
Peers, the heads of great Whig families in Scotland
—as Argyle and Hay—Loudoun and Leven—Rosebery
and Stair—combined as one man against it, and seem
to have carried far greater weight than their brethren
in the Commons. It was determined to take the trial
of strength on the Third Reading, which was fixed for
1708. the 7th of February ensuing.

The two Ministers meanwhile had brought to a
point their difference with Harley. It was no light
matter for Marlborough especially to relinquish a
colleague with whom he was connected by ties of early
friendship and long continued political agreement. It
was foreseen both by the Duke and Godolphin that if
Harley were dismissed the other Tories still in office
would at once resign, and that the administration would
be entirely under Whig control. Harley himself endeavoured by a personal interview with Godolphin to
clear himself from the suspicions under which he
laboured. For a long time the Lord Treasurer, weighing
one cause of alarm against another and quivering at

each, paused and hesitated. But the political necessity which has already been explained finally impelled him onward.

CHAP.
X.
1708.

There was another incident at this juncture greatly to the disservice of Harley. A clerk in his office, William Gregg by name, had been employed by him as a spy in Scotland and elsewhere. More recently this man had entered into a treasonable correspondence with M. de Chamillart, the French Secretary of State. He was wont to slip his letters into the packets which Marshal Tallard as a prisoner in England used to send unsealed to the Secretary's office to be there examined and then forwarded. One of these packets being on some suspicion opened in Holland was found to contain the copy of a draft, which Gregg transmitted, of a letter which it was designed the Queen should write in her own hand to the Emperor, requesting him, according to the wish expressed in Parliament, to appoint Prince Eugene to Spain. Gregg had even been able in the copy to mark those passages first written by Harley as Secretary of State, and those others added by Godolphin as Prime Minister.

In consequence of this discovery Gregg was taken into custody and examined before the Privy Council when he acknowledged his guilt. On the 19th of January he was brought to trial at the Old Bailey, found Guilty on his own confession, and condemned to death. At the same time two smugglers named Bara and Vallière were also committed to Newgate. Harley had taken them into pay as spies, and frequently sent them over to Calais for that object, but they betraying his protection had carried counter-tidings to the French. It was thought that the intelligence which they were able to collect in our ports as to the sailing 'or the situation of our convoys might have been the cause of the heavy losses which we had recently sustained at sea.

In consequence of these transactions doubts of Harley's own fidelity were expressed without scruple by his political opponents. Meanwhile the two great Ministers having surmounted their own repugnance to his dismissal were labouring to overcome the repugnance of the Queen. But Anne continued firm. She acted on a religious feeling, overstrained no doubt but as certainly sincere. In her zeal for the Church she desired to retain Harley as a zealous Churchman in her service, which in her opinion did not at that period comprise too many such.

It must be felt, I conceive, even by those who admit the prejudice of Anne, and have no sympathy of feeling with the Tories of her reign, that the poor Queen was at this time sore beset. For several months past her husband had been slowly sinking under a mortal malady. Never did she intermit the most affectionate care. Never did she cease to share his bed, even though he was compelled by the violence of asthma to raise himself sometimes for great part of the night while his consort had to watch and tend him. By day she would sit at his side hour after hour as he painfully panted for breath, and she remained in the adjoining apartment ready to be called in when he snatched an uneasy slumber in the afternoons. It was during these intervals, while herself oppressed with sorrow and weariness, that she had to withstand the sharp and reproachful representations of Godolphin for the removal of a Minister whom she trusted and esteemed.

Godolphin and with him Marlborough finding their complaints unheeded had recourse, as they had often before, to the threat of resignation. The Queen, as Bishop Burnet tells us, seemed not much concerned at Godolphin's offering to lay down, but she was greatly touched at the impending loss of Marlborough, and studied with some soft expressions to dissuade him. It would seem however that the Duke's intention to resign applied only to his offices at home and did not extend to his foreign command. This is not expressly stated at the time, but may be probably deduced from his correspondence with the Duchess during the last campaign. Thus he wrote: "For my own part I am out of heart and wonder at the courage of Lord Treasurer; for were I used, as I do not doubt but I shall, as he is, by the Whigs who threaten to abandon him whenever the Queen displeases, I would not continue in business for all the world could give me; and I believe they would be the first that would have reason to repent. . . . . . When I say this I know I must go on in the command I have here as long as the war lasts, but I would have nothing to do anywhere else."[2]

Harley on his part protested that he had no other view than to continue the administration with the very basis upon which it had been founded, a combination of moderate Tories and moderate Whigs, so that neither party should have the entire ascendant and control. The Queen had the same desire, and it was hoped that the remaining members of the Cabinet or most of them, acting on this principle, would acquiesce in the secession of their two most powerful colleagues.

---

[2] Coxe's Marlborough, vol. III. p 376.

CHAP.
X.
1708.

The Duchess of Marlborough also came forward at this juncture. Suddenly one morning she appeared before the Queen. "Since" she cried with tears and sobs "Lord Marlborough is now about to be forced from your Majesty's service, I cannot in honor remain any longer at Court;" and she then proceeded to implore a Royal promise that whenever she did retire the numerous offices which she held might be divided between her two elder daughters. Anne endeavoured to elude compliance, repeating several times with apparent kindness, "you and I must never part." But the Duchess was not to be diverted from her purpose. She continued to press her suit with so much importunity that the Queen at last gave way and made the promise required; and the Duchess then took her leave kissing the Queen's hand.—This story might well have been regarded as a calumny of one of the Duchess's enemies were it not recorded by a narrative in her own handwriting. [3]

Such was the situation of parties on Saturday the 7th of February when there was moved in the House of Lords the Third Reading of the Bill to render the Union with Scotland more complete. An amendment was brought forward that the Privy Council of Scotland should determine on the 1st of October next instead of the 1st of May; the opponents of the measure feeling that if they could but gain time they might probably defeat it altogether. But in its support was raised the eloquent and authoritative voice of Somers. There are still on record the ample minutes of the speech, fraught

---

[3] See a summary of this manuscript in Coxe's Marlborough, vol. IV. p. 43. From the short corresponding passage in the "Conduct" (p. 254) it might be supposed that the promise was spontaneous.

with unanswerable arguments, which he addressed to CHAP.
X.
1708. the House in this debate. [4]

Godolphin and Marlborough appear on this occasion to have regarded themselves as virtually out of office and no longer bound to support the measures of their own administration. They found the opponents to this Bill far more numerous and far more vehement than they had foreseen; and they may have desired by siding with them to gain the future adherence of the Scottish people. Under these circumstances they gave their votes for the amendment, which on the division was rejected only by the narrow majority of five, the numbers being 45 and 50. But further still on the consequent passing of the Bill a Protest against the whole measure was immediately entered on the Journals, and among the signatures we may observe with some surprise the names of three of its authors, Godolphin, Marlborough, and Cowper.

The political crisis however was determined by a Cabinet Council which had been summoned to meet on the following day, namely Sunday, the 8th of February. It was usual in that age, I may observe in passing, for the Cabinets to meet upon the Day of Rest, and usual also for the Sovereign to preside at them. That same morning Godolphin and Marlborough waited on the Queen to state that, Harley still continuing in office, they could not attend the Cabinet, nor take any further part as Her Majesty's Ministers. Anne allowed them to depart and went to the Cabinet as usual. There Harley produced his papers as Secretary of State and began to open the business of his department. But around him he saw grim faces and

---

[4] They are published in the Hardwicke State Papers, vol. II. p. 473.

he heard half-muttered complaints. As he paused the Duke of Somerset rose and said, "I do not see how we can deliberate to any purpose when neither the General nor the Treasurer are present." This observation he repeated twice, and with some vehemence, while the other Ministers expressed their agreement by their looks. The Queen remained silent but presently withdrew, leaving the business of the day undone.

It was plain from the proceedings at this Cabinet that Harley had desired to continue in office with the aid of certain of his colleagues. It was possible that he might still be intent on forming a wholly new administration. A whisper of these circumstances was not slow in spreading among the principal Whigs, and had considerable influence on the proceedings of the House of Lords next day. Then, that is on Monday the 9th, we learn from the lists in the Journals that both Marlborough and Godolphin were present. Then it appears that the House resolved to appoint by ballot a Committee of Seven Lords to examine William Gregg, lately convicted of High Treason and under sentence of execution in Newgate. It was well understood on all sides that this Committee was designed as a menace against Harley, and with the hope of involving him in a criminal charge. Such an object was still more apparent when, as the result of the ballot for the Committee, there came forth seven names of zealous Whigs, namely Devonshire, Somerset, Bolton, Wharton, Townshend, Somers and Halifax. The extreme unfairness of seeking to try any statesman by a body consisting solely of his political opponents seems to have been overlooked amidst the political passions of that time.

Harley however had no intention of prolonging the CHAP.
X.
1708. contest for power. He considered the result of the last Cabinet as decisive against him, and he pressed the Queen next day to accept his resignation. With much hesitation and still more reluctance Anne at last complied, and his resignation took place accordingly on the 11th of the same month. With him retired Henry St. John, Secretary at War, Sir Simon Harcourt, Attorney-General, and Sir Thomas Mansell, Comptroller of the Household. Thus was the Tory Opposition reinforced by two powerful chiefs, the plausible Harley and the "all-accomplished St. John," during the very month in which Death deprived them of Sir Edward Seymour, so long in their front ranks, though of late confined by his infirmities to his country-house and even to his chair.

On the other hand the two great Ministers, "the Treasurer and General" as they were often called, were restored to the Queen's presence and Councils though certainly not to her favor. The Seals of Secretary of State were given to Henry Boyle, the Chancellor of the Exchequer, a zealous Whig, but greatly esteemed by all parties. He was succeeded at the Exchequer by the Speaker, John Smith, although his formal appointment was deferred until after he should leave the Chair at the end of the Session. The successor of St. John at the War Office was Robert Walpole, the most rising man in the Whig as was St. John in the Tory ranks. Earl Cholmondeley became Comptroller of the Household; but the office of Attorney-General remained vacant during several months, since the Queen could by no means reconcile herself to Sir

James Montagu, a brother of Halifax, whom Godolphin pressed upon her.

The seven Whig Lords assembled in the Peers' Committee were more assiduous than successful in their task. They went to Newgate to examine Gregg; they had also before them the two smugglers, and other witnesses. But with all their pains nothing was elicited in any quarter to impeach the loyalty of Harley. At the same time however, it was clearly proved against him that he was negligent and slatternly in his transaction of business. All the papers of state, said Gregg, used to lie so carelessly about his office, that every one belonging to it, even the door-keepers, might have read them, and it was in this manner that Gregg himself had obtained his information.

The Committee having concluded their inquiries and presented their Report, Gregg after some further respite was left to undergo his doom. A paper which he gave in at his execution contains these words: "And I do sacredly protest that, as I shall answer it before the Judgment Seat of Christ, the gentleman aforesaid (the Right Hon. Robert Harley, Esq.) was not privy to my writing to France directly nor indirectly." [5] Nevertheless the rage of party was not on either side appeased. The Whigs continued to whisper that, though Gregg had been staunch, Harley had shared in his treason. The Tories did not scruple to affirm that the Committee had tampered with the prisoner, and held out to him a hope of pardon if he would but accuse his chief.

[5] See the whole Declaration in the Complete History of Europe, 1708, p. 172.

While thus torn by faction at home, we found our- CHAP.
selves exposed to some loss of influence with our near- X.
est and best ally.   An opportunity to rouse against us 1708.
the jealousy of Holland occurred to Louis the Fourteenth.   It came from a Treaty of Commerce signed
at Barcelona on the 10th of July preceding, between
General Stanhope as the Queen's Minister and Prince
Lichtenstein and others on the part of Charles.   Diminution of duties and simplification of forms were
therein stipulated in a manner no doubt greatly to the
benefit of England, but which, according to the larger
views of Adam Smith as they have since prevailed,
would have been no less for the benefit of Spain.

But besides the stipulations in the Treaty there was
a separate and secret Article of much greater importance.   This provided that after a General Peace there
should be formed a Company of Commerce to the
Indies, that is, to the Spanish dominions in America,
the Company to consist conjointly of the subjects of
Spain and the subjects of Great Britain.   In case however of unforeseen accidents or obstacles the Article
further declared, that during any interval between the
conclusion of such a Peace and the establishment of
such a Company the subjects of Great Britain might
send every year to the Spanish Indies ten ships, each
of five hundred tons, with liberty of trade, the subjects of France to be for ever excluded from any like
privilege.[6]

This Treaty had been negotiated by Stanhope with
anxious care during many months, and it was warmly
approved by the Ministers in England.   Thus as Secre-

---

[6] The entire Treaty appears in Lamberty's collection, vol. IV. p. 592, and
there is a summary of it in Tindal's History, vol. IV. p. 415.

tary of State wrote to him Lord Sunderland: "I am very glad the Treaty of Commerce is so happily concluded, and that you have had the honor of it. . . . . As it is certain notwithstanding our misfortune at Almanza no Englishman can ever think of putting an end to this war but by settling King Charles upon the throne of Spain, so it is very fortunate to have this matter concluded whilst they are yet in adversity, for I am afraid their gratitude would hardly effect it."[7]

The satisfaction was not quite the same upon the other side. Charles and his Ministers had no sooner concluded the Treaty than they were seized with doubts and qualms. So jealous were the Spaniards of any even the smallest participation in their South American trade, that great popular disfavor would undoubtedly ensue from terms so liberal, accorded to aliens and to heretics. The Separate Article was indeed to be kept a secret, but how long would that secret be preserved? Under these apprehensions Charles did not ratify the treaty for six months, that is not till January 1708. By that time Stanhope had returned to England on leave of absence. The ratified Treaty was at once sent after him, being embarked at Barcelona to go on by land from Genoa. As it chanced the sloop that bore it was captured on its way by a French frigate; and the captain who had been apprised of the importance of his freight rather than allow it to be taken threw it over-board. But the sea being shallow in that part, the secret packet was recovered by the aid of divers, and transmitted to the Marquis de Torcy at Versailles. By order of his Royal Master Torcy found means to lay it before the States General, foreseeing that it could

7 To General Stanhope, July 8 and August 5, 1707 (MS.).

not fail to irritate and inflame them in a high degree against their English allies.

Louis was in hopes at this period to strike a blow against Great Britain in what he deemed its most vulnerable part. Carefully concealing his design he planned an expedition to Scotland. There was made ready at Dunkirk a squadron of five men-of-war with transports and frigates, the command of the whole being assigned to the Chevalier de Forbin, the best seaman of France at that time. From St. Germain's would be sent over that young Prince whom his adherents called King and his enemies Pretender, but whom both could mention as on common ground by the title which he took at this period, the Chevalier de St. George, or more shortly the Chevalier. With him as his guide and Mentor was to go an experienced officer, Gacé de Matignon, raised on this occasion to the rank of Maréchal de France. The number of the troops embarked would scarcely exceed 4,000, but Louis had means of obtaining through the Stuart emissaries, an exact account of the English force in Scotland, which at this time consisted only of two regiments of Dragoons wanting their full complement and of the depôts of five battalions of foot, making altogether less than 1,700 men.[8] There was therefore every prospect that the French troops on landing would be able to maintain their ground against what may be termed the garrison of the established government, and allow time for the partisans of James to rise. And if even the expedition had not the full success that was desired, it might serve to draw Marlborough and great

[8] In a speech of Lord Haversham founded on the papers laid before a Select Committee the number is stated as only 1,500 (Parl. Hist. vol. vi. p. 768), but Mr. Burton computes 150 more. (Hist. of Scotland, vol. ii. p. 13.)

part of the British forces from Flanders, and thus achieve an all-important diversion for the arms of the French King.

All preparations were made accordingly. James was to set out from St. Germain's on the 7th of March, to be at Dunkirk on the 9th, and to embark on the morning of the 10th. So scrupulously was the secret kept that it was not till the 4th that Madame de Maintenon writing to Princess Orsini had permission to announce it through her to the Court of Spain.[9] But at the very point of departure the young Prince, then less than twenty years of age and not robust in constitution, fell ill of the measles. It was necessary to postpone his journey, and he did not actually embark till the 17th of the month. By that time the alarm had been given. An English fleet commanded by Sir George Byng and three-fold stronger than the French came in pursuance of previous orders off the harbour of Dunkirk. Some regiments English and Dutch were summoned over in haste from Flanders. Other of our native troops, such as could at once be mustered—some 7,000 foot and 1,800 horse—were appointed to meet at York, and designed if necessary to march across the Tweed.

On the 17th however the English ships having been driven from their station by high winds, Forbin was able to sail out of Dunkirk harbour with his small Armada. Making for the Firth of Forth they a little overshot the mark and first sighted the land at Montrose. Thence turning southwards to their real destination they anchored at the Isle of May. They made certain signals which had been agreed upon between Colonel

---

9 Letter of March 4, 1708, in her published correspondence with "la Princesse des Ursins."

Hooke and his Scottish friends, but received no signals in reply from the shore, showing clearly that the northern Jacobites after all their boasts and promises were not yet prepared. Under such circumstances Forbin felt that he could not venture to land the troops committed to his charge. Nor was there much leisure for deliberation; early next morning the man at the mast-head called out that the English fleet was in view. With but five ships against Byng who had at least sixteen Forbin could hazard an engagement even less than a landing; so without delay he cut his cables and made all sail to the north. One of his ships the Salisbury, a former capture from the English, having ventured too far into the Firth of Forth, was taken in returning, with about 400 men; but the rest held on their course, the hindmost being not far pursued and but slightly attacked by Byng.

The Mars was the French Admiral's ship. On board her besides the Chevalier de St. George were some of the principal exiles of his cause from Scotland, the titular Duke of Perth, Lord Middleton, Colonel Hooke, and several more. These gentlemen earnestly advised that a landing might be made in Aberdeenshire. It was the country of the gallant Gordons and the Hays of Errol; and the appearance of the young Prince might work wonders. James himself when consulted joined in their request. He several times entreated Forbin to be put on shore, even if it must be so without the French troops, and although none were to follow him but his domestics. Forbin on the contrary declared that his instructions left him no such latitude, and that they having received no signal nor invitation from their friends on land there was nothing left for them but to return as they came. They had already rounded Buchan Ness when Forbin accordingly gave orders to steer back. Partly by his good seamanship and partly perhaps by his good fortune, he avoided any encounter with the English fleet, and brought back his Armada safe to Dunkirk harbour on the 7th of April. Thus ingloriously ended an enterprise from which so much had been expected.[1]

The Parliament showed great zeal against it. No sooner was it known and announced than both Houses voted loyal addresses to the Queen and passed two Bills to strengthen Her Majesty's Government. The first Bill empowered Justices of the Peace in any part of Great Britain. to summon before them any suspected person and tender to him an oath abjuring the Pretender; a person who declined such oath to be adjudged "a Popish· recusant convict." The second Bill was to suspend the Habeas Corpus until the month of October following. Under this last enactment numerous arrests were made; the Duke of Hamilton, the chief amongst them. His Grace was found by the Queen's Messenger in Lancashire on his way south from Scotland, but so cautious and reserved had been his whole conduct to the disaffected, who nevertheless relied on him as leader, that he had nothing now to dread beyond the inconvenience of a short imprisonment.—A third Bill of greater stringency was brought in by General Stanhope seconded by Sir David Dalrymple; it was to discharge the Clans of Scotland from their vassalage to such of their

---

[1] For the proceedings on board this squadron see especially two narratives, one by M. d'Andrezel who gives many minute particulars, as for instance the precise day "when His Britannic Majesty became very sick," and the other by Marshal Matignon. (Secret History of Hooke, &c. p. 153 and 159, ed. 1760.)

chiefs as should take up arms against the Queen; but
this Bill, which might have gone far to avert the events
of 1715 and 1745, was, it would seem, allowed to drop,
when the invasion itself collapsed. Anne herself showed
great resentment at the audacious attempt to dethrone
her; and a consequent variation in her style was observed. She had never in any previous Speech mentioned
"the Revolution" by that name; now on the contrary
the phrase appeared in two of her answers to Addresses.
And when on the 1st of April, she closed the Session
with a Speech from the Throne, she willingly gave in-
sertion to a paragraph denouncing "the designs of a
Popish Pretender bred up in the principles of the most
arbitrary government." Hitherto she had not been so
ready to refer to her brother in such terms.

Louis, however much disappointed at the result of the
Scottish project, was only the more intent on achieving
some successes in the next campaign. He had resolved
to concentrate his main forces on his Flemish frontier,
and instead of there remaining as of late on the defensive,
to make a forward movement and recover by surprise
the great towns of Brabant. To inspirit the troops he
would place at their head his grandson the Duke of
Burgundy, a young Prince of no mean ability and heir-
apparent to the Crown; while at his side would stand
one of the ablest of the Marshals, the Duke de Vendome.
But whatever advantages of military ardour might attend this junction were much more than counterbalanced,
as will presently be seen, by the evils of divided command. Along the Alps of Piedmont would be stationed
Villars to contend against the Duke of Savoy. The
Duke of Orleans would be sent back to Spain. Berwick
on the other hand would be retained in France to share

with the Elector of Bavaria the command upon the Rhine.

On the part of the Allies, we may observe in the first place that both Das Minas and Galway were recalled from Catalonia, and in the course of February came back by sea to Portugal. There, Das Minas was permitted to retire into private life, while Galway, by the favor of his friends in England, was still maintained in command. He was left to head the scanty forces remaining on the Spanish frontier in conjunction with another chief appointed by the Court of Lisbon. Stanhope was named in his place to command the British force in Catalonia, retaining at the same time his post as British Minister at the Court of Charles. It had been found impossible to prevail upon the Emperor to send Prince Eugene to Spain. Instead of that great General who would have ruled the whole, His Majesty appointed Count Guido Staremberg to command the Imperial as Stanhope would the British troops. Count Guido was born in 1657, and trained by the Jesuits for the priesthood, but his destination changing he had entered the army, distinguished himself in the Turkish wars, and in 1704 attained the rank of Field Marshal.[2] Both chiefs—the one from England and the other from Italy—arrived at Barcelona in the course of May, shortly after the decease at a great old age of the General for the Dutch Count Noyelles. Count Belcastel became the successor of Noyelles in that post.

While Eugene was not to be spared for Spain he could as little be employed in Northern Italy. The differences between him and his cousin the Duke of

[2] Geschichte des Hauses Stahremberg, von J. Schwerdling, p. 323, ed. Linz, 1830.

Savoy had risen after the siege of Toulon to such a
pitch of hostility that it was impossible for them to
serve together in the next campaign. The Duke was
therefore left to cope singly with Marshal Villars, receiving from Vienna large promises of reinforcements,
but in truth a most scanty supply. The post intended
by the Emperor for Eugene was on the Moselle with a
new army to be formed in great part by detachments
from that recently assigned to the Elector of Hanover
upon the Rhine.

The excellent diplomacy of Eugene was at this period
almost as requisite for the cause of the Allies as were
his talents for war. Not one of the smaller German
Princes but had now, since the German reverses of last
year, some fresh grievances to allege or some further
advantages to claim. Such was the case more especially
with the Elector Palatine, the Landgrave of Hesse, and
King Augustus as Elector of Saxony. The Elector
of Hanover also was vehemently chafing against any
diminution of the army which he was expected to
command. It might be requisite for Eugene to visit
each of these Potentates at their own little Courts before
the military operations recommenced. Still more was
it essential that he should have a meeting with Marlborough and determine the plan for the new campaign.
With this view he repaired to the Hague and impatiently
awaited the arrival of his English colleague.

Marlborough on his part was of course detained in
England until the prospect of invasion had wholly
passed away. Then at once taking his departure he
reached the Hague in the first days of April New Style.
Acting in the closest concert with Prince Eugene these
two great men also called into their counsels their tried

friend in Holland, Pensionary Heinsius. It was agreed between them that there should be two plans of campaign, the one ostensible to guard against murmurs and objections and the other real. The ostensible project was that the army on the Scheldt under Marlborough and that on the Moselle under Eugene should cooperate from different sides as though for the invasion of Lorraine. The real project was to unite these two armies by a rapid march and give battle to the French in the Netherlands.

The Deputies of the States being duly consulted on the first of these designs gave it their assent. It was as important, and it seemed more difficult to obtain the concurrence also of the Elector of Hanover. Eugene knew that His Highness already viewed him with great jealousy and would allow but little weight to whatever arguments he might adduce. He warmly pressed that Marlborough should meet him at Hanover and there exert his usual powers of persuasion.

At this very period however a new Court feud had broken forth in London, and in order to allay it Marlborough was full as eagerly called back by his consort and his colleagues. Nothing can paint in stronger colours the ascendency of this great man. He could by no means be spared from the Continent whenever there was a Prince to be reclaimed or a battle to be fought, and as little could he be spared from England, if the Ministers required guidance, or if there was a point to carry with the Queen.

Seeing the urgency of the case Marlborough yielded to the entreaties of Eugene. He travelled with all speed, being only twelve days absent from the Hague and remaining but forty-eight hours at Hanover; yet even that short stay proved sufficient for his purpose. As he writes to Godolphin on the 3rd of May having returned to the Hague the night before: "After a very great deal of uneasiness the Elector has consented to the project for three armies; but we have been obliged to leave on the Rhine two Imperial regiments more than we designed: so that Prince Eugene will have 2,000 horse less on the Moselle; and as for the joining the two armies we thought it best not to acquaint the Elector with it, so that I expect when that is put in execution he will be very angry; but since the good of the campaign depends upon it I know no remedy but patience." And the Duke adds upon another subject: "The burgomasters of Amsterdam were above two hours with me this morning to convince me of the necessity of a sudden peace. This, from the most zealous part of the Dutch, has very much alarmed me." Once again at the Hague the Great Duke, instead of thanks for his most successful exertions, received only upbraiding letters from the Duchess and Godolphin, who blamed him for not allotting his spare time to themselves. He had given them some promise of a visit after he should have come back from Hanover, but this was precluded by the calls of the service and the necessity for him to repair to Brussels and collect his army. Prince Eugene on his part had visited the Elector Palatine at Düsseldorf on his way to Hanover; and from Hanover proceeded to the Court of King Augustus at Dresden. To these two Princes as also to the Landgrave of Hesse he was able to hold out assurances that the Emperor had complied with most of their demands, and thus could he retain them within the pale of the Grand Alliance.

CHAP.
X.
1708.

5 *

From Dresden Eugene returned for a brief space to Vienna to give the Emperor in person an account of his recent conferences and to quicken the preparations for the coming campaign. Thence he hastened to put himself at the head of the force not as yet fully formed on the Moselle. Marlborough meanwhile from his head-quarters at Brussels wrote as follows to Godolphin on the 14th of May: "The great want of rain (and consequent want of forage) will oblige me to put off the assembling of the army till the 21st of this month."— And again on the 24th: "To-morrow I shall march towards Hal, where we shall join the English and the rest of the troops which came from Flanders. You know already my intention of gaining time till Prince Eugene can act with his army, which I am afraid cannot be till about the middle of next month."

Vendome on his part had been reinforced, according to the resolution taken at Versailles, by considerable detachments from the other French armies; and he was joined not only by the Duke of Burgundy and his brother the Duke of Berri but also by the Chevalier de St. George. That young Prince had a natural desire for military distinction, but from that wish committed the great error of drawing his sword against his countrymen where his own cause was not·concerned. Having mustered their army at Mons, Vendome and his Princes marched forward and took up an advanced position at Braine-la-Leud. Marlborough foresaw that a general action might ensue, and sent an express with all speed to Eugene, whose forces, from the slow forms at Vienna, were still lagging in the rear. The Duke exhorted the Prince if he could not yet bring up his foot to press onward with his cavalry and to join him without delay.

The advance to Braine-la-Leud, being to the right of Marlborough's army, seemed to threaten either Brussels or Louvain. But such was not the real design of the enemy. In their further course they relied on the popular aversion to the Provisional Government. That Government of foreigners, as established by the Dutch after the conquest of Brabant, to endure while their own Barrier was depending, had run counter to all the prepossessions religious and political of the native race. Vendome knew that he could in consequence depend upon their sympathy, nay more, on their cooperation. Already in the month of May there had been a plot to betray Antwerp to the French, a plot which only the vigilance of Marlborough had in good time detected. Now, at day-break of the 5th of July, a detachment of French having marched all night suddenly appeared before Ghent; and the foremost men representing themselves as deserters obtained by that stratagem possession of the gate. Then the main body of the French rushed in, and obtaining the aid of the citizens they made themselves masters of the city, after which they surrounded the garrison of only 300 men in the citadel and compelled it to lay down its arms, in two days. Six hours after the surprise of Ghent another French division came beneath the walls of Bruges, which surrendered almost on the first summons. Thus easily were the two chief cities of Brabant recovered by the French. Other like losses might well be feared. As Marlborough wrote: "The States have used this country so ill that I no ways doubt but all the towns will play us the same trick as Ghent has done whenever they have it in their power."

So far successful in their objects the French proceeded to carry out the entire scheme which they had formed, by investing Oudenarde. This fortress, built on the left bank of the Scheldt and in a strong position, would be of great importance to them in securing their recent conquests, and would form the connecting link between the French frontier and Brabant. For that very reason the news of this siege, which was commenced on the 9th of July, spread the greatest alarm among the Dutch and Imperial authorities, and even in the midst of Marlborough's army at the quarters of Marshal Overkirk, the Dutch commander.

Marlborough as ever with quick intuition saw that, both on military and political grounds, he must at all hazards strike a blow for the relief of Oudenarde. His army was inferior in numbers to the French. It was computed at the beginning of the campaign as of 112 battalions and 180 squadrons, while Vendome had 124 of the first and 197 of the last, making altogether, it was roughly reckoned, almost 100,000 men. Nor could Marlborough expect timely aid from the Emperor's side. As he had written to Godolphin more than a month before: "I would not willingly blame Prince Eugene, but his arrival at the Moselle will be ten days after his promise." The delay in fact proved to be of many more days than ten. But it was no fault of that gallant Prince. So far from partaking in the slowness of the Court which he served he was at this very time pressing forward from the Moselle with his cavalry only; and on hearing when he came to Maestricht of the French advance he outstripped even his horsemen, and scarcely rested until he reached Marlborough's quarters. The two friends embraced with their wonted cordiality, and that entire elevation above all petty jealousies,

which in long subsequent years distinguished on a like
occasion Wellington and Blücher, as it now did Marlborough and Eugene.—Marlborough had also been
joined by the Electoral Prince of Hanover, the future
George the Second. "It would have been more natural
for him" writes the Duke "to have served with his
father, but I suppose they have a mind he should make
acquaintance with the English officers."

For the investment of Oudenarde the French had
hitherto employed only one division of 16,000 men.
They designed to cover the siege by occupying with
their principal forces the strong post of Lessines upon
the Dender. Here however they were anticipated by
the promptitude of Marlborough. He sent forward a
large detachment under General Cadogan to march by
night and to seize upon Lessines, and he followed with
his entire army the next day. By this bold and unexpected movement the enemy found Marlborough interposed between them and their frontier. They relinquished the investment of Oudenarde, and fell back
to Gavre lower down the Scheldt.

The object of Marlborough was now, by another
bold march to reach the Scheldt opposite Oudenarde
—to effect his passage before the French could return
to oppose him—and to give them battle on the left
bank as they came. Eugene when consulted had
warmly approved the scheme, and expressed his joy
that he had arrived in time to take part in the coming
conflict. "My troops" said Marlborough very modestly
"will be animated by the presence of so distinguished
a commander."

In pursuance of these resolutions the English army
was in movement soon after dawn on the memorable

11th of July, Cadogan as before leading the vanguard.
Reaching the Scheldt after a toilsome march of fifteen
miles, Cadogan began to construct bridges of pontoons
which were completed soon after midday, and then the
whole English army passed. The French were on the
left bank already, their bridges at Gavre having been by
previous orders made ready for them before they reached
the river. They had a good defensive position a little
to the north of Oudenarde, protected by some swelling
uplands, which in that part of the country are called
"Couters." One of these, the Bosen Couter, was especially strong.

It might well seem rashness in the English General
to assail a gallant army thus advantageously posted
with soldiers much inferior in number, and wearied by
fifteen miles of march. But Marlborough, who had so
often suffered from the evils of divided command and
jarring counsels, was now to reap the benefit of these
when displayed in the ranks of his opponents. The
Duke of Burgundy and the Duke of Vendome were
not only competing in authority but opposite in character. Take first His Royal Highness. A devout
Catholic, with a due horror of Protestants and Jansenists
as became a grandson of Louis the Fourteenth, with
many accomplishments and many virtues as became a
pupil of Fenelon, he was however shy, reserved, and
inexperienced. Vendome on the other hand was a
scoffer at religion and notorious for abominable vices.
His countrymen, the most polished people in the world,
might stare at his filthy person and neglected dress;
they might smart under his roughness nay sometimes
brutality of language; they might condemn those
sluggish habits from which he only roused himself on

some great occasion; but they were compelled to ac-
knowledge his great genius and energy in war.

In this army Monseigneur the Royal Duke held the supreme command as his rank seemed to require. It was intended at Versailles that he should mainly rely upon Vendome. But from personal alienation the young Prince was disposed to trust other and less able advisers, as M. de Puységur. The result was a fatal confusion of orders in the battle which ensued. Once for example when Vendome had commanded the brigades of Picardy and Piedmont to charge across a small intervening plain the Duke of Burgundy as chief bade them halt, saying that he knew that plain to be impassable. "Your Majesty" says Vendome in his report to the King "will be so good as to observe that this plain which was called impassable was passed by the enemy without hindrance, and had not upon it either a thicket or a ditch.[3]

But here I am anticipating. Should I not sooner have said that the battle was commenced towards three in the afternoon? Should I not have related how at the outset Marlborough seeing two of the French brigades in advance sent against them De Rantzau with eight squadrons of Hanoverians and Cadogan with twelve squadrons of English? Should I leave untold how in the gallant charge which ensued the Prince of Hanover bore his part bravely and had a horse shot under him? By degrees as the troops came up the battle grew general. Marlborough and Eugene remained for a while together; then separating the Prince received from his friend in compliment the command of the right wing which was strengthened to almost

3 Mémoires militaires de la Succession d'Espagne, vol. VIII. p. 390.

CHAP.
X.
1708.

sixty battalions and comprised the British troops. The Duke retained under his own direction no more than twenty battalions, some Dutch, some Hanoverian, and some Prussian. Thus advancing they pressed the enemy from different sides and carried the scene of conflict to the uneven ground where the cavalry could not engage. At one point it seemed to Marlborough that the right of the French might be turned and cut off from their main body; and he entrusted the execution of this bold manœuvre to the veteran Marshal Overkirk who had brought up the rear with twenty battalions of Dutch and Danes. Overkirk, though weighed down by years and for some months past in languishing health, showed all the spirit of a young man in the discharge of so welcome a duty.

During several hours the battle though most irregularly fought was well sustained. But when the shades of that summer evening deepened, victory had everywhere declared for the Allies. The French chiefs, after a fruitless consultation in which Vendome alone maintained that the battle might be renewed in the morning, gave orders for retreat in the direction of Ghent. Several detachments however and large parties not being duly apprised or missing their way in the darkness were surrounded and brought in as prisoners by thousands the next day. The loss of the Allied army was about 3,000 in killed and wounded. That of the enemy has been sometimes stated as no larger though more probably twofold. According to Marlborough's report "we have taken 95 colours and standards besides three the Prussians keep to send to their King."[4]

[4] To the Lord Treasurer, July 26, 1708. It is therefore surprising to

There are several letters from Marlborough on the morrow of his victory. Thus to Godolphin: "I must ever acknowledge the goodness of God in the success He was pleased to give us, for I believe Lord Stair will tell you they were in as strong a post as is possible to be found; but you know when I left England I was positively resolved to endeavour by all means a battle, thinking nothing else would make the Queen's business go on well." With this public motive in the Duke's mind another more domestic might not unworthily mingle. For on the 4th of May he had written to Sunderland as follows: "For my own part I shall endeavour to do my duty this campaign, after which I should be glad to see my place well filled, and that for the remaining part of my life I might have a little quiet and be sometimes with my children."

A few days after the battle the troops of Prince Eugene some twenty-five or thirty thousand strong came up from the Moselle. On the other hand Marshal Berwick had been observing and following them with the best part of his army from Alsace, so that the relative force of the contending parties was but little changed. It was now for Marlborough and Eugene to consider what steps consequent upon their victory they should next take. Marlborough formed the scheme of masking Lille and other fortresses on the frontier, and marching with his main army past them, into the heart of France. It need scarcely be shown how much this idea was in advance of the military notions of his age, and how, although conceived by the genius of

find it stated in General Pelet's able compendium, "Nous ne perdîmes ni artillerie, ni drapeaux, ni étendards, ni bagages, et nous prîmes aux ennemis un drapeau." (Mémoires militaires, vol. viii. p. 38.)

Marlborough, it was left to be carried out a century afterwards by other Allies combined against another monarch of the French.

In 1708 at all events the scheme was thought too bold. Godolphin fully concurred in it, but as Marlborough writes to him in reply, "I have acquainted Prince Eugene with the earnest desire we have for our marching into France. He thinks it impracticable till we have Lille for a PLACE D'ARMES and a magazine." Far less could the Great Duke prevail with the Dutch chiefs. "I have spoke of it" he says "to nobody but the Prince, for by several observations I have of late made of the Deputies of our army, I am afraid the States would not be for this expedition nor any thing else where there is a venture." It was therefore necessary for Marlborough to confine himself to the humbler task of besieging Lille, and even this was deemed to be an enterprise of extraordinary daring.

The city of Lille was one of the earliest conquests of Louis the Fourteenth. Since that time Vauban himself had been employed in strengthening the fortifications, adding to them also a new citadel, until they became one of the master-pieces of his skill. At the first thought of any danger from the arms of the Allies, Marshal Boufflers who held the rank of Governor hastened to his post, and gathered round him a garrison which by divers reinforcements rose to nearly 15,000 men. Beyond his walls there were French armies amounting at the very least to 100,000 men, all excellent troops, and with able chiefs ready it was supposed to discover and to profit by any even the slightest error of Marlborough and Eugene.

There were other and most serious obstacles. So

long as the French retained possession of Ghent they could command the course of both the Scheldt and the Lys, and entirely prevent the conveyance by water of the cannon and provision required for the siege of Lille. To transport these by land would call for vast exertion and expose them to considerable risk. Still Marlborough persevered. "We have ordered" he writes "twenty battering pieces to be brought from Maestricht; and we have taken measures for sixty more to be brought from Holland. The calculation of the number of draught horses to draw this artillery amounts to sixteen thousand, by which you will see the difficulties we meet with . . .; but we must overcome them or we shall have very little fruit of our victory."

To assail the huge convoy which was gradually prepared at Brussels and amounted to 94 pieces of artillery with 3,000 ammunition waggons, or on the other hand to forward and protect it, was now the aim of the opposite chiefs. Vendome sent out from Ghent a division of 18,000 men, and Berwick advanced with part of his army to Mortagne, each in the hope during its slow progress to profit by some vulnerable point. But the precautions of Marlborough and Eugene proved too good. The unwieldy mass was conveyed in perfect safety from Brussels to Ath, and thence to the ground before Lille, where Eugene was enabled to open the trenches on the night of the 22nd of August. It was agreed that Marlborough, who had recently encamped first at Werwick, then at Helchin, should command the covering army, while the operations of the siege should be directed by Eugene.

The siege of Lille now commencing raised extraordinary interest in Europe. Men of high rank or high renown, present or to come, hastened to attend it. King Augustus late of Poland and the Landgrave of Hesse appeared in Marlborough's camp as volunteers. There came Maurice of Saxony, then only a boy of twelve, who in his eagerness had escaped on foot from his tutors at Dresden, but destined to be in after years the victorious leader of French armies. There came Schwerin and Munnich, both subsequently Field Marshals of much fame, the one preceptor in arms of Frederick the Great, the other, rival of Biren in the sway of Russia. It was known that Marlborough and Eugene would make the most strenuous exertions for the reduction of the place. It was known that Louis the Fourteenth had set his whole heart on its relief.

As the first step to this latter course the French armies now combined. The Dukes of Burgundy and Vendome, leaving a corps of 20,000 men for the protection of Ghent, marched from it to the Dender at Lessines, where Berwick had advanced to meet them, and where accordingly on the 30th of August the junction was effected. Then returning within their own frontier they moved against the besiegers' lines before Lille with the intention of hazarding a battle as Louis had enjoined. But far from that cordial union which so constantly prevailed between Marlborough and Eugene, the three French chiefs were hopelessly at variance. Whatever one suggested was certain to be bitterly opposed by the other two. Thus they could not come to any clear decision as to either the time or the place for an attack. It was in vain that Louis renewed his orders. It was in vain that Chamillart posted down from Versailles to inspect the ground and to reconcile the Generals. By these delays Eugene

had been enabled to intrench his position so strongly
that the French chiefs could discern no opening to
assail it. With bitter mortification they found themselves reduced to be only spectators of the siege.

During this time De Boufflers as chief within the
walls had displayed admirable skill and spirit, infusing
his own zeal into the troops, nay even into the towns-
men, over whom he held sway, disputing every inch of
ground, repelling attacks, repairing breaches, making
frequent and courageous sallies. The besiegers while
sustaining heavy losses gained but little ground, and
the Deputies advised that the enterprise should be
relinquished. On one occasion Eugene himself was
wounded in the head; and Marlborough found it necessary for some days to perform a double duty: the command of his own army, and the superintendence of the
siege. Towards this period also the Allies lost one of
their most honoured chiefs by the death of Marshal
Overkirk, whose health had sunk under the labours of
this campaign.

At this juncture, since the enemy contrived to debar
all water carriage and had recently cut off the land
communication with Brussels, the Allied army could
only obtain its supplies slowly and with risk, by way of
Ostend. Here at least the French commanders hoped
to strike a blow. They formed a design against the
largest and most important of these convoys. They
stationed Count de La Mothe at Bruges with a strong
division, and with orders to dart forward against the
train of waggons as soon as it drew near. On the other
hand Marlborough had sent General Webb and a body
of foot for its protection.

On the 27th of September the large convoy thus

attended set out from Ostend. Next day it was sharply attacked by La Mothe at the wood of Wynendale. The French troops were far more numerous than the English but may have lost something of their spirit by their enforced inaction before Lille. They were on all points repulsed by General Webb, supported towards the close of the action by General Cadogan who came up with some squadrons of horse; and the convoy on which so much depended pursued its progress without further hindrance. As Marlborough's letter states it: "Webb and Cadogan have on this occasion, as they always will do, behaved themselves extremely well. The success of this vigorous action is in a great measure owing to them. If they had not succeeded and our convoy had been lost, the consequence must have been the raising of the siege the next day."

Since the reverse of the French arms at Wynendale the Allies made more rapid progress at Lille. The breaching batteries were augmented, and poured in an almost incessant fire of artillery. At length on the 22nd of October, after sixty days of open trenches, Boufflers beat a parley. From respect to his most gallant defence Eugene allowed him to dictate his own terms. He was allowed to withdraw into the citadel, which he determined to maintain with the rest of his garrison now reduced to 5,000 effective men, while 'his sick and wounded were to be conveyed beyond the French lines to Douay. Thus the Allies became masters of the city and proceeded without delay to invest the citadel.

But while the siege of the citadel was thus depending peril to the Allies arose in another quarter. The Elector of Bavaria, who had been called from his station on the

Rhine, thought the opportunity auspicious for a COUP
DE MAIN on Brussels where there was a strong party to
befriend him. Suddenly marching from Mons at the
head of 15,000 men he appeared before the gates of
Brussels and summoned the city, sending in also emissaries to stir up a revolt; but he could not induce either
the garrison to surrender or the inhabitants to rise.
He was therefore obliged to begin a siege in regular
form and leave leisure to Marlborough and Eugene to
concert their measures. By a well-timed surprise they
forced the passage of the Scheldt near Oudenarde, and
Marlborough then marching full on Brussels compelled
the Elector to raise the siege with much precipitation,
and to hurry back to the French frontier. Then Marlborough also retraced his steps to his camp near Lille,
and took part in the capitulation of the citadel, which,
after prodigies of skill and valour on the part of Boufflers,
ensued of necessity on the 9th of December. Sooner
than lose even another day at this late season, they
granted to the Marshal the most advantageous conditions.   He marched forth with all the honors of war
at the head of his faithful soldiers, and was with them
escorted to his countrymen at Douay. Thence proceeding to Versailles he was greeted by the King as his
admirable defence so well deserved, with the warmest
thanks and also with the highest rewards.

It was now almost the middle of December and the
campaign might be thought concluded.   But Marlborough and Eugene were determined to allow themselves or their troops no rest until after Ghent and
Bruges had been recovered. Not an hour was lost in
the requisite movements. Ghent was invested by Marlborough's army on the 18th of the month; and on the

24th the trenches against it were opened under his direction by the Prussian chief Count Lottum. La Mothe who commanded in the place was not able to emulate the example of Boufflers. With no effort beyond a single sally he sent out a trumpet on the 30th to demand an honourable capitulation, which Marlborough granted, to spare his soldiers who were already suffering from the frosts. In writing to Godolphin the Duke could announce a still further and final success. "As soon as the French knew I had possession of the gate of this town, they took the resolution of abandoning Bruges. This campaign is now ended to my own heart's desire; and as the hand of the Almighty is visible in this whole matter, I hope Her Majesty will think it due to Him to return public thanks, and at the same time to implore His blessing on the next campaign."

During this year there was nothing of importance achieved upon the Rhine. The Elector of Hanover, after much procrastination, had taken the command of the army assigned him, but it was only to utter complaints and show his jealousy of Prince Eugene. Thinking his dignity offended he declined to make any offensive movement, although the detachment of so many bodies of French troops to Flanders, and the departure first of Berwick and next of his brother Elector might well have tempted an advance.

It was much the same in Italy. The Duke of Savoy had been joined by the Austrian General, Count Daun, but still confined himself to a war of outposts with Marshal Villars; and his main exploit during the campaign was the reduction of the small fort of Exiles.

In Catalonia the nuptials of the King seemed the

all-absorbing event. Charles had in the spring of this CHAP.
X.
1708. year married by proxy at Vienna a Princess of Brunswick, who changed her religion for the sake of Royalty. In the month of July following the new Queen landed at Madrid, and Charles desiring, as we are told, to see her for the first time incognito was admitted among other gentlemen to kiss her hand. After this he discovered himself to his consort, and then as the annalist assures us "many compliments passed." [5]

Meanwhile the war around him languished. The Court of Vienna had indeed, tardily complying with Marlborough's urgent representations, sent a few thousand additional men to Barcelona. Still however, the Duke of Orleans headed a force far superior to any Staremberg and Stanhope could bring against him, so that these were reduced to a strictly defensive system. They could not hinder the investment and reduction by the Duke of the important town of Tortosa, but they so far obstructed and delayed him that this proved to be his only exploit during the campaign. In the Spanish seas the Allies had better fortune. Admiral Sir John Leake having come to Barcelona with a British squadron, planned with Staremberg and Stanhope an expedition to Sardinia. There was no resistance to be apprehended. The Marquis of Jamaica, who commanded in the island for King Philip, had scarcely even a handful of troops, while the people were disposed to make common cause with their Catalan neighbours. No sooner then had the Admiral appeared off Cagliari and thrown a few bombs into the town, than the inhabitants compelled the Governor to lay down his arms and surrender

---

5 Complete History of Europe, 1708, p. 184 and 247.

at discretion, while the whole island declared in favor of King Charles.

But Stanhope's great object was Minorca. Its harbour Port Mahon was the best in the Mediterranean, and, even in the most stormy winters, would afford secure anchorage to any British fleet. For this reason, its importance in the contest for the Crown of Spain was from the first well understood both by friend and foe. Lord Peterborough had at one time resolved to attempt it, but was withheld by the strong objections of the naval officers. The project though acknowledged to be arduous was now resumed, and earnestly pressed upon Stanhope both by Marlborough in private letters, and by Sunderland in public despatches. There were however great obstacles to overcome. The entrance to Mahon was defended by a fortress of considerable strength named St. Philip's Castle, which Louis had not left to the negligent administration of the Spaniards, but on the contrary had caused to be carefully repaired. He had stationed there a garrison of about 1,100 men, half French and half Spanish; at their head Colonel La Jonquière, a Frenchman and an experienced officer.

Stanhope was further pressed upon this subject by letters from the Lord Treasurer, whose notions of the war in Spain were certainly a little wild: "In my last I was very pressing with you on the importance of getting Toulon, and I still insist that we cannot winter a squadron in the Mediterranean without having Port Maon" (for so he spells it) "or that place. But I look upon being masters of Toulon as being masters of Madrid, for one is the infallible consequence of the other." Stanhope when thus exhorted from home was at the camp of Cervera, but at once taking his resolu- CHAP. X. 1708. tion hastened back to Barcelona to attempt Mahon. It was with great difficulty that he could prevail on Staremberg to spare him about 700 Spaniards and as many Portuguese. It was only by a stratagem that he could induce some of the sea-captains to assist him. Using however great exertions he was able on the 14th of September to effect a landing in Minorca with a battering train of forty-two great guns, and a force of 2,600 men, nearly one-half of whom were English, including the marines from the fleet who served on shore.

Twelve days were required for the toilsome transport, of no more than two miles, but through a most rugged country, before the cannon could be brought to bear, or St. Philip's Castle be invested. The strength of the works was found to be fully equal to their reputation; it was only the spirit of the Governor that had been falsely estimated. On the 28th however, the besiegers' cannon made several breaches in the new line wall; and some of their grenadiers rushing in pell-mell were promptly supported by Brigadier Wade and two battalions; then Stanhope coming up and driving the enemy from the two flank towers pursued his advantage, and made good a lodgment before night on the glacis of the main castle. Next day he disposed his men for another onset, but at the first ball that fell the heart of La Jonquière failed him. Contrary to the advice of several of his officers, he beat a parley and proposed a capitulation, which was concluded the same afternoon. When on the 30th, the English marched into the fortress they found it to contain above a hundred pieces of cannon, three thousand barrels of powder, and all other supplies that La Jonquière could have needed had he resolved to continue his defence.

There were two other walled towns on the opposite coasts of the island, Fornells and Ciudadella, but they were of no strength and immediately surrendered. The entire conquest cost the Allies less than fifty men, among whom was the General's brother, Captain Philip Stanhope, of the Milford, an officer of much promise who was serving on shore with his marines. The French soldiers of the garrison were kept prisoners as hostages for the English and Dutch of about equal number taken in Xativa, and detained by Asfeld, in defiance of their terms of capitulation; but La Jonquière and the other officers were permitted to return to France. La Jonquière had little cause to congratulate himself on this exception. No sooner had he landed at Toulon than he was brought to trial for his misconduct in the siege, found guilty, and not merely dismissed the service but sent to prison.[6]

So strongly impressed was Stanhope with the great importance of Minorca as a station for the British fleet that, on the very day after the capitulation of St. Philip's, when writing his despatch to Sunderland with an account of his conquest, he presumed to "offer it as my humble opinion that England ought never to part with this island, which will give the law to the Mediterranean both in time of war and peace." And thus again on the 9th of November: "Whether we have

---

[6] Mém. de St. Simon, vol. VII. p. 4. The strength of St. Philip's Castle is fully described in Armstrong's History of Minorca, p. 23, ed. 1752, the author himself an engineer.

war or peace I cannot but hope we shall think of pre- serving Port Mahon and indeed the whole island." Sunderland and the other Ministers adhered to Stanhope's counsel, and sent him the authority he asked to negotiate with Charles's Ministers for the eventual cession of the island. He had certainly a strong plea to urge in behalf of such a grant, from the large subsidies which the Court of St. James's had paid and was still paying to the Court of Barcelona. Nevertheless Stanhope was met, as he says, by "an unspeakable reluctancy." It was only after some months of diplomacy, that he succeeded in sending home Mr. Craggs with powers from King Charles to the Austrian Count Gallas to sign a treaty for engaging on certain conditions the island to the Queen. Such were the first steps to its absolute cession at the Peace of Utrecht, and to our sovereign possession of it during the greater part of the eighteenth century. Mahon was not forgotten when, ten years after its conquest, Stanhope was promoted to an Earldom; and we may reckon. it as among the curious vicissitudes of human affairs, that the name first given by a Carthaginian chief Mago, the brother of Hannibal, should now be borne by the eldest son of an English Peer.

Having remained some days in Minorca to settle the government of the island, Stanhope designed to proceed to Denia and secure that fortress from attack. But his way was barred by some French men-of-war which cruised along the coast; and Denia shortly afterwards yielded to the Chevalier d'Asfeld, Captain Carleton being among the prisoners of that little garrison. Asfeld next turned his arms against Alicant and reduced the town with little difficulty; but the castle, which was held by two English regiments, was long and valiantly defended.

Soon after Stanhope's return to Catalonia from his Minorquin enterprise, he was greeted by a singular negotiation. The Duke of Orleans employed two agents, named Flotte and Renault, to make some secret overtures to the English General, with whom during his youth he had been on familiar terms. The object was to inquire whether, as weary of the war, the French might not relinquish their King Philip and the Allies their King Charles, and whether then by way of compromise, the Duke of Orleans might not be accepted by both parties as monarch of Spain. Stanhope at once declared that England would not break faith with her ally nor desert King Charles, but he proceeded with the assent of the Cabinet at home to hold out some hopes to the Duke that, if there were another rising in the Cevennes with the Duke's connivance, the Allies would be inclined to form for him an independent sovereignty, made up of Languedoc and Navarre.

It is by no means clear even yet, after so many secret documents of the period have come to light, how far the first of these overtures was made with the private sanction of Louis. As to the second, if ever the Duke did lend an ear to it, we may fairly conclude that he intended only by prolonging the negotiation to bring back the Allies to the first. But Princess Orsini, who at this time entirely directed Philip and Philip's kingdom through his Queen, obtained some clue to the intrigue and took her measures accordingly. In the winter, after the Duke had returned to France, she caused both his agents to be seized. Their papers

when examined gave at least sufficient grounds for injurious imputations on their master, and vehement
complaints from the Court of Madrid to the Court of
Versailles.   Louis after some hesitation did his best to
vindicate his nephew, but felt that it was impossible to
send him back to Spain.[7]

7 An impartial summary of this involved transaction, as deduced from
different sources, will be found in Sismondi.   (Hist. des Français, vol. xxvii.
p. 67.)

CHAPTER XI.

THE Parliament which had been prorogued on the
1st of April was dissolved on the 15th. In the English
elections which ensued, the influence of the late attempt
on Scotland was strongly felt, and that influence was
almost everywhere to the advantage of the Court. For
even among those who inclined more or less decidedly
to the exiled Prince, by far the greater number at this
time looked to the succession of the Queen and not to
her dethronement. To plunge the kingdom in civil
war for this latter object, and by the aid of a foreign
enemy, was generally viewed as a criminal and unjustifiable enterprise; and its abettors real or supposed
found no favor at the hustings.

But Godolphin as Prime Minister had at this time
other and deep causes of alarm. The dismissal of
Harley with St. John and Mansell in his train had by
no means sufficed to the ambition of the Whigs. They
regarded it as only another step, in the ladder which
they sought to climb. No sooner was it accomplished
than they came forward with a new demand—that the
Presidency of the Council should be bestowed on
Somers. Godolphin himself was willing but the Queen
was much distressed. Besides that she entertained at
that time—however unjustly yet sincerely—an ill-
opinion of Lord Somers from his conduct during the
late reign, she knew that his appointment would give
great pain to her Consort, who regarded Somers as the

real author of the recent attacks upon the Admiralty measures. At first then the Queen evaded the request, declaring that she did not wish to see Lord Pembroke removed. But this plea did not long avail her. Two Whigs already in office, the Dukes of Newcastle and Devonshire, came one day to her without previous notice and again pressed the appointment of Lord Somers. The Queen again alleged the hardship to Lord Pembroke. Then, at least, said the Dukes, let your Majesty call Lord Somers for the present to the Cabinet Council without any post at all. Taken by surprise the Queen replied after some delay that she thought the Cabinet Council was full enough already. The Dukes took their leave in great discontent, and proceeded to terrify Godolphin, who on his part urged new representations on the Royal Lady.

Thus pressed from divers quarters, Anne thought that her prejudices—or as she would say her principles —might claim some regard from the earliest and most constant object of her favor—the Duke of Marlborough. She wrote to His Grace, then just returned from Hanover, to Holland, and gave him an account of what had passed, "looking upon it," she adds, "to be utter destruction to me to bring Lord Somers into my service. And I hope you will not join in soliciting me to do this thing, though Lord Treasurer tells me you will, for it is what I can never consent to. You are very happy to be out of the disagreeable and vexatious things that I am more or less continually made uneasy with, which makes me not wonder at your not coming back as you promised. I pray God bless and direct you in every thing." Marlborough in his answer made it clear that he was firmly linked with Godolphin and

CHAP.
XI.
―――
1708. must press quite as ardently this concession to the Whigs. But still the Queen refused to yield. "So perverse and so obstinate ――――," her Prime Minister writes.

The Whig chiefs, much incensed at the inability of Godolphin which they mistook for unwillingness, planned a bold manœuvre in sign of their resentment. The Election of the sixteen Scottish Peers at Holyrood, the last of all the elections in order of time, was still to come. It might be possible by a sudden COUP DE MAIN to defeat the candidates brought forward by the Court. But for this purpose the Whigs by themselves were not sufficiently strong; they must combine with some leading Tories, nay even Jacobites of Scotland. A fitting instrument for this design appeared in the Duke of Hamilton. He was now, as we have seen, a prisoner in the Tower, as strongly suspected of dealings with the exiled family. Three great Whig noblemen, Newcastle, Halifax, and Wharton, now declared to the Government their conviction of his innocence and their readiness to be his bail; and on their bail accordingly the Government consented to release him. The Duke at once set out for Edinburgh well provided with secret instructions from his new allies. It is not at all to the credit of Sunderland, that although one of the Cabinet Ministers he appears to have been a party to this whole intrigue.

By the time, however, that the Duke of Hamilton arrived in Edinburgh and concerted measures with his friends, another Duke—His Grace of Queensberry, as Secretary of State for Scotland—had obtained some clue to the design, and was able so far to counteract it that it only in part succeeded. Of the candidates favoured by the Whigs and Tories in alliance, no more CHAP. XI. than six were elected; the other ten were supplied from the Court list. 1708.

This party entanglement in Scotland was the more perplexing to the Ministers, since that country then afforded so many other elements of strife. A great ferment had of course prevailed among the people while invasion was in prospect, and it continued long after all idea of invasion passed away. The Government on the suspension of the Habeas Corpus had made numerous arrests. Edinburgh Castle was crowded with prisoners, who were sent off to London in three detachments, each guarded by a body of dragoons. They comprised some of the men of most mark in the country, as for example the Duke of Gordon, the Earls of Errol, Seaforth, and Nithisdale, Cameron of Lochiel, and Stirling of Keir.[1] Nearly all were, it may be said, more than suspected of secret dealings with the Court of St. Germain's.

It was certainly most justifiable in the English Ministers, after their recent and great alarm, to seize these well known adversaries, and seek for proofs to convict them of their treason. But there was one case for which no such defence can be pleaded, the arrest of Lord Belhaven. We have seen how bold and how able was the part which he took against the Scottish Union. He stood forth on that occasion as the uncompromising opponent of the Ministers. But it required such tremulous nerves as Lord Godolphin's to suppose him on that account a plotter against the throne. Neither in this reign nor in the preceding had he ever

[1] The entire list (upwards of forty in all) is given in Tindal's History, vol. IV. p. 554.

swerved from his loyalty to the Sovereign or his zeal for the Hanover Succession. To cast him into prison as though a Jacobite conspirator was a wanton insult to the old adversary of Dundee, the soldier of Killie-crankie; and he felt it deeply. His confinement was not indeed long protracted, since, after two months, being brought up to London he was recognised as innocent and released on bail. But the insult had preyed on his ardent spirit, while his burly frame had suffered from the want of exercise. On the very day of his release he was seized with a brain fever, and in four days more expired. He was but fifty-one years of age.[2]

As regards the other prisoners it was found that no overt act could be brought home to them, and that their confinement must be terminated as soon as the Habeas Corpus Act revived. Under these circumstances, and after some delay, nearly all were admitted to bail. Only Stirling of Keir, Seton of Touch, and a few other gentlemen of Stirlingshire, were put on trial for High Treason. It was shown that they had assembled in arms towards the time of the expected landing; but still their purpose was not manifest, and the Jury returned a verdict of "Not Proven."[3]

Besides these prisoners there were others taken on board the Salisbury, and sent like the rest from Scotland to London. They comprised Lord Griffin, Colonel Francis Wauchope, and two sons of the Earl of Middleton. Lord Griffin had already been attainted by outlawry for High Treason during the last reign; and

---

[2] A good sketch of Lord Belhaven's life and character will be found in the Complete History of Europe, 1708, p. 436-445.
[3] State Trials, vol. xiv. p. 1395.

sentence of death was now in due form passed upon CHAP. XI. him. But it was not thought desirable to inflict that extreme penalty on a man already advanced in years 1708. and of high personal character. He was not expressly pardoned, but he received a respite, which was continued from month to month until he died a natural death in the Tower, about two years afterwards.

This clemency however gave great offence to the Whig chiefs. Incensed as they grew, more and more, at the continued non-acceptance of Somers, they looked on all Ministerial measures with jaundiced eyes. We find Sunderland in a confidential letter at this period inveigh bitterly against what he calls "the villainous management of Scotland, and in particular the pardoning Lord Griffin." And he adds: "These are such proceedings that, if there is not a just spirit shown in Parliament, we had as good give up the game, and submit to my Lord Treasurer and Lord Marlborough's bringing in the Prince of Wales."[4]

The accusation comprised in the last few lines may well astonish the reader who bears in mind the twofold relation in which the accuser stood to the accused. Sunderland was not merely the son-in-law of Marlborough but also his Cabinet colleague. Was there then the least shadow of ground for the suspicions which he had formed? Certainly not, if he intended to imply any design against the reign of Anne. But as regards the state of things after her decease it seems likely, considering the past connection of both Marlborough and Godolphin with the Court of St. Germain's, that they

---

4 Earl of Sunderland to the Duke of Newcastle, Aug. 1708. This document which was first published in the Second Series of Original Letters by Sir Henry Ellis, has been appended as a note to the later editions of Burnet (vol. v. p. 351).

may have regarded the succession of her brother as a chance not wholly unwelcome. There was a singular conversation of Marlborough which took place about a month before this letter, but of which it is scarcely possible that Sunderland can have had any knowledge. Lieutenant General de Biron, subsequently a Marshal of France, was among the prisoners of Oudenarde. On the day after the battle, the Duke with his invariable courtesy to captives invited him to dinner. When thus at table, Marlborough suddenly turned to him and asked him news of the Prince of Wales as serving with Vendome; and added his apologies for giving that Prince no higher title. "We shall' not quarrel upon that" said Biron in great surprise, "for even in our army he is called only the Chevalier de St. George;" and he then proceeded to speak of James in the highest terms of praise. The Duke listened to him very attentively and answered, "You give me great pleasure by telling me so much good of him, for I cannot help feeling a great interest in that young Prince;" and having said so much he began at once to talk of something else. Biron went back to Paris on his parole a few days afterwards and repeated this conversation in confidence to his friend the Duke de St. Simon.[5]

The Whig chiefs with unabated perseverance were still pursuing their favourite object of Somers. Their next step was to threaten the Queen, that if she did not yield upon this point they would, as soon as Parliament met, bring up again the question of inviting to England by an Address some member of the House of Hanover; and to propose this time, not the Dowager

<hr>

5 Mém. de St. Simon, vol. vi. p. 262.

Electress but her grandson the Electoral Prince, who
as young and active would be able to cause Her Majesty much greater uneasiness. Anne was much· distressed. She had a conversation upon this threat with Lord Haversham. "I told him" she says "if this matter should be brought into Parliament, whoever proposed it, whether Whig or Tory, I should look upon neither of them as my friends; nor would ever make any invitation neither to the young man, nor his father nor his grandmother ... it being a thing I cannot bear to have any successor here though but for a week."[6]

But Anne, however harassed, was still firm against Somers. Then at last, other expedients having been tried and failing, the Whig chiefs with sure sagacity discerned the vulnerable point. They intimated that unless the Queen would call their chief to her counsels, they would at the meeting of Parliament not only assail Admiral Churchill but bring a direct charge by name against Prince George for mismanagement of naval affairs. Then indeed the Queen's resolution gave way. Any thing rather, she thought, than that the threat of personal accusation should embitter the last hours of her dying husband. She announced to Godolphin her consent to accept Somers as one of her Ministry, so that the great object of the Whigs at this time was carried through, and complete success attended their well-timed, though certainly most unfeeling, manœuvre.

The concession of the Queen took place towards the 20th of October; and the event which she endeavoured to soothe was not long delayed. The Prince then and for some time past at Kensington was rapidly

---

[6] The Queen to Marlborough, July 22, 1708.

sinking. On the 28th of the same month he expired. "Nature" so writes Godolphin "was quite worn out in him and no art could support him long." The Duchess of Marlborough as Mistress of the Robes was present at his death, and supported her Royal Mistress during her first burst of anguish and removal to St. James's. The Queen's heart was softened towards her former favourite, whom we find that she once more addressed in her notes as her "dear Mrs. Freeman." But the reconciliation did not endure.

The death of the Prince however cleared the way for the time in public affairs. No further objection was offered by the sorrowing Queen. Admiral Churchill fell of course with his chief and patron. Lord Pembroke was transferred to the Admiralty, while two of the Whig Junto, Somers and Wharton, were appointed the one President of the Council and the other Lord Lieutenant of Ireland. The place of Attorney-General so long vacant was filled by Sir James Montague as Godolphin had proposed.

Parliament met on the 16th of November, and was in the Queen's absence opened by Commission. A gentleman of high character and moderate Whig principles, Sir Richard Onslow, was chosen Speaker on the recommendation of the Government, instead of Mr. Bromley as the Queen had wished. The ascendency of the Whigs at this time was undisputed; and little was done during the short remainder of this Session beyond the passing of loyal Addresses and the requisite Supplies. There was however a motion from one member of the Opposition, namely Sir Thomas Hanmer, of a vote of thanks to General Webb for his victory at Wynendale. The motion was carried unanimously

and was well deserved by that gallant chief, but it was CHAP.
also designed as a side-blow against Marlborough, who XI.
had inadvertently given the chief praise to Cadogan, 1708.
in the hurry of his first despatches.

The Christmas holidays having passed there was 1709.
further an attempt in both Houses—which in both
proved abortive—to arraign the Government for connivance in the lately intended invasion. Lord Haversham made on this occasion, what his contemporaries
call, his "annual speech"—most amply reported by
himself. In one passage he was understood to reflect
on the Lord Treasurer with especial bitterness. "Remember" he said "that he among the Apostles who
bore the bag proved the traitor!"

In the same month there was also an expression
of Parliament, which in those days was looked upon
as most loyal and becoming, but which at present
would certainly be deemed an unjustifiable intrusion
upon private sorrows. On the 28th of January, exactly
three months from the death of the Prince, the two
Houses sent up a joint Address to the Queen, praying
"that she would not suffer her just grief so far to
prevail, but would have such indulgence to the hearty
desires of her subjects as to entertain thoughts of a
second marriage." The Queen in her reply observed,
that the frequent marks of duty and affection from her
Parliament must needs be very acceptable to her. She
said that the provision she had made for the Protestant Succession would always be a proof how much
she had at heart the future happiness of the kingdom.
And Her Majesty added: "The subject of this Address
is of such a nature that I am persuaded you do not
expect a particular answer."

7*

It had been rashly supposed that the Whig chiefs would be satisfied with the large concessions which they had obtained on the Prince's demise. But this did not prove to be the case. They seemed as on former occasions to regard the grant of a favor as only a step to the enforcement of another. Of the members of their famous Junto three, namely Sunderland, Somers, and Wharton, were now placed in some of the highest offices of state. But there remained Halifax and Orford. Immediately then after the Christmas holidays, Halifax put forth in haughty terms his claim to be joint Plenipotentiary at the Congress expected to be held for the negotiation of peace. When told by Godolphin that this appointment was already promised to Lord Townshend he uttered the most violent invectives, levelled especially at the Marlboroughs—both Duchess and Duke.

In like manner the Whig chiefs now insisted that Lord Orford should be placed at the head of the Admiralty. The Queen, who had by this time resumed her attention to business, felt a strong repugnance to his character—not more strong however than impartial historians have expressed. Thus Mr. Hallam, when referring to Lord Orford in his earlier course as Admiral Russell, denounces what he terms "his infamous neglect of duty and contemptible excuses." And Mr. Hallam adds, I think very truly: "It is one thing to prefer the Whig principle; another to justify as an advocate the party which bore that name."[7]

Thus during the remainder of this Session—it did not close till the 21st of April—both the Treasurer and General were grievously harassed. "I must give

7 Constitutional History, vol. III. p. 126 and 202, ed. 1855.

myself the vent of saying"—so writes the former to the latter—"that the life of a slave in the galleys is Paradise in comparison with mine." There was one transaction, or rather chain of transactions, which especially disquieted Godolphin. They are related in the Parliamentary History with very little clearness, and as if only on vague hearsay; but I can here supply a secret narrative as given in confidence by an actor in the scene. For thus did the elder Horace Walpole write to General Stanhope then in Spain:

"This Session of Parliament had like to have been happily determined without any difference between Court or country, or new improvements in Government; but at last something fell out to exercise the spirits and inclinations of all sides. The Lords, in considering how to improve the Union of the two Kingdoms, passed a Bill for making the laws in cases of Treason the same throughout the United Kingdom, which was strenuously opposed by the whole body of the Northern Peers, notwithstanding they themselves by the Articles of Union, at their own desire, are to be tried by their Peers, and according to the Laws of England. The North Britons, in the Lower House, were as violently and unanimously determined to be against any such Act, and their pretence was that their laws in treasonable cases are more for the security of the subject than those of England; as giving more time to the prisoner to be informed of the witnesses that are to swear against him, and upon conviction not making their entailed estates liable to forfeiture, because a tenant in tail there cannot, by any fiction in law, cut off the entail as he can here by a common recovery. But the darkness of their laws in cases of treason, their manner of proceeding in trials, and the power of the Ministry in Scotland in almost all cases where the law is concerned, were thought by some here greater inconveniences to the subject than the aforesaid objections. When the Bill came to the Commons the Tories had no consideration but to oblige so great a body as the Scotch. The old Whigs, either for the same reason, or in hopes of getting a Clause added to take away their forfeitures in treason in case the Bill should proceed, joined with the North Britons, first in opposing the Bill, and then upon the commitment got a sufficient party to add such a Clause; which the Court opposed; but it was carried, and the Bill passed with it in the House. The Scotch were here mightily deceived, for they were so complaisant to their friends, the Whigs, as to vote for passing the Bill, thinking it would certainly with the clause of taking away the forfeitures be rejected by the Lords, and so their friendship preserved in one House, and their aim of keeping up a distinct government in their own kingdom, and by that measure making themselves of greater weight to every party on occasion, would be obtained in the other. But when the Bill with the Amendment, that no estates should be forfeited upon conviction of treason, nor the crime of the father visited upon the son, was returned to the Lords, they prudently, rather than lose an Act of such consequence to the United Government, let the Clause stand, with this Amendment, that it should not be in force till after the Pretender's death. Yesterday this Amendment was considered by the Commons, and agreed to by a majority of five votes; upon which the North Britons left the House, in a body, very much enraged; and

the Commons proceeded in the Bill, and added an- CHAP.
other Amendment to the Lords', that the forfeiting XI.
Clause should not take place till after three years after 1709.
the death of Her present Majesty, to which I hear just
now that the Lords have agreed, so that the laws in
cases of treason will be in the united nation the same
as they are in England."[8]

It was greatly feared, on the passing of this Bill,
that by the aid of its provisions divers acts of vengeful
retrospect, of severity and persecution, might be set
on foot. Under these apprehensions the Ministers
found themselves enabled, ere the Session closed, to
propose and carry through an Act of Grace and Free
Pardon, which the Queen sent down, and which the
two Houses confirmed. It was the first in this reign
and the fullest since the Revolution. The Royal for-
giveness was now granted to all treasons committed
before the passing of the Act, excepting those only
done on the high seas; by which limitation it was
intended to shut out those who in the previous year
had embarked with the Pretender.

This beneficent Act had a much larger scope than
at the time was fully apprehended. It ensured the
safety and it allayed the fears of very many who within
the last twenty years had held correspondence with the
Court of St. Germain's. No stronger proof can be
given of its wide-spread influence than that the two
chief men in the Queen's service—Marlborough and
Godolphin—were in truth affected by it. Both had
formerly bound themselves by secret engagements to

[8] Letter dated Whitehall, April 19, 1709 (MS.). The proviso that the
Clauses as to forfeiture should not take effect until after the Pretender's death
was moved by Lord Somers. (Parl. Hist. vol. VI. p. 797.)

the exiled King; both had made themselves liable on detection to all the penalties of High Treason until within the shelter of this Act of Grace which was framed and carried by themselves.

Marlborough had remained upon the Continent long after the close of the campaign and beyond the commencement of the year. His great object was to watch the progress of the French overtures for peace. Louis had grown more and more eager to conclude, even at the cost of low submissions and heavy sacrifices, a to him disastrous war. He had seen General after General defeated, fortress after fortress reduced. He had seen Desmarets, whom he had lately in the room of Chamillart placed at the head of his ruinous finances, wholly unable to retrieve them, or to wring fresh imposts from the overburthened people. But great as the public distresses were already they rose during this winter to the direst pitch of suffering. On the 5th of January there commenced, and there continued during many weeks, a frost of such intensity as had no parallel in France. Not only were the rivers congealed, but ice in some places formed on the sea along the shores—ice so thick as to bear a waggon's weight.[9] The fruit-trees throughout the kingdom—the apple-trees of Normandy no less than the olive-trees of Provence—withered away and died. Blight fell on Anjou with its rich corn-lands, and on Gascony

---

9 Mém. de St. Simon, vol. VII. p. 100. Though with less severity the same frost extended to England as is commemorated by Swift in his Prophecy of Merlin for this year.

> "Tamys rivere twys y-frozen,
> Walke sans wetyng shoes ne hozen,"

(Swift's Works, vol. XIV. p. 92.)

with its budding vines. The hope of the harvest was
gone, and famine stared the people in the face.

In a streight so grievous the King, deeply touched
with compassion for his suffering subjects, felt that he
should do everything, and bear everything, to obtain a
peace. He renewed his overtures at the Hague in a
private form, first through Mesnager, a deputy of the
merchants at Rouen, and a man well skilled in business,
and next through Pettekum, the Minister in Holland of
the Duke of Holstein. It was found impossible to draw
the Dutch into any separate negotiation; a peace, if
made at all, must be made with the whole of the Allies.
Pensionary Heinsius moreover declared that it was
useless to discuss the question any further, unless the
French, at the very outset and previous to other
demands that would be made on them, were prepared
to offer Spain and the Indies, with the Milanese and
the Netherlands; a Barrier of strong towns to the
Dutch; and a treaty of commerce in their favor.

Hard as these conditions were deemed at Versailles,
as not even preliminaries but only the foundation of
preliminaries, M. de Torcy was instructed to allow
them. To carry on the negotiation by directly accre-
dited agents he requested that passports should be sent
from the Hague for two Ministers on the part of
France; the one to be a French subject, the other
Bergheyck, late Intendant for Spain in the Low
Countries. A passport was sent to the Frenchman,
but refused to the Spaniard. Louis, suppressing all
resentment at this slight, made choice for his sole negotiator of Rouillé, a President of the Parliament of Paris,
who had shown much ability and address in former
diplomatic missions. He was instructed to stipulate

the best terms he could, especially if possible the kingdoms of Naples and Sicily as a compensation to Philip of Spain, but above all to obtain a suspension of hostilities, so as to avert from France the only too probable disasters of the next campaign.

With no further delay Rouillé set out for Holland. There he was received with great coldness and exposed to many mortifications. He was not permitted to come to the Hague, but ordered to confine himself first to Moerdyke and afterwards to Worden; and to hold no communication except with the two Deputies assigned him, Buys and Vanderdussen.

Marlborough, on the other hand, had repaired to London in the first days of March to concert measures with his colleagues. It was felt strongly, and above all by the Whig members of the Cabinet, that the recent attempt at invasion rendered necessary three new claims upon France. In any treaty of peace that was concluded Louis must own the Queen's title and the Protestant Succession. He must further engage to send the Pretender out of the French dominions, and to demolish the fortifications and the harbour of Dunkirk. The two former propositions, in the shape of an Address to the Queen, were moved by Somers in the House of Lords, and passed Nem. Con. Being sent to the Commons for their concurrence the third point as to Dunkirk was added, on the motion of Mr. Secretary Boyle. The Lords agreed, and the three points went up to Her Majesty as the unanimous recommendation of both the Houses. Few things could be conceived more galling to the pride of Louis, once so uncontrolled, as the injunction to banish from France a Prince whom he had so long cherished and protected,

and to destroy with his own hands the works con-
structed by him on the coast of his own dominions.

With these instructions however did Marlborough return to the Hague, and was joined by Lord Townshend as the second plenipotentiary on the part of England. On the same errand came Prince Eugene and Count Sinzendorf from Vienna. A crowd of Envoys from the smaller Princes followed in their train, each armed with some new pretension, each hungry for some fragment of France.

Thus at each succeeding conference, President Rouillé found to his despair the demands upon his master step by step enlarged. Besides the terms which Pensionary Heinsius had already framed, Louis was required to cede a line of ten fortresses on the Flemish frontier as a Barrier to the Dutch, comprising not only places which he had lost such as Lille, but others such as Tournay which he still possessed. He was to relinquish some of his most highly prized possessions held by him before the commencement of the war, Strasburg with its province of Alsace, and Luxemburg with its Duchy, while at the same time nothing was clearly promised in return; neither as yet a suspension of hostilities, nor any portion of Italy for King Philip on his resigning Spain. The negotiation was suspended until Rouillé could refer the subject to his Court. On the 28th of April his last despatches were read at a Council which was held at Versailles, the King himself presiding; with him the Dauphin and the Duke of Burgundy and five Ministers of State. Hard, most hard, as these terms appeared to them, the Duke of Beauvilliers supported by the Chancellor Pontchartrain, and even it is said by the Duke of Burgundy, urged their acceptance from the absolute necessity of peace. Others though more silent were not less convinced. Then M. de Torcy, as Secretary for Foreign Affairs, offered to go himself to Holland, with the passport of a common courier, the only ones that the Dutch had sent. He undertook to struggle where there was any prospect of success; where there was none to yield; to carry concession to its furthest limits, and to sign a peace with the least possible delay.

Setting off accordingly as in disguise with his courier's pass, the Minister reached the Hague on the evening of the 6th of May and drove straight to the house of Heinsius, who was greatly surprised at the appearance of this eminent and very far from expected visitor.[1] Both Marlborough and Eugene had availed themselves of the recent lull in diplomacy to leave the Hague, and had gone, the one to his colleagues in England, the other to the army in Flanders; but on their return a few days afterwards the conferences were resumed, and Torcy was permitted to summon Rouillé to his aid.

Heinsius appeared to Torcy a cold and resolute man, plain in his habits and unostentatious in his temper. Although the first man in his Republic, his household, as Torcy noticed, consisted only of a Secretary and a coachman, a single lackey and a single maid-servant. By no motive of personal interest could he be swayed. But of Marlborough the Frenchman had better hopes. It was resolved at Versailles, that when alone with the Duke Torcy should venture to offer him what we English coarsely call a bribe but the French with far greater elegance of language a DOUCEUR.

[1] Mémoires de Torcy, vol. i. p. 232, ed. 1757.

Torcy was instructed to engage the word of his Royal CHAP.
Master that Louis would transmit to Marlborough a — XI.
present of two millions of livres, if through his in- 1709.
fluence Naples and Sicily, or even Naples alone, could
be reserved for Philip, or if France could be spared
either the cession of Strasburg or the demolition of
Dunkirk. The present was to be increased even to
four millions if Marlborough should be able to obtain
all these objects together.

It is painful to think that such offers were actually
made. But we may rejoice that the Great Duke met
them exactly as his warmest admirers could have
wished. Torcy informed the King that whenever, in
their private interviews, he reverted to these points of
personal emolument he saw Marlborough redden and
without reply change the conversation. On the public questions however the Duke spoke frankly and
strongly. He declared that he was most desirous to
see a peace concluded, since his sole remaining thought
was to live quietly at home and look only to the
manifest hand of God in explaining the wonderful success of the Allies. "You also" he continued "ought
to desire peace for France. You should make it as
soon as you can. But if you really wish it, be assured
that you must yield to us every single portion of the
Spanish monarchy. On that point my countrymen are
unanimous. Never will the English people allow that
Naples and Sicily, or even one of those two kingdoms,
should remain in the hands of a Bourbon Prince.
Never will any English Minister dare to entertain such
a scheme."[2]

It was supposed by the French negotiator, to whom

* Mém. de Torcy, vol. 11. p. 62 and 79.

the demands relative to Dunkirk and to the Pretender had been already explained by Heinsius, that Marlborough had nothing further to ask on the part of England. The case proved otherwise. The Duke informed him that he had positive orders from his Royal Mistress to insist on the restitution of Newfoundland. "That is a point" he added "which Lord Townshend who is come with me as my colleague will more particularly urge," and as to all these points Marlborough pressed with much earnestness that the French should yield.

Several times during these discussions did the Duke express his great respect, nay almost attachment, to Louis the Fourteenth; always remembering he said that it was in the French service and under M. de Turenne that he had learnt the Art of War. Torcy hoping still further to engage him let fall an intimation that he knew all the circumstances of the Duke's secret correspondence with King James in exile and subsequently with the Duke of Berwick. The face of Marlborough flushed but he made no reply. Yet in other parts of the same and the next ensuing conversations he adverted to the young Chevalier in terms of warm regard. "I much wish" he said "to serve the Prince of Wales. He is son of a King for whom I would have given my blood and my life. And I think that it will be for the Prince's real interest if he now leaves France, which my instructions have directed me to urge as a condition of the peace."

"But where is he to go?" Torcy asked. "Any where he pleases," Marlborough answered. "He may fix his residence in any other country and enjoy full security and freedom." "And how subsist" continued

Torcy "when removed from the King my master's bounty? Could not the English Government in such a case undertake to pay the dowry which it owes to the Queen his mother?"

In reply to these last questions Marlborough pointed out that any payment to the Exiled Queen would encounter great obstacles from the state of the law in England. But he advised Torcy to insist strongly on this point whenever the Duke with Townshend as his colleague came to hold their joint conference with him. "In Lord Townshend" continued Marlborough "I have now a kind of SURVEILLANT or watcher over me. But he is a very honest man, named to this office by my own selection. He belongs to the party of the Whigs, and in his presence I am obliged to speak like an obstinate Englishman; but I wish with all my heart to serve the Prince of Wales; and I shall be very glad if your 'instances' with him shall afford me the present means to do so." — Torcy adds that in these declarations the Duke spoke with great emphasis and earnestness, several times calling God to witness for the sincerity of his words.[3]

In the further negotiations which ensued', Torcy was greatly guided by the wise counsel which he had received from Marlborough. He went to the furthest limits of his powers to obtain a peace. He was willing to admit the several demands of England. He was willing to give up ten fortresses in Flanders as a Barrier to the Dutch. He was willing to yield Luxemburg, Strasburg, and Brisach to the Empire, and

[3] Despatch of Torcy to Louis XIV., May 22, 1709, and his Memoirs, vol. ii. p. 68 and 89. All this is much softened down in Coxe's Marlborough, vol. iv. p. 395.

moreover (subject to further instructions) Exiles and Fenestrelles to the Duke of Savoy. Above all he consented to relinquish the whole of the vast inheritance of Spain. But this last concession however indispensable gave rise to a difficulty of another kind. The Duke of Anjou, as the Allies continued to call him, was King Philip in nine-tenths of Spain. He seemed to have taken firm root in Castille. He was at this time relying almost wholly on his own subjects and his own resources, since his French auxiliaries were now under notice of withdrawal and left only for a limited time. What authority then had Louis to promise, or what power to enforce, the resignation of his grandson?

Already in announcing the withdrawal of the French auxiliaries from Spain, Louis had authorised his ambassador at the Court of Madrid to make known to Philip that the exigency of his own affairs might compel him, in any treaty of peace, to cancel his first recognition and forswear his further aid. It was desired in this manner to prepare his mind for his voluntary retirement from Spain. But the answer of the young Monarch addressed to Louis himself was most lofty and uncompromising in its tone. "God" he said "has placed the Crown of Spain on my head; and I will maintain it so long as a drop of blood flows in my veins."[4]

It did seem to Louis however that so long as Philip had the prospect to continue King though of a much smaller kingdom he might be expected to resign. If France made peace he could scarcely hope single-handed to maintain himself against the united efforts of

---

[4] This letter, which bears date April 17, 1709, is printed in the Mémoires de Noailles, vol. IV. p. 45, ed. 1777.

the High Allies. The certainty even of Sicily would be preferable to so slight a chance of Spain. But if no compensation at all were held out to him as the price of his compliance what motive had he to comply? What more could he lose by resisting and wherefore not resist?

On these grounds it was earnestly impressed by Torcy upon the other negotiators, that, since they insisted on obtaining the entire succession of the Spanish monarchy, Louis could not undertake to answer for his grandson. He could only promise to withhold every succour of men and money, and leave Philip to his fate. But here the chiefs of the Allies suspected some design of deception, as though the object were only to amuse them and gain time. The ill faith of Louis had been experienced on former occasions in the course of his long reign; and certainly if a Prince has broken his plighted engagements his enemies may be forgiven for mistrusting his solemn asseverations. Perhaps however they did not sufficiently discriminate the cases. In this case the depression of France was a pledge for the sincerity of Louis.

The party of war however was just then in the ascendant at the Hague, or to speak more accurately the party of peace on the hardest terms; and Marlborough was in like manner overruled by his instructions from England. On the 27th of May Pensionary Heinsius in the name of the Allies presented to Torcy their project of Preliminaries in forty articles. These comprised all the concessions on the part of France which have already been enumerated and a few besides, to England, to Holland, to the Emperor, and to the Duke of Savoy, but they did not give to France a treaty

CHAP.
XI.
1709.

of peace in return.   They provided only for a suspension of arms during two months commencing on the 1st of June.   Within those two months, the Duke of Anjou was to relinquish Spain and retire into France with his principal adherents, and if he failed to do so, Louis was to enter into concert with the Allies for his compulsion; that is, in other words, join the league against his grandson.   During these two months Louis was to place in the hands of the Allies some of the most important fortresses which he still possessed, as Mons and Namur, Luxemburg and Strasburg, and to raze the works at Dunkirk.   In the Congress intended to be held meanwhile at the Hague, the smaller Princes of the confederacy might put forward their pretensions, and if a peace were not agreed upon within two months, the hostilities might recommence.

On seeing these Preliminary Articles, Torcy declared to Heinsius that he had no sufficient powers to sign them, and that, as he believed, they would not be accepted by his master.   He undertook however to convey them with all despatch for the King's decision, leaving meanwhile Rouillé at the Hague.

With these Articles accordingly did Torcy re-appear at Versailles, and a Council was forthwith summoned to decide the momentous question which he brought. There, on the 2nd of June, appeared the majestic presence of Louis;   there were his son and his grandson; there was his nephew of Orleans;   there was every Minister of State.   All with one voice declared the treaty inadmissible.   It was not so much the vast amount of the concessions which deterred them.   For these they were in great measure prepared, by what they knew of the distresses of France and the claims of the Allies. But it was felt that these concessions gave them in fact no peace and only a truce of two months, when France, after having surrendered some of her best fortresses and demolished her works at Dunkirk, might have to recommence the contest at still greater disadvantage. Louis was moreover deeply pained by the Article which, in the event of Philip's non-compliance, might require him to join the Allies. "If I must wage war" he said "I would rather wage it against my enemies than against my children."

The decision of his Counsellors concurring with his own, the King on the same day addressed a letter to President Rouillé, commanding him to return to France. First however, he was to signify to Heinsius that His Majesty rejected the Preliminaries and declared null the offers he had made. At the same time by the advice of Torcy, and for the first time during his reign of fifty years, Louis made an appeal to his people. He issued a Circular to the Governors of the Provinces designed to be made public, and explaining the great sacrifices which he had been willing to make for peace, while only a short truce was tendered in return, and calling on his faithful subjects to support him in the prosecution of now a necessary war. The result of this appeal was such as to exceed his highest hopes. It roused from deep depression the martial spirit of the French. Famine-struck and wasted as they were and cast down by a long succession of disasters, the call upon their pride of country was to them like the sound of the trumpet to the steed. They felt that their Sovereign had gone to the furthest lengths to give them peace, and they girded themselves up to renew the contest, even though with a bankrupt Treasury and with starving armies.

To set an example of the sacrifices which the time required, the King sent his plate, gold and silver, to the Mint, and the same course was adopted by nearly all the great Lords of his Court. There was another measure by which Louis sought to gratify his people. Rightly or wrongly they with one voice imputed great part of their reverses in the field to the fault of Chamillart. He had already some months since been permitted at his own request to resign one of the two great offices which he held as Minister of the Finances. Now he was dismissed from the other, or the War department, his place being supplied by Voisin, formerly Intendant at Maubeuge.

The demands of the Allies in these negotiations do not, when fairly reviewed, seem liable to the charge of injustice which the French historians have alleged. [5] There was no injustice after such victories as those of Blenheim and Ramillies in demanding that France should relinquish whatever she had gained since the Peace of Westphalia in 1648—and it was to that limit that the claim for cessions was confined. But if not of injustice the Allies may be accused of impolicy. By taking a stand on their extreme right and urging conditions so harsh, they kindled as we have seen in France a flame of resentment and resistance, and supplied to their enemy a new weapon for the war.

During these negotiations the political foes of Marlborough both in Holland and in England renewed the malicious charge against him, that he endeavoured to

---

5 "Les conditions aussi injustes qu'humiliantes," says, for example, Sismondi. (Hist. des Français, vol. XXVII. p. 80.)

prolong the war for the sake of his own emoluments. But the facts were directly otherwise. The secret letters of Marlborough to Godolphin and the Duchess, and not merely his conversations with Torcy, make it manifest that he was striving for peace—that he was hopeful of it—that he was fettered far more than he wished to be by the stringency of his instructions from home. Above all the pretensions of the Dutch as to their Barrier seemed to him exorbitant. So strongly did he feel this that when, on the failure of the negotiations with France, the Dutch desired a Treaty of guarantee with England for their eventual claims in that respect Marlborough peremptorily refused to sign it, and it was signed by his colleague only. The superior sagacity of the Great Duke was proved by the event, when in less than three years, the Tories being then in the ascendant, that colleague Lord Townshend was for his share in the obnoxious Treaty censured by the House of Commons in the severest terms.

The hopes of peace having vanished hostilities were now to recommence. Marlborough and Eugene put themselves at the head of the army in Flanders amounting to 110,000 men. To oppose them Louis sent Marshal Villars, the only French chief who during this war had been constantly fortunate. The troops that he found were not only inferior in numbers to those of the Allies, but half clothed, half armed, half fed. "Only imagine" says the Marshal in one of his letters "the horror to see an army in want of bread. To-day it was not delivered till the evening and late in the evening too. Yesterday, that I might supply the brigades which had to march, I was obliged to impose a fast on the brigades which stood still." Under these circumstances Villars could only remain on the defensive. He entrenched himself to the best advantage on the plains of Lens. Marlborough and Eugene came to reconnoitre his position but deemed it too strong to be assailed, and changing their plans they suddenly invested Tournay. Trenches were opened on the night of July the 7th. The town was strongly fortified and held a garrison of several thousand men, but it was ill defended and yielded by capitulation so early as the 29th, the French retiring to the citadel which they continued to maintain.

During this time the troops of Villars had received some considerable reinforcements, and were animated by the rising zeal among their countrymen which the Circular of Louis produced. Nor was it a slight advantage to be joined by Marshal Boufflers. He was greatly the senior of Villars in military rank, but from a most noble spirit well worthy the defender of Lille, and feeling how much might depend upon a single life, he had offered to the King to go, and he had come to serve as second in command. There came also, as a volunteer, the Chevalier de St. George.

It was hoped by Marshal Villars that he might find some opportunity to relieve the citadel of Tournay, but he was constantly baffled by the vigilance of Marlborough and Eugene. The citadel surrendered on the 3rd of September, and the Allies then prepared for the investment of Mons. That important city, the capital of Hainault, was ill supplied both with troops and stores; and Villars felt that he must make an effort to prevent if possible the siege. He broke up from the plains of Lens and reached the heath and hamlet of Malplaquet. There after some preliminary movements he took post at a "Trouée," or cleared space, between the wood of Lanière and that of Taisnières with its prolongation, the wood of Sars. The Allied chiefs on the other hand beheld his advance with joy, as trusting to bring him to a battle. Both armies cannonaded each other during great part of the 10th of September, and the Allies were meanwhile rejoined by the troops which they had left at Tournay. In the evening and night which ensued, Villars threw up some intrenchments and abbatis of trees, hoping in this position both to secure himself and to cover Mons.

Marlborough and Eugene however had resolved to attack him on the morrow. At three o'clock in the morning of that morrow, the 11th of September, Divine Service was solemnly performed in their camp, and the divisions then moved in silence to their appointed posts. But their assault was delayed not only until the sun had risen, but until the morning mists had cleared away. Eugene commanded their right having Villars opposed to him; Marlborough the left and centre confronted by Boufflers. According to the most careful computation the two armies were very nearly equal in numbers; each more than 90,000 strong. And as equal in numbers so they were alike in spirit. The French were disposed to forget their late reverses and rely on their new commander. As he mounted his horse at seven in the morning he was greeted with shouts along the line: "Vive le Roi! Vive le Maréchal de Villars!" Many of the men, ill supplied with food as they had recently been, threw aside their rations of bread in their eagerness to begin the engagement. Among the Allies, on the other hand, the soldiers were told how on this very day, the 11th of

September twelve years before, Prince Eugene had signally defeated the Turks in the plains of Hungary. They looked with some disdain at the field-works and intrenchments of their foes, which might remind them of a siege rather than a battle, and they were heard to mutter, "So we have still to make war upon moles!"

The onset of the Allies was begun by two columns of Marlborough's division; the one under the Prince of Orange; the other under Count Lottum. There ensued a fierce conflict, which raged especially in the centre beyond the little wood of Tiry. Ere long the engagement became general. There were strenuous exertions on both sides, and the slaughter of the assailants was terrible. The troops of Eugene advanced till close upon the French intrenchments, where they were received by so murderous a fire of small arms that they recoiled in disorder, but they were rallied by Eugene himself who took post in the very front of the line. On the centre of the Allies, in like manner, Count Lottum's column was thrust back, though bravely supported by Lord Orkney with fifteen battalions. Then to recover the ground Marlborough in person charged at the head of d'Auvergne's cavalry three thousand strong.

To the left, the column of the Prince of Orange though a little later was fully as gallant in its onset. It comprised troops of various nations, but nearly all in the pay of the Republic, the Dutch themselves being led by Spaar and Oxenstiern. Heading this column was the Scottish brigade under the direction of Major-General Hamilton; it consisted in great part of Athol Highlanders commanded by Lord Tullibardine, eldest son of their chief. As they advanced a terrible shower both of musketry and grape-shot was poured upon them, and whole ranks were swept away. Oxenstiern fell dead by the side of the Prince of Orange, and His Highness's horse was shot under him, but the Prince with the spirit of his race still pressed forward on foot. At length by a steady rush the intrenchments on this point were carried, both the first and second line, but they could not be maintained. The Prince had no reserve to bring up, and Boufflers with some fresh troops charged fiercely on his front, while a battery with grape-shot opened in flank. Tullibardine was slain upon the redoubt which he had so gallantly won, and Hamilton was borne away wounded. The slaughter of the Allies did not cease as they wavered and fell back, and the veteran Spaar also was left dead upon the field.

Meanwhile upon the right, Marshal Villars, having drawn from his centre the Irish brigade and that of Brittany, sallied from his works and fell with fury upon the English and Prussians at the wood of Taisnières. But by this movement the French in the centre were weakened, and besides being hotly pressed by Marlborough, were thrown into confusion by the fall of their immediate commander General Steckemberg. Thus in spite of their resolute resistance, Marlborough was enabled to carry the intrenchments on that side, and began to pour his men through the opening into the open plain beyond where the French cavalry was ranged.

Prince Eugene on his part was rallying his men and leading them to another charge when one of the enemy's musket-balls struck him behind the ear. The officers in his train entreated him to retire that his wound might be dressed, but he answered calmly: "If I survive it will be time enough this evening," and he remained in the front ranks. Far more severe was the wound of Marshal Villars. As he was directing a charge with the bayonet on the advancing troops of Eugene, he was struck by a musket-ball above the knee. Like Eugene's his high spirit at first sustained him, and he called for a chair that he might continue on the field, but fainting from the anguish of the wound he was borne away senseless to Le Quesnoy.

Marshal Boufflers, on whom the chief command devolved, made the most strenuous exertions to retrieve the fortune of the day. But his position, as already pierced through in the centre, was in truth untenable, and some desperate charges headed by himself proved in vain. Ere long loud shouts, which burst forth to the left of the Allies, announced that in this quarter also the French works were finally carried. It only remained for Boufflers to make a retreat in good order, and this he accomplished falling back upon Bavay. His soldiers left the field not scattered nor singly nor as men defeated, but in serried ranks and compact masses as men ready at any moment if need were to renew the conflict. In the whole action which had lasted seven hours they had lost less than 500 prisoners and very few pieces of cannon. Of standards and colours they had taken full as many from the Allies as the Allies had taken from them. As to the slain it will presently be shown that they had inflicted a loss far more heavy than they had sustained. On the whole then, after so many and such great reverses in their campaigns against Marlborough and Eugene, a defeat so well contested by themselves and so dearly bought

by their opponents seemed to them almost an equivalent of victory. Thus Marshal Villars in one of his
reports to his King, dated a few days afterwards,
thought himself justified in saying: "If God in his
goodness should vouchsafe to us to lose such another
battle your Majesty may consider your enemies an-
nihilated!"[6]

With respect to the numbers we cannot indeed assent to the exaggerations of Villars, whose undoubted
gallantry was only too often dashed with gasconade.
He goes the length of declaring that the Allies had lost
30,000 men and his own army only 6,000. The most
careful computations derived from different sources
make out that the French loss was not less than
12,000, while that of the Allies exceeded 20,000. Such
as it was however the disproportion afforded an argument to those politicians in England who desired to
prove how much of nerve and vigour the French armies
still retained. As Bolingbroke wrote: "A deluge of
blood was spilt to dislodge them, for we did no more,
at Malplaquet."[7]

If we trace the mind of Marlborough during these
events as revealed in his most secret correspondence,
we shall find a strange amalgam of the petty and
heroic—the most insignificant vexations commingled
with the highest public cares. The Duchess had written
to him lately in her usual strain of imperious violence,
reproaching him bitterly because he had not, as she
demanded, reproached the Queen. The passion of his
wife struck with tremor that great chief whom no peril

---

[6] Lettre au Roi du 14 Septembre 1709. Mémoires militaires de la Succession d'Espagne, vol. IX. p. 377.

[7] Letters on History from Chanteloup, 1735. Letter VIII. For the computation of the numbers see especially Coxe's Marlborough, vol. v. p. 64.

in the field could discompose. He answered her on the day before the battle with expressions such as these: "I can take pleasure in nothing so long as you continue uneasy and think me unkind. I do assure you, upon my honor and salvation, that the only reason why I did not write was, that I am very sure it would have had no other effect than that of being shown to Mrs. Masham. . . . In the meantime I cannot hinder saying to you that though the fate of Europe if these armies engage may depend upon the good or bad success, yet your uneasiness gives me much greater trouble."

The battle being fought and over, Marlborough added a postscript as follows the same evening: "I am so tired that I have but strength enough to tell you that we have had this day a very bloody battle; the first part of the day we beat their foot and afterwards their horse. God Almighty be praised it is now in our power to have what peace we please, and I may be pretty well assured of never being in another battle, but that, nor nothing in the world, can make me happy if you are not kind."

But Marlborough was not content with compliments like these; he offered also an unconditional surrender. He wrote to his consort a few days afterwards undertaking to do what he had hitherto declined—namely despatch a letter to the Queen of the purport that the Duchess had asked. Nay more, lest Her Grace should consider him lukewarm in his language, he sent her a draft of his intended letter, that she and Godolphin might correct it as they pleased, and that he might afterwards transcribe and send it—which they and he did accordingly.

It is more pleasing to contemplate another feature by which the character of Marlborough was at all times most highly distinguished—his tender care of the wounded. As he rode over the field of Malplaquet next morning he surveyed with deep emotion the numbers of the dead and dying as strewed along the plain or heaped upon each other. He could not sleep on the two ensuing nights, and was seriously indisposed for some days; and, as is observed by himself in a letter of the time to Godolphin, "the lamentable sight and thoughts of it has given me so much uneasiness that I believe it the chief cause of my illness." But his sympathy had been shown in deeds. He had at the first despatched Cadogan to the outposts, there to hold a parley with one of the French officers, and propose a suspension of arms for two days during which the dead might be buried, and the wounded be relieved. This was readily agreed to, and Marlborough gave most careful directions for seeking out and assisting the French wounded, many of whom, officers and soldiers, had crept away into the neighbouring woods where they would certainly have perished but for this timely aid.

It was probably from the great number of the slain at Malplaquet and from the severe illness of Marlborough immediately afterwards, that a rumour of his having fallen in the battle spread through some of the French provinces. Thence appears to have arisen the well-known ditty "Malbrook s'en va en guerre," which relates how the tidings of his death were brought to his consort from abroad. But the great popularity of this song dates only from 1781, when a village nurse used it as a lullaby, at the cradle of an infant Dauphin.[8]

Mons became the prize of Malplaquet. The investment of that city was as soon as possible commenced by the army of Eugene, and covered by the army of Marlborough. While they vigorously pressed the siege divers plans to raise it were discussed in vain by Marshal Boufflers who continued in command, and Marshal Berwick who had recently joined him from the frontiers of Savoy. The breaches being declared practicable on the 20th of October the Governor beat a parley and the garrison capitulated. With this success ended the campaign. Marlborough and Eugene having disposed their troops in winter-quarters repaired to Brussels and from thence to the Hague.

On the Rhine, the Elector of Hanover had been as before, most tardy in taking the field and most inactive after he had taken it. A detachment of his army was indeed sent to the southward under Count Mercy; it crossed the Rhine near Basle, and attempted the invasion of Alsace. But a counter-detachment of the French army under Count de Bourg engaged it near Neuburg, when Mercy was totally defeated and compelled to fall back to Germany with heavy losses.

In Dauphiny there was in truth no campaign at all. The Duke of Savoy was offended at the slackness of the Court of Vienna in sending him supplies, and at its jarring pretensions to certain districts in the north of Italy. He sullenly remained in his palace at Turin

---

[8] Notice par P. L. Jacob: Chants populaires de la France, vol. III. M. Jacob adds of Marlborough: "Faute de pouvoir le vaincre on essaya de le chansonner."

leaving the command of the troops to Count Daun, who attempted little, and did nothing.

Nor yet in Spain was there much achieved. The siege of the citadel of Alicant had continued ever since the close of the preceding year. Stanhope was eager to relieve it and went to Port Mahon there to expedite the fleet. With about 4,000 troops on board he appeared in Alicant Bay, but was baffled by tempests and contrary winds, and succeeded only so far as to obtain favourable terms for the two English regiments which formed the garrison, and which had defended the place with the greatest gallantry. These regiments he embarked and brought back to Barcelona. In the summer Staremberg and Stanhope mustered their army on the Segre, but found it too feeble for any offensive operations. They could do little more than maintain one bank of the river, while Marshal Bezons with the French and Spaniards held the other.

On the frontier of Portugal, the Allied troops, English and Portuguese, had as chiefs conjointly the Earl of Galway and the Marquis de Fronteira. Advancing from Elvas and passing the river Caya, they had in front the Spaniards commanded by the Marquis de Bay. On the 17th of May and on the plain of La Gudina the two armies met. It proved another battle of Almanza on a smaller scale. The Portuguese cavalry was routed with but slight resistance, and it left exposed two battalions of English foot, which were thus cut off and compelled to lay down their arms. Lord Galway, who had a horse shot under him, narrowly escaped being taken with them. The rest of the foot however, English and Portuguese, made an orderly retreat with little loss to Elvas, and were able to maintain their position during the rest of the campaign.

The political state of Northern Europe underwent at this time not only a vicissitude but a total revolution. Charles of Sweden had for many months been warring against the Czar. He had wintered in Muscovy amidst hardships of every kind, while his troops wasted more and more under the twofold influence of stubborn enemies and inclement skies. In the summer of 1709 he was lured to the invasion of Ukraine and the siege of Pultawa. There on the 8th of July the Czar gave him battle at the head of a far superior army. Notwithstanding the great bravery of the Swedes they were entirely defeated; the soldiers for the most part taken and sent as prisoners to Siberia, while Charles himself had to ride for his life and seek shelter within the Turkish dominions. At these tidings the party which he had overthrown in Poland raised its head. King Augustus declared that his renunciation was null and void as having been extorted from him, and he marched back to Warsaw; while King Stanislas was in his turn exiled and dethroned.

Reverting to home politics, we find the cabals continued. Mrs. Masham retained her ascendency at Court. The Duchess of Marlborough had several times forced herself into the Royal presence, and made some desperate attempts to recover her lost ground. She had yet to learn that friendship is not like a fortified town to be carried by assault. Finding other means fail she transcribed sundry extracts from the "Whole Duty of Man" and also the injunction from the Book of Common Prayer, bidding us be in charity with all men before the Holy Communion is received. To these extracts she added a long memorial in praise of her own conduct and enclosed the whole to the Queen, with a letter beseeching Her Majesty's perusal of these bulky documents. In return she had only a note, in which Anne briefly said that when she had leisure to read all the papers she would send an answer to them.

It is said that an arrogant act on the part of the Duchess tended to precipitate the scale against her. It is said that one day in a ceremonial at Court Her Grace, as though by inadvertence, spilled a whole glass of water on the gown of Mrs. Masham. This anecdote is for its truth mainly dependent on tradition, nor is it clear at what precise period it occurred. But it seems the rather entitled to credit as being expressly recorded by Voltaire, who was in London not very many years afterwards, who had access to the best companies, and who found means to collect the most authentic information.[9]

The Queen through all these altercations with her former favourite continued to refer to Marlborough in the terms of respect and gratitude due ·to his public services. Still the Duke might foresee as possible the decline, nay even the downfall of his influence. Were there then no means by which that influence might be maintained? Was there no expedient to render Marlborough, and as under Marlborough the army, independent of the power of the Crown? Such an object

---

[9] "Quelques paires de gants d'une façon singulière que la Duchesse refusa à la Reine, une jatte d'eau qu'elle laissa tomber en sa présence par une méprise affectée sur la robe de Madame Masham, changèrent la face de l'Europe." Siècle de Louis XIV., vol. 1. p. 371, ed. 1752. On this story Scribe has framed his comedy, "Le Verre d'Eau," first acted November 17, 1840.

CHAP.
XI.
1709.

would be fully accomplished if the Duke could obtain a patent for life of his present office as Captain General or Commander in Chief, and to that patent for life Marlborough now aspired.

The first difficulty was to find any precedent for so unconstitutional a claim. Marlborough, before he set out for the campaign in Flanders, had spoken to the Lord Chancellor upon the subject, but Cowper assured him that this high office had never been granted otherwise than during pleasure. Since however this answer was given in conversation only, it did not satisfy Marlborough, who requested the Chancellor to search the public records. This was done accordingly but with no other result. Not yet convinced, Marlborough next deputed Craggs to examine especially the commission of General Monk, who, from his eminent service as restorer of the monarchy, might perhaps afford some warrant for Marlborough's exorbitant pretension. Here again it appeared that Monk's commission was made during pleasure only; and the Chancellor added his opinion that a patent for life would not merely be an entire innovation, to which he would not put the Great Seal, but moreover be liable to malicious imputations.

With or without a precedent Marlborough was determined to proceed. He addressed a letter to the Queen in the course of the campaign praying to be made General for life. It was a most ill-timed request when a cry was already raised against Marlborough's ambition, and the vast accumulation of offices in his own and the Duchess's hands. Nor can it be thought surprising that the Queen was both offended and alarmed. After consulting, as is supposed, her private advisers she answered the Duke with a positive refusal. Marlborough, who in the whole of this transaction seems to have been transported far beyond the bounds of his customary prudence, rejoined by another letter of angry reproach and remonstrance, which only increased the indignation of the Queen.

Through the whole of this summer Anne had been warmly pressed with solicitations upon another subject. It was to place Lord Orford at the head of the Admiralty. The Queen having slowly and reluctantly yielded, there arose another contest on the composition of the Board. Her Majesty desired to exclude from it those naval chiefs whom she regarded as the late Prince's ill wishers, especially Sir George Byng and Sir John Jennings. But these being zealous Whigs were no less warmly urged by Lord Sunderland's party, and the Queen could prevail only as to the latter name, for which Sir John Leake's was substituted. Thus amidst a thousand difficulties the list was settled. Lord Pembroke was recompensed for the loss of office by the enormous pension of £3,000 a year; and the new Commission was issued on the 8th of November the very day on which Marlborough landed in England.

Parliament met on the 15th of the same month. The Royal Speech referred to the attempts which the French had made to create divisions or jealousies among the Allies. "But" added the Queen "they were entirely disappointed in their expectations. . . . God Almighty has been pleased to bless us with a most remarkable victory. . . However, the war still continuing, I find myself obliged again to desire you, Gentlemen of the House of Commons, to grant me such Supplies as may enable us to put the last hand to this great work." Nor was there any remissness in the House of Commons. Within a few weeks it voted upwards of 6,000,000*l.* of Supply, including an augmentation of forces.

Parties seemed at rest and the dominion of the Whigs might be thought securely established. They had struck down the Tories. They had overpowered the Queen. They had dictated their own terms to the Treasurer and the General in chief. They had conquered the last remaining stronghold in the administration by the appointment of Lord Orford and his Admiralty Board. Yet so strange are the vicissitudes of Fortune that in almost the very same month in which the Gazette announced this final conquest, this new Admiralty Board, they took a resolution upon another subject which at no long interval produced the eclipse of their party, and the downfall of their power.

CHAPTER XII.

HENRY SACHEVERELL was grandson of a Presby- CHAP. XII.
terian Minister at Wincaunton and son of a clergyman 1709.
of Low-Church principles, the incumbent of a church
at Marlborough. For himself, on entering Holy Orders
he attached himself to the school of Archbishop Laud.
After some years of obscurity, in a country retirement
and as Fellow of Magdalen College at Oxford, he attained the rank of Doctor in Divinity, and also by
popular election the benefice of St. Saviour's in South-
wark. There he could preach to large congregations
his favourite doctrines of non-resistance and passive
obedience. In the discussions which these occasioned
among the London people he was commonly pitted
against Mr. Benjamin Hoadley, then Rector of St.
Peter-le-Poer in the City, who carried the opposite
doctrines to the very furthest extreme. But in the
eyes of all discerning judges, Sacheverell was on these
occasions and on every other far more distinguished
by zeal and noise than by either ability or learning.

It so chanced that in the August of this year
Dr. Sacheverell had preached before the Judges at
the summer assizes of Derbyshire. The subject of this
sermon was described by himself as the "Communication of Sin." On the 5th of November following he
preached before the Lord Mayor and Aldermen of
London at St. Paul's, and this second discourse he
entitled "the perils of false brethren both in Church

and State." In both these sermons, but in the latter more especially, he gave the rein to his hostility against the principles of the Revolution, by denying that resistance was lawful to any form of tyranny. He inveighed with bitterness against the Dissenters, and still more against what he termed "the toleration of the Genevan discipline." And he argued that, in consequence of such toleration to Calvinists, the Church of England was "in a condition of great peril and adversity" even in Her Majesty's reign. Nor did he refrain from personal allusions, glancing above all at the Lord Treasurer under his well-known nickname as the Old Fox or Volpone.

The Lord Mayor of London at this time, himself an ardent High Tory, greatly admired these sentiments as he heard them delivered from the pulpit at St. Paul's. He invited the Doctor to dinner that same afternoon, carrying him home in his coach, gave him thanks for his good sermon, and told him that he hoped to see it in print. "I am afraid" said Sacheverell "that I have spoken some bold truths which might displease some people." The Lord Mayor nevertheless undertook to propose to the Court of Aldermen that they should return Sacheverell thanks for his sermon and desire him to print it. The motion so made was rejected by the Court of Aldermen. But Sacheverell, relying on the Lord Mayor's connivance, proceeded to publish the sermon as also his former discourse at Derby. The one at St. Paul's being greatly the superior in audacity excited far the most attention. It was disseminated far and wide by those who wished well to its doctrines, and, as was commonly computed, the number of copies sold or sent round amounted to 40,000.

The Whigs were much incensed, and justly so. They apprehended the popular impression which might be made, and they rejoiced that the preacher had by his publication brought himself within reach of their resentment. The Ministers meeting in Cabinet discussed the question in the first days of December. Somers with his usual sagacity advised, that if the sermon were noticed by the Government at all, it should only be by prosecution according to the ordinary forms of law. In this counsel he was, after some hesitation, supported by Marlborough. But Sunderland came forward with the more vigorous proposal, that Sacheverell should be made the subject of an impeachment by the House of Commons and a trial by the House of Lords.

It was this last proposal which commended itself to the judgment of Godolphin. Like many timid men he would sometimes rush into the very rashest courses as a relief from his own fears. He seems to have looked upon Sacheverell as so dangerous a monster that no means could be too potent to subdue him. Moreover he was stung to the quick by the nickname of Volpone. Under this affront, or, as Lord Macaulay says of him, "inflamed with all the zeal of a new-made Whig,"[1] he pressed for the most vindictive measures, and by his influence as Prime Minister appears to have turned the scale.

The determination thus taken was promptly carried out. On the 13th of December Mr. John Dolben, seconded by Mr. Spencer Cowper, made complaint in the House of Commons of the two published discourses, some paragraphs from which were at their desire read

---

[1] On the War of the Succession in Spain. Collected Essays, or Edinburgh Review, No. CXII. p. 534.

CHAP.
XII.
1709.

forth by the Clerk at the Table. After some debate the House resolved that these sermons were "malicious, scandalous, and seditious libels, highly reflecting upon Her Majesty and her government, the late happy Revolution, and the Protestant Succession." It was further ordered that Dr. Henry Sacheverell and Henry Clements his printer should attend at the Bar of the House next day.

Next day accordingly the Doctor and the printer came. Sacheverell freely owned the authorship of the two sermons, said that he was very sorry to have fallen under the displeasure of the House, but expressed no contrition for his doctrines. Under these circumstances Clements was allowed to slip through. As to Sacheverell on the contrary the House resolved that he should be impeached by them of high crimes and misdemeanors. A Committee comprising Mr. Secretary Boyle and other Ministers was appointed to draw up the Articles of Impeachment, and it was ordered that the Doctor should be taken into the custody of the Serjeant at Arms.[2]

The House of Commons in the same sitting gave another token of its resentment against Sacheverell by a recommendation of his rival. It was moved and carried that the Rev. Benjamin Hoadley had done good service in often justifying the principles of the late happy Revolution; and that the Queen should be entreated to bestow some dignity in the Church upon him.

A few days later Sacheverell sent a Petition to the

---

[2] Compare the Commons Journals, Dec. 13 and 14, 1709, with Howell's State Trials, vol. xv. p. 1. The Parliamentary History (vol. vi. p. 805) is here very inaccurate.

House praying to admit him to bail that he might have CHAP.
an opportunity of making his defence. This request XII.
was referred to the Committee upon the Impeachment 1709.
to search for precedents, and some such appeared;
nevertheless after sharp debate the prayer of the Petition was rejected by 114 votes against 79.

While these things were passing in the Commons 1710.
the first days of the new year were troubled by a conflict at Court. The Earl of Essex having died, there fell
vacant two offices that he held as Constable of the
Tower and Colonel of the 2nd Regiment of Dragoons.
In disposing of these Her Majesty evinced her continued alienation from her principal Ministers. Without consulting them she bestowed the place of Constable upon Earl Rivers, a General Officer of merit and
service but on no terms of confidence with Marlborough.
The Duke was much mortified, but after some strong
remonstrances submitted. As regards the regiment, the
Queen next commanded him to confer it upon Colonel
Hill the brother of her favourite. Here Marlborough
conceived that he might make a stand. Having first
through the Duchess assured himself of the support of
his Whig colleagues, he asked an audience of the
Queen and pointed out the prejudice which would
ensue to the Service by promoting so young an officer
as Colonel Hill over others of superior rank. He
added that he should feel it a personal mortification,
as a sign of his own declining influence, were he
forced to bestow that or any other favor on a brother
of Mrs. Masham. But the Queen received his representations very coldly. She adhered to her request
and closed the interview by saying "You will do well
to advise with your friends."

Much incensed Marlborough took the resolution to retire from Court. He set out with the Duchess for Windsor Lodge, omitting the usual ceremony of taking leave and selecting the very day on which a Cabinet Council was to be held. But this secession did not produce a like effect to that of 1708 which compelled the resignation of Harley. At the Cabinet the customary business was transacted; the Queen who was present took no notice of Marlborough's non-attendance; and Godolphin struck with tremor did not venture, either there or at an audience which ensued, to make the slightest allusion to his absent and dissatisfied friend.

Nor did any success attend a letter which Marlborough had left in draft for the consideration of his colleagues. It declared to the Queen his fixed intention of resigning unless Mrs. Masham were removed; and it asked Her Majesty to choose decisively and once for all between her and him. But the Treasurer, in an agony of apprehension, shrunk from so bold a course, and he prevailed with some of his Whig friends to join him in pressing that Marlborough should modify his draft and desist from his pretension. Finally there was a compromise effected. The Duke and Duchess were to return to Court. Mrs. Masham was to remain as before. Colonel Meredith obtained the regiment instead of Colonel Hill; and the latter was gratified with a pension of 1,000*l.* a year; for a pension, according to the ill practice of that age, was it may be said a salve for every wound.

During this time the Impeachment Committee had prepared their heads of accusation, comprised in four articles with an argumentative preamble. These being reported to the House gave rise to a warm debate.

Harley above all insisted on leaving out the word "seditious," alleging a precedent from the reign of Charles the First, in the prosecution of Prynne. He was supported by Bromley and others; and it was moved that the Report be recommitted, but this passed in the negative by 232 against 131. Then the Articles of Impeachment were agreed to and ordered to be sent to the Lords, while Sacheverell was transferred to the custody of their House, that is to their officer the Deputy Usher of the Black Rod. But in this new jurisdiction he was dealt with differently as to the matter of Bail. It had been refused in the Commons; it was granted in the Lords; fixing however a very high amount, Sacheverell himself in 6,000*l.* and each of his two sureties in 3,000*l.* One of these two sureties was Dr. Lancaster, Vice-Chancellor of the University of Oxford—no slight token in itself of the increased support which the Doctor was now receiving.

On the 25th of January Dr. Sacheverell delivered in his Answer to the Articles; it was bold and uncompromising in its tone. The Commons were allowed a Replication; and the Lords were then proceeding to the Trial at their Bar. But the most vehement opponents of Sacheverell in the Commons thought that they should add to the solemnity of the proceedings by a motion, that not merely the Managers of the Impeachment but the House as a body desired to be present; thus for better space transferring the scene to Westminster Hall. This motion was supported by the friends of Sacheverell also. They knew that the necessary arrangements would require time to complete; and from the rising ferment in the country they foresaw that delay would be most advantageous to their cause.

With this combination of parties the motion was carried on the 4th of February by 192 against 180. The Lords accordingly appointed Westminster Hall as the place for the Trial, and postponed its commencement until the 27th of the month.

Marlborough from the first appears to have looked coldly on this ill-advised impeachment. It was noticed that he was scarcely ever present at the preliminary discussions of the House of Lords.[3]   In this girding up for the contest of two warring parties he became an object of suspicion to both. Both, though for different reasons, came to desire his absence. A pretext, nay even a reason, was soon found. The King of France having renewed his overtures for peace and the States General being inclined to hearken to them, Sir Gilbert Heathcote on the 18th of February moved an Address to the Queen praying that she would order the Duke of Marlborough's immediate departure for Holland, "where" it was added "his presence will be equally necessary to assist at the negotiations of peace and to hasten the preparations for an early campaign." This Address, unanimously voted in the House of Commons, was as unanimously agreed to by the House of Lords. The Queen returned a gracious answer and the Duke set out accordingly.

The nearer the Trial approached, the more its gross impolicy appeared. There has always been a tendency in England, whenever a political prosecution is urged to an extreme, to favor the side of the weak even where the weak are clearly wrong. Such was the case for example with Sacheverell, with Wilkes, with Caroline of Brunswick. In the case now before us, the large ma-

[3] Coxe's Marlborough, vol. v. p. 124.

jority of the English clergy were far, I conceive, from CHAP. XII. holding the doctrine of Passive Obedience as Sacheverell held it. But they disliked still more the semi-republican tendencies which Hoadley put forth upon the other side; and above all seeing the solemn attempt to crush one of their own body, they stood up in defence of their Order. In like manner the country gentlemen of that period were for the most part of the Cavalier and High Church school, yet attached to the Revolution settlement and zealous for the title of the Queen. They would certainly have owned at the outset that the sermons of Sacheverell went much too far. When however they saw him so hotly assailed by the Whigs they thought themselves bound to defend him with an equal zeal. Thus it happened that not merely the Passive Obedience men, or the Jacobites and Non-jurors, but the entire Tory party espoused his cause. The ablest of the Tory writers, Dr. Atterbury, placed his pen at the Doctor's disposal. The ablest of the Tory lawyers, Sir Simon Harcourt, was one of the five counsel assigned him.

On the 27th of February at last the Trial commenced. It lasted three weeks, during which, as an eye-witness has remarked, it took up all men's thoughts, so that other business was at a stand.[4] As Chancellor Lord Cowper presided. The Commons had ordered. that the members of the Committee which had framed the Articles should be the Managers of the Impeachment. They were twenty in number but only eighteen appeared in Westminster Hall. According to Bishop Burnet "their performances were much and justly commended. Jekyll, Eyre, Stanhope, King, but above all Parker, distinguished themselves in a very particular manner." By

---

[4] Burnet's History, vol. v. p. 440.

none of them perhaps was the great doctrine of justifiable resistance laid down more clearly than by General
Stanhope. "I believe" he added "one may further venture to say, that there is not at this day subsisting any
nation or government in the world whose first original
did not receive its foundation either from resistance
or compact; and as to our purpose it is equal if compact be admitted. For wherever compact is admitted
there must be admitted likewise a right to defend the
rights accruing by such compact."[5]

On the other side Sir Simon Harcourt and the other
counsel for the Doctor were far too skilful to maintain,
as he had seemed to do, the doctrine of unconditional
submission to any form of tyranny. They freely acknowledged the lawfulness of resistance in extreme
cases. They plainly justified the Revolution and our
deliverance by King William. But they took their
stand on the admitted truth, that obedience ought to
be the rule and resistance only the exception. Hence
they argued that it was not fit to name such an exception in a sermon, and that the duties of morality ought
to be delivered in their full extent without supposing
an extraordinary case. And beyond doubt there are
some parallels that might be plausibly urged. Thus
a preacher might most properly enforce the general
duty of truthfulness without being expected to allege
certain especial instances—as of a band of robbers inquiring the direction of their prey—in which deception
would be justifiable, nay even entitled to praise.

It was clear from the very outset of the Trial that
the popular favor was wholly on the Doctor's side. He
lodged in the Temple and came every day in solemn

5 Howell's State Trials, vol. xv. p. 127.

procession through the Strand to Westminster Hall. As he passed great crowds gathered round his coach, striving to kiss his hand and shouting "Sacheverell and the Church for ever!" Those who would not join in the shouts were often insulted or knocked down. The ardor of the multitude was even less justifiably shown by their attack upon some meeting-houses, in which the pews were demolished and burned. They threatened a like execution upon the house of Bishop Burnet, a prelate at all times most obnoxious to High Churchmen, but they were in good time met and dispersed by a party of the Guards. Some few of the rioters were apprehended and subsequently brought to trial. It is plain that the people of London at this time, as the people of Birmingham eighty years later in the Priestley riots, were loud for "Church and State," as was the cry, although they showed their zeal in a manner which the Church could not approve nor the State let go unpunished.

Thus also when the Queen impelled by curiosity went several times—"incognito" as it was termed—to hear the Trial, the people pressed about her sedan-chair exclaiming "God bless your Majesty and the Church. We hope your Majesty is for Dr. Sacheverell." Such was not at the outset the inclination of the Queen. When Bishop Burnet came to town soon after the impeachment had commenced, the Queen said to him of Sacheverell and his pulpit oratory: "It is a bad sermon, and he well deserves to be punished for it." When however Anne found the Clergy of the Church of England almost as a whole and excepting the Whig Bishops espouse his cause—when she saw some of her own chaplains and other chief Divines—as Atterbury and Smalridge soon afterwards raised to the Bench, Dr. Robert Moss, and Dr. George Stanhope Dean of Canterbury—stand by his side in Westminster Hall as though making his cause their own—there is reason to believe that her secret wishes changed.

It was thus surrounded that, at the close of the Trial and after his Counsel had spoken, Sacheverell read to the Peers a speech in his own defence. He read it, says Bishop Burnet, "with much bold heat." Yet his tone was not that of his sermons but rather that of his Counsel. He justified his intentions towards the Queen and her Government; he spoke with respect of the Revolution, and with zeal of the Protestant Succession. And he added some pathetic touches likely to move the feelings of the Peers. So superior was this speech in composition to any thing which Sacheverell had hitherto produced, that it was well understood to be no offspring of his brain. Its merit was in general and probably with reason ascribed to Atterbury.

The Doctor having ended, the Managers of the Commons replied, one of them, Mr. William Thompson, adducing in his speech a most quaint comparison.[6] Then the Peers after first resolving the doubt upon a point of form which Lord Nottingham had raised, proceeded to debate the question at large. Five of their speeches have been preserved by the care of the speakers, namely, Lord Haversham for the defence, and four Bishops—Salisbury, Oxford, Lincoln, and Norwich

---

6 "Since the Doctor does still presume to defy and arraign the Resolution of your Lordships and the Commons, I may apply to him the saying of a goat browsing on a vine :

'Rode caper vitem, tamen hinc cum stabis ad aras
In tua quod fundi cornua possit, erit.'"

—for the impeachment. The well known Tory leaders
—Rochester, Buckingham, Nottingham—were warmly
on the Doctor's side. But inclining to him with more
or less of openness there were also some dissatisfied
Whig Peers. First there was the Duke of Somerset.
For some time past he had been estranged from Marlborough and Godolphin and striving to form a separate
cabal of his own. And at this juncture as Godolphin
reports: "The Duke of Somerset labours hard against
us and makes use of the Queen's name to North and
South Britain with a good deal of freedom. I doubt
he is pretty sure of not being disavowed." Then there
was the Duke of Shrewsbury. After several years of
sojourn at Rome he had come back to England bringing
with him an Italian wife, and in some degree discredited
by her, yet still by degrees regaining a portion of his
former influence. There was also His Grace of Argyle
who sat in the House of Lords as Earl of Greenwich,
and who made common cause with his brother, Earl of
Isla. He had greatly distinguished himself in Flanders
during the last campaign, and his promotion had been
eagerly pressed by Marlborough, to whom he might
seem bound by ties of gratitude; but gratitude and
constancy were not among the virtues of this accomplished man.

The debates having concluded, the Lords were prepared to give their votes on Monday the 20th of March.
Then in due form the Chancellor, beginning with the
lowest in rank among the Peers, called upon them in
succession to pronounce Guilty or Not Guilty. It was
found that 69 voted Guilty and 52 Not Guilty. Among
the latter none perhaps were more attentively observed, or more freely discussed than the Duke of

CHAP.
XII.
1710.

Shrewsbury, Dr. Sharp Archbishop of York, and Dr. Compton Bishop of London, so conspicuous in the Revolution as one of its principal leaders and the adviser of the Princess Anne. The Duke of Somerset did not vote at all.

So far then the Ministers prevailed. But when, the Doctor being thus found Guilty, the question arose next day as to the sentence to be passed upon him, the majority dwindled away. Argyle and Isla for example left their friends and joined the other side. The first vote that Sacheverell should be prohibited from preaching for the three years next ensuing was carried only by six. The subsequent motion that he should be incapable during that time of taking any preferment in the Church was lost by one. No higher and more rigorous penalties could be even proposed. There was added only a Resolution that his two ser- mons should be publicly burned by the hand of the common hangman, and together with them the Decree of the University of Oxford passed in July 1683, which maintained the absolute authority of Princes, and which had been alleged by Sacheverell in his defence.

"And so"—exclaims Godolphin as he reports the event to Marlborough—"so all this bustle and fatigue ends in no more but a suspension of three years from the pulpit, and burning his sermon at the Old Ex- change!"—Well indeed might the Treasurer look with sorrow to this issue. Well might he rue an impeach- ment so unpopular in its progress and so ridiculous in its result. Well might he repent his own rashness in overruling the sagacity of Somers, and attempting at every hazard to silence the buzz of a single in-significant priest. The fable of the bear that hurled a heavy stone at the head of its sleeping master on purpose to crush a fly upon his cheek is a type of the service which on this occasion Godolphin rendered to his party.

Marlborough on his part was greatly moved. His resentment fell especially on that comrade in arms whom he had so recently befriended. As he writes to the Duchess: "I do with all my heart wish I had not recommended the Duke of Argyle; but that cannot now be helped; nothing is good but taking measures not to be in the power of ungrateful people." ·

On the other hand the friends of Sacheverell in England considered and with good reason the mild sentence of the Lords' as almost equivalent to an acquittal. As such it was celebrated through the country. There were bonfires and illuminations, there were huzzas and addresses, not in London only but in many other places. The zeal for Sacheverell prevailed as we are told especially among the ladies. They flocked in crowds into the churches where he read prayers (since it was only from preaching that he was debarred), they often sent for him to baptize their children, and several were christened of his name. As the spring advanced the oak-leaf—dear to loyal hearts since the days of Charles the Second—was frequently assumed and worn. And when in June the Doctor set out to take possession of a considerable living bestowed on him in Wales, his journey became a festal pro-gress. Thus at Banbury and again at Warwick he was met by the Mayor and Aldermen in their robes of office; thus at Shrewsbury a crowd of five thousand people poured forth to greet him. [7]

A fortnight after the sentence upon Dr. Sacheverell the Session was closed by the Queen. Her Majesty referred as follows to the recent trial. "The suppressing immorality and profane and other wicked and malicious libels . . . they being an evil complained of in all times, it is very injurious to take a pretence from thence to insinuate that the Church is in any danger from my administration. I could heartily wish that men would study to be quiet and do their own business rather than busy themselves in reviving questions and disputes of a very high nature." From these words it was too rashly concluded that there was no ground for the common rumours of the Queen's inclination to Sacheverell. It soon appeared that Her Majesty's expressions were Ministerial only.

This Prorogation took place on the 5th of April. Next day the Duchess of Marlborough having written to the Queen followed her letter to Kensington, and was, though not very willingly, admitted by Her Royal Mistress. She had explained that her object in forcing an interview was to clear herself of some imputations which, she added, would have no consequence in obliging Her Majesty to answer. The Queen availed herself of these last words, and amidst the torrent of expostulations and the flood of tears which the Duchess now poured forth, repeated again and again, "you desired no answer and you shall have none." The Duchess in her own account of this interview accuses herself of some disrespectful language, but observes

---

[7] Complete History of Europe, 1710, pp. 455 and 494. Burnet's History, vol. VI. p. 11.

that the circumstances might well excuse it. Finally, as she would not go, Her Majesty quitted the room. This was the last time that the Duchess ever saw the Queen.[8]

A week later Queen Anne took a step of considerable boldness. She sent for the Marquess of Kent, Lord Chamberlain, and ordered him to give up his Staff of Office, promising in compensation to bestow on him forthwith the rank of Duke. On the same afternoon, and without consulting any of her Ministers, she conferred the vacant office on the Duke of Shrewsbury. Godolphin, who was then betting at Newmarket, was only apprised of this event so nearly touching his administration by a letter from the Queen. Then was the time to show vigour. Then was the time to throw up office with effect. As Sunderland had written a few weeks before under other circumstances but with the same character to comment upon, "If Lord Treasurer can but be persuaded to act like a man—."[9] But that was the very thing Godolphin could not do. He exhausted his whole energy in one reproachful letter to the Queen, and even before concluding that letter submitted unconditionally to her Royal will. For he says at the end that "For my own part I most humbly beg leave to assure your Majesty I will never give the least obstruction to your measures." Somers and Sunderland, though no doubt with much heartburning, and after them the other Ministers, followed the guidance of their chief. All continued to hold office, tamely hoping that no fresh dismissals would assail them. Thus, according to a

---

[8] Conduct of the Duchess of Marlborough, p. 281, ed. 1742.
[9] Letter to Marlborough, dated Feb. 21, 1710.

CHAP.
XII.
1710. jest which was current at the time, the enemies of Passive Obedience now became passive themselves.

A step taken at this period by Marlborough, then in Holland, was, as I conceive, by no means to his credit. More than once he had been offered, either indirectly through the Emperor or directly from King Charles, the government of the province he had conquered—the Low Countries. The emoluments of the post, according to Marlborough's own computation, were no less than 60,000*l.* a year.[1] Marlborough howeyer, as we have seen, declined the glittering prize, finding that the very rumour of it roused vehement jealousies at the Hague, and put to hazard the stability of the Grand Alliance. There was no reason to suppose that at this later juncture the jealousies would be less rife, or the Grand Alliance less imperilled. Nevertheless, at this later juncture, the Duke feeling the insecurity of his offices in England, applied for that foreign appointment. He addressed himself to King Charles, through Mr. Craggs, at Barcelona. Charles at first drily replied, that he would give his answer through General Stanhope when the General arrived. The answer as announced to Stanhope was, at last, that His Majesty would be well pleased to grant His Grace's wish, "so it might be with the general consent, and particularly of the Dutch." This, in fact, was only a refusal in a civil form.[2]

During this time the Great Duke at the Hague was intently watching the French negotiations. They had been renewed mainly through the active zeal of Pettekum who went to Paris for that object. But the

---

[1] Letter to Godolphin, July 6, 1706.
[2] Compare in Coxe's Marlborough, vol. 11. p 387. and vol. v. p. 385.

Dutch States would agree to them only on condition CHAP.
that the King of France should accept the Preliminaries XII.
of the preceding year except the thirty-seventh article, 1710.
which provided for the cession of the Spanish monarchy
by Philip within the space of two months; and as to
that article Louis expressed his readiness to offer a
satisfactory equivalent. On this footing then the conferences of 1709 were resumed. Gertruydenberg was
appointed the place for them; and for negotiators the
States sent as before the Deputies Buys and Vanderdussen, while Louis named the Abbé, afterwards Car-
dinal, de Polignac and the Marshal d'Huxelles.

In the interviews that followed, it was again urged
on the part of Louis and with considerable force, that
if no fragment however small of the Spanish inheritance
as Naples or Sicily were allowed to Philip, the King of
France had no prospect of inducing Philip to relinquish
Spain. Even with such compensation it was very
doubtful that Philip would yield; and if in any case he
would not, what power of compulsion was there in
Louis's hands? He, the King of France, had already
withdrawn his troops; and his feelings revolted at the
thought of himself declaring war against his grandson.
But he went great lengths in his offers. He proposed
to issue an edict recalling his subjects of whatever
rank and under severe penalties from the Spanish service.
He proposed to contribute by monthly subsidies to
the prosecution of the war against Philip if Philip persevered. He was even willing, as a pledge of his good
faith, to give up four cautionary towns which should
meanwhile be held by the Allies. On the other hand
the Allies still insisted that Louis must make himself
answerable for the issue, that within the space of two

months he must either compel or induce his grandson to resign the throne of Spain.

In the course however of these conferences, the Dutch statesmen came to acknowledge to each other that more was claimed from Louis than he had really power to perform. Their thoughts reverted to the first idea of some lure or compensation to Philip, and the Pensionary did not scruple to own among friends that it would be a happy thing if peace could be purchased by the cession of Sicily. Both Godolphin and Somers being consulted by letter were found to be of the same opinion—altogether different from that which they had hitherto with much warmth expressed. On the other part Count Sinzendorf presented a Memorial at the Hague, declaring in the strongest terms, that the House of Austria would never suffer the smallest portion of the Spanish territories even out of Spain to be ceded to a Bourbon Prince. The like opposition was announced on the part of Savoy. Thus it was clear that even Sicily could not be granted without imminent risk to break asunder the Grand Alliance. "I am afraid"—so writes Marlborough to Godolphin—"the French are not ignorant of these two opinions, by which they are the better able to amuse and cheat us."[3]

In these transactions it is wholly false to allege of Marlborough, as his enemies have sometimes done, that he strove by all the means in his power to prolong the war. So far from it, that in his correspondence we find him incline to the conciliatory counsels of Heinsius by complying with which a peace would have been signed. But at this juncture he was greatly on his

---

[3] Letter dated Hague, March 18, 1710.

guard. Looking back to England he felt how much CHAP. his influence had declined, and how probably his acts XII. might be questioned. Therefore he confined himself 1710. strictly within the limits of the instructions he received. As was said by himself at this period he was "white paper" upon which the Treasurer and his friends might write whatever they pleased.

Upon the whole of this matter, waiving for the time the question whether the Allies did not urge their points too far, and looking only to the vast extent of the offers that Louis made, we may be permitted to exult at the proud position which—mainly by Whig policy and by treading in the footsteps of King William—England had now attained. We may echo the contrasted terms in which that position was set forth by Stanhope when he addressed the Lords on the Sacheverell trial. "Our Henrys and our Edwards have justly left behind them immortal fame for having broke and subdued in their times the power of France. Queen Elizabeth will be ever glorious for having humbled the pride of Spain. These two great monarchies have each in their turn aimed at the universal monarchy of Europe; and each hath been near compassing it, notwithstanding that the one always opposed the other. But it was never imagined that if once they became united any force in Europe could have disputed with them. Yet we have lived to see those two formidable Powers united and threatening destruction to all the liberties of Europe. It was a task reserved for Her Majesty to encounter this united force. She has attacked and reduced them to sue for peace." [4]

The conferences at Gertruydenberg were continued

----

[4] Howell, State Trials, vol. xv. p. 133.

till near the end of July.· But long before that time it became apparent to close observers that they would lead to no practical result. There being meanwhile no cessation of hostilities concluded Marlborough and Eugene prepared for an early campaign. They hoped to effect great things in the Netherlands, and with that view prevailed upon the Emperor to send them considerable reinforcements from the army upon the Rhine. The lessening of that army however led to a change in its chief. His Highness of Hanover resigned a command which he had found both irksome and inglorious, and which thus curtailed appeared to him unworthy of his rank. In his place there was appointed a subaltern General, who could do no more than maintain his ground.

So early as the 19th of April and anticipating Villars by three weeks, Marlborough and Eugene joined at Tournay and put themselves at the head of the army which ere long amounted to near 120,000 men. They had before them lines which during the winter the French had fortified with care, and which were held by a strong division under M. d'Artagnan, now a Marshal of France with the title of Montesquieu. As their first object, the Allied chiefs sought to force the lines and besiege the important fortress of Douay. But they had further in view, another and more mysterious enterprise in reference to which Godolphin had desired Marlborough to adapt so far as possible his movements. This is more fully explained in a letter not hitherto published. "By Mr. Stanhope's safe hand I may acquaint you that yesterday my Lord Sunderland had a letter from the Town-Major of Calais,5 by a messenger

---

5 Not the Mayor, as stated in Coxe's Marlborough, vol. v. p. 177.

who had been ten days coming over by way of Ostend, because of contrary winds. The business was to represent to the Queen that both Calais and Boulogne with all the whole country were so oppressed and in such misery, the garrisons of these places so weak and the inhabitants so disposed to put themselves under Her Majesty's protection, that he had it in his power and was ready, upon the assurance of a good reward, to deliver them up to the Queen. He did not desire any help of troops or ships till he had actually made himself master of them, and then he would come over hither himself and remain an hostage for the security of the garrison Her Majesty should think fit to send thither. . . . . . The man was sent back immediately, with a fair wind and the assurance of the reward he desired." [6]

The French lines were passed without loss since the enemy at once retreated from them, and Douay was then without delay invested. It held a garrison of nearly 8,000 men with an excellent chief, Albergotti, and it made accordingly a valorous resistance. Meanwhile Marshal Villars, having set out from Paris and reached his head-quarters at Cambray, advanced at the head of an army little if at all inferior to that of the Allies. Three other Marshals of France had joined him in expectation of a battle. Marlborough writes: "If their resolution holds of venturing one, this country being all plains it must be very decisive. . . . . In all the former actions I did never doubt of success, we having had constantly the great blessing of being of one mind. I cannot say it is so now; for I fear some are run so far into villanous faction that it would give

CHAP.
XII.
1710.

---

[6] Secret letter, dated March 16, 1710. Coxe's Transcripts, Brit. Mus.

them more content to see us beaten. .... The discourse of the Duke of Argyle is, that when I please there will then be a peace. 'I suppose his friends speak the same language in England; so that I must every summer venture my life in a battle and be found fault with in the winter for not bringing home peace though I wish for it with all my heart and soul." [7]

Marshal Villars however was resolved not to offer battle unless with some advantage of position over the Allies; and such was precluded by the skill and vigilance of their two chiefs. Thus Douay was left to its fate; and on the 26th of June the garrison having continued its defence to the utmost, agreed to a capitulation on favourable terms.

While Marlborough was warring in Flanders his enemies were caballing in England. The Queen, more than ever estranged from her Ministers by the danger to which, as she believed, they had exposed the Church, was wholly guided by Mrs. Masham and through Mrs. Masham by Harley; and the rising ferment in the nation gave confidence both to her and to them. About a month after the appointment of the Duke of Shrewsbury Anne sent for Robert Walpole, who was acting as Secretary at War, and insisted that of the vacant regiments two should be bestowed on Colonel Hill the brother and Mr. Masham the husband of her favourite. It was with difficulty that Walpole obtained a respite till the Great Duke could be consulted. Marlborough was much perplexed though inclining to stand firm. But he was plied with earnest representations from Godolphin who hoped to avert a breach in the administration by his compliance. "The question" he

<hr>

7 Letter to Godolphin, June 12, 1710.

wrote "is not so much what is wrong and what is right, but what gives a handle to the Duke of Somerset to tell lies and make impressions." To such arguments Marlborough yielded. He endeavoured to make a virtue of necessity and to claim some merit with Colonel Hill by sending for him at once, and announcing to him his advancement before the commission itself arrived.

Contrary to Godolphin's expectation these timid counsels did not prevent the breach he feared. The secret advisers of the Queen prepared for a more important blow. They determined to strike next at Sunderland, conspicuous alike as Secretary of State and as son-in-law of Marlborough. Yet he was the easier prey since his own ardent temper had done him some disservice. He had altogether failed, since her first objection, to reconcile the Queen to his presence in the Cabinet; and he had frequently offended other members of that Cabinet, even the Great Duke himself, by blunt representations and reproaches. When therefore the rumour grew—for Harley did not conceal his object—that Sunderland would ere long be dismissed, several of his colleagues seemed to be but lukewarm in his cause.

On the 13th of June the expected blow was struck. The Queen apprised Godolphin that she should direct Mr. Boyle as joint Secretary of State to go to his colleague and fetch away the Seals; and next day she wrote again declaring her intention to give them to Lord Dartmouth. This was a nobleman of high character and good ability, the son of a keen high Tory or rather Jacobite, and himself a keen High Churchman.

At these unwelcome tidings a meeting of the men

in office was held at the Duke of Devonshire's house. Neither Godolphin nor yet any of the Whig Ministers showed any desire to resign. On the contrary they drew up and signed a joint memorial to the Duke of Marlborough entreating him to forego his resentment and to retain his command. This they urged partly for the welfare of England and of Europe as involved in the successful prosecution of the war, and partly because they thought his continuance at the head of the army the only measure that could avert an entire dismissal of the Ministry, and a dissolution of the Parliament which they above all things apprehended.

Marlborough, deeply as he was offended, felt the duty of yielding to these representations. But he also felt the importance of the utmost caution in all his further steps. We find him write as follows to the Duchess: "For God's sake let me beg of you to keep your temper, for you are in a country amongst tigers and wolves." And again two days later: "Keep your temper"—no needless caution—"and if Parliament continues we will make some of their hearts ache. I am heart and soul yours."

At home the fall of Sunderland roused to a high pitch the ardour of the opposite parties. The Tories, full of exultation, showered praises on their Sovereign for having with so much firmness asserted her authority. "Your Majesty is now Queen indeed"—so said to her the Duke of Beaufort. In the same spirit there came in loyal addresses in which the determination was declared to support against all gainsayers the cause of Church and Queen. On the other hand the monied men, who were for the most part of the Whig connection, gave signs of alarm. The Funds fell and public

credit seemed to be affected. A deputation from the
Bank, headed by the Governor Sir Gilbert Heathcote,
himself a zealous Whig, waited on Her Majesty to represent the injurious effects which the dismissal of the
Secretary had produced, and to deprecate any further
changes. Anne replied as follows: "I have for some
time resolved to remove the Earl of Sunderland for
particular reasons of State. I have no present intention
to make any farther changes, but should I alter any of
my Ministers it shall be no prejudice either to the Bank
or to the common cause."

Some similar remonstrances came to the Queen from
M. Vryberg the Dutch Envoy and Count Gallas the
Imperial Minister, and some similar assurances were
given in return. It appears from the private correspondence, that these remonstrances were in secret
prompted by Godolphin. Marlborough, with a truer
instinct, foresaw that the further interference of Foreign
Powers would serve only to irritate the Queen. He
therefore took pains to dissuade it. Still less could he,
or his friends in politics, expect any advantage from
the headlong anger of his consort. At this very juncture the Duchess had revived an acrimonious correspondence with the Queen, committing in the course
of it an unpardonable breach of trust, by inclosing a
confidential letter which the Duke of Somerset had
formerly addressed to herself, and in which the Queen
was treated with little ceremony. This correspondence,
after much passion on Her Grace's part, came to a
close only because the Queen, who for some time past
had returned but very short answers, returned at last
no answers at all.

In his military movements no less than in his diplomatic correspondence, Marlborough saw the necessity of great caution at this time. A single false step, and even a trifling failure might lay him open to the machinations of his enemies. At another period he would probably have run some hazard for the object of securing Calais; for although there had been a premature disclosure of the plot within the town, there was on foot another project for a landing at the mouth of the Somme, and a conquest, as was hoped, of the entire district comprising not only Calais but Boulogne. Now however Marlborough deemed it most expedient if not to relinquish at least to postpone the scheme. He had hoped as did Eugene that, after taking Douay, they might besiege Arras. But Villars with great skill drew together his whole army on some new-constructed lines, and the Allied chiefs considered it impracticable either to attack him in that strong position, or to invest Arras while he continued to hold it. Obliged therefore to content themselves with a lesser object they sat down before the small town of Bethune, which so bravely prolonged its resistance that it was the 28th of August before its capitulation ensued.

On the frontier of Italy the continued differences between the Emperor and the Duke of Savoy withheld the latter from attempting anything considerable; and there is little to record beyond a series of marches and counter-marches, on the part of Count Daun and of Marshal Berwick. There had been planned however a descent upon the coast of Languedoc to connect itself if possible with a rising in the Cevennes. A body of troops, about two thousand strong, were accordingly sent by sea from Barcelona and landed at Cette on the 25th of July. Though in great part English they had

for their chief a French Protestant, born in that very
province; but they received no encouragement, not
even in words, from the hill-country, while intelligence
came that the Duke of Noailles was marching against
them from Roussillon with all the forces he could
muster. Within four days they were content to reembark, leaving behind them some fifty men who were
taken prisoners. The French, it is said, lost but one
grenadier who was killed by chance with his own
musket.[8]

It was only in Spain that the war was vigorously
waged. There both parties had a strong motive to
press it. The fact that all French troops had been
withdrawn from Philip's service and summoned home
was intelligence most encouraging of course to the
Ministers of Charles in Catalonia. Now or never must
be the time to renew the conquests of 1706 and to plant
his standards once more at Zaragoza and Madrid. On
the other hand the very same fact—the withdrawal of
the French auxiliaries—tended to arouse in Philip's
favor the national spirit of Castille. The Spaniards of
his party were eager to show if possible that even
without the aid of the "Gavachos," as the French in
Spain have been always for some unknown reason
termed, they could not only hold their own but overpower their antagonists. Even the two Princes, arrayed
against each other, and who though opposite in interests
were much alike in character—each inclining to uxorious ease and a dreamy indolent seclusion—caught in
some degree the enthusiasm of the hour, and were disposed to take the field.

8 Complete History of Europe, 1710, p. 541. Sismondi, Hist. des Français, vol. XXVII. p. 104.

General Stanhope, as we have seen, had returned to England for the Session of Parliament. In the middle of March he set out again for his scene of command. First he visited the camp of the Duke of Marlborough, to whom he brought the secret plan for the surprise of Calais. Next he repaired to Genoa, where he intended to await some considerable reinforcements that he had succeeded in obtaining. But being apprised that the enemy had already taken the field, he embarked at once with a thousand recruits and moreover a good sum of money—still more welcome to the needy Court of Barcelona. On the 26th of May, he reached the camp which Marshal Staremberg had pitched on the left bank of the Segre, and a few days later they were joined by Charles himself, who as titular monarch assumed the chief command. On the day after his arrival there was a general review. According to one eye-witness "everybody says our army makes a very fine appearance, but I believe nobody can tell by the King's countenance when he is pleased."[9]

Maintaining the opposite bank of the river now stood the Bourbon army; with its King Philip to confront King Charles. This army had been augmented by levies throughout the kingdom, by volunteers from France, and by detachments from the frontier of Portugal. Earnest entreaties had been addressed to Louis that he would allow the Duke of Vendome to lead it, but Louis, as we have seen, could give no such permission while the negotiations at Gertruydenberg were still proceeding. Failing Vendome the command was entrusted to the Marquis of Villadarias, the ablest of

9 Journal of Mr. Lenoir, comprised in the Stanhope Papers, and printed in the War of the Succession in Spain, Appendix, p. cxxi.

the Spanish Generals of the time, while Don Antonio CHAP.
Amezaga, an officer of some note in the former XII.
Valencian campaigns, had the special charge of the 1710.
cavalry.

At the outset the superiority seemed to be with
Villadarias. He had already received all the fresh
troops that he expected, while the reinforcements due
to the Allies were still upon their way. Thus mustering
about 20,000 foot and 6,000 horse he much outnum-
bered the present army of Staremberg and Stanhope,
and he crossed the Segre to give them battle, but found
them strongly intrenched near the bridge of Balaguer.
On the 13th of June the advantage was with them, in
both a cannonade and a skirmish. In the latter Stanhope, who headed the cavalry, fell upon the rear of
the Spaniards which had been incautiously exposed,
and a spirited action ensued, the horse of the English
General receiving two wounds under him, and the
enemy at last retiring with the loss that day of several
hundred men.

It was not long moreover ere the combatants upon
both sides had to sustain the two never-failing in-
cidents of a Peninsular campaign—scarcity of provision
and sickness both of man and horse. The journal
kept at this time by Mr. Lenoir, the Acting Military
Secretary to the British troops, has several entries like
the following: "The people of the country that come
in say that the enemy ransack all the villages round
about for corn for bread, and oblige them even to beat
and grind new corn for them, and are nevertheless in
want."—"Provisions, especially flesh, are very dear
with us."—"Both armies very sickly and the flux reign-
ing among them."

There was another difficulty which at this time was confined to the Allies. While the regular troops under Philip were wholly Spanish, and with no Frenchman among them beyond some volunteer officers, there was a Babel-like confusion of tongues in Charles's camp. There, besides the English and Germans, were some Catalan levies, some Valencian refugees, several Portuguese regiments under the Conde of Atalaya, and several Dutch under Count Belcastel. There was also in consequence a whole host of jarring pretensions. To reconcile these as far as possible we learn from Mr. Lenoir, that only two days after Charles had joined the army it was "given out in Orders that all officers shall roll by the commission they have from their own Prince."

Through the month of June the two armies were engaged in divers marches and manœuvres. Thus on one occasion, writes Mr. Lenoir: "We have been all À L'EVEILLÉ these five days past, during which time nobody has had their clothes off." In July, the Allies were joined by the expected reinforcements, chiefly Germans, which made them as strong in foot as their enemies, although the latter still exceeded them in horse to the amount of twelve or fifteen squadrons. Stanhope pressed eagerly to fight, since, as he argued, delay would bring further succour to the Spaniards, "whilst" he said "we moulder away by sickness and desertion." Staremberg however, and under his guidance Charles also inclined to more dilatory counsels. The question being referred to a Council of War, the majority was clear against them. Even then the King and Marshal would only yield so far as to consent that the troops should cross the Segre and Noguera. At

that time the Spaniards had called in their outposts, CHAP.
and concentrated their army round the fortress of XII.
Lerida.   1710.

Having crossed the Segre by the bridge of Balaguer
the next point for the Allies was to secure in time the
passage of the Noguera. Their vanguard, chiefly of
horse and with Stanhope at its head, began its march
at midnight. Villadarias had sent out a stronger force
to intercept it, but his men were too late. When at
nine in the morning of the 27th of July they came in
sight of Stanhope, they found that he had already
three hours before crossed the river and made his
stand at Alfaraz. Then they also took post on some
high ground at the village of Almenara two miles
lower down the stream.

As the day advanced the two armies came up
squadron by squadron and battalion by battalion on
either side; and both the Kings appeared upon the
ground. As Stanhope relates it, "the Marshal was
pressed several times to attack the enemies' horse
which was before us, their foot marching a great distance behind them in the valley, where they could be
of no use." The Marshal seemed still determined not
to hazard anything, and Charles when appealed to by
the English General was equally immoveable. At six
in the evening however the enemies, with the view of
a defiance, marched several of their squadrons down the
slope of the Almenara hill, upon which a loud cry of
"Shame!" burst forth in the English ranks. Then,
though not without some further pressing and consequent delay, the leave to charge them was at last extorted from Staremberg and Charles. It wanted then
but half an hour of sunset; and there was not a mo-

ment to lose. Stanhope, as bursting free from his shackles, did not pause to muster his whole force but gathered round him in haste only sixteen squadrons, namely six English, four Dutch, and six Palatines; and with these he darted straight at the enemy. Seeing his intention the advanced squadrons of the Spaniards retired up the hill and rejoined their main body of horse, which Stanhope found to consist of twenty-two squadrons in the first and twenty in the second line; at their head their General of the cavalry Amezaga. As the English neared them the two chiefs closing together engaged in single combat; and Stanhope raising his sword hewed down Amezaga who fell dead from his horse. This exploit, which recalls the warfare of far earlier ages, is modestly omitted by Stanhope in his own relation, but is told in detail by other writers, and portrayed upon the medal which by the Queen's orders was struck in honor of the day.

The ardour of the onset carried everything before it. On the left of the Spaniards their horsemen, mostly new levies, fled at once; on the right the Royal Guards made some resistance but were also borne down. Philip himself was nearly taken prisoner, and only rescued through the intrepidity of his General, Villadarias, and another officer. It is asserted, perhaps a little too confidently, that with two hours more of daylight not one foot-soldier of their army could have escaped. As it was the darkness favoured them. They retired in headlong haste and broken ranks to the walls of Lerida, throwing away their tents, and leaving behind them some cannon with great part of their baggage. Their killed, wounded, and missing amounted to 1,500 men. On the other part the Allies had lost

400 only. Both the first and second in command of the English troops, Generals Stanhope and Carpenter, were slightly wounded; and two young officers of great promise, Lord Rochford and Count Nassau, were among the slain.

CHAP.
XII.
1710.

The consequence of this battle was the immediate retreat of the Spanish army. Philip, leaving only a garrison in Lerida, fell back in great haste first to the line of the Cinca and then to the line of the Ebro. At Zaragoza he was joined by the Marquis de Bay, the victor of La Gudiña in the last campaign, on whom dismissing Villadarias he now bestowed the chief command. The Allies on their part followed in the track of Philip by painful marches through an arid country, undergoing in that sultry season great distress for want of water and as great for want of bread. One of themselves describes as follows their last day before they reached the river: "With violent thirst and heat we had not a drop of water; and to incommode us the more the enemy had set fire to a very long heath we were to pass over. It is not to be conceived what we suffered upon such a march, smothered all that day with clouds of ashes, especially the foot. About five in the evening and not before, the horse of both lines got to the Ebro whose waters did not a little refresh us."[1] As Mr. Lenoir writes: "The men have wanted bread but do not complain; and the horses straw and corn and yet hold out."

While thus toiling forward in Aragon, General Stanhope, who commanded a separate division of 2,000 horse, succeeded, by a night march to Sarineña, in

---

[1] MS. narrative of the campaigns in Spain, embodied in Tindal's History, vol. v. p. 290.

surprising and putting to the rout two regiments of the enemies. During their further retreat he pressed closely on their rear. So near indeed were the two armies that once, as is recorded, King Charles supped in the house in which on the same day King Philip had dined.

The counsels of the Allies at this time were by no means unanimous. Both Staremberg and Charles still inclined to cautious counsels, and showed themselves unwilling to advance. Entreaties and remonstrances to them had to be renewed day after day. Even when they reached the Ebro, they would have desired to remain on the right bank. It was with reluctance that they suffered Stanhope and Carpenter to ford the river with the cavalry, between Pino and Osera in the night of the 17th of August. But that point being accomplished, the other Generals who with Stanhope had formed the majority at the Council of War—as Wills from the English, Belcastel from the Dutch, and Frankenberg from the Palatines—repaired to the Marshal's quarters, and urged the necessity of supporting their friends beyond the stream. After a long consultation they prevailed. It was agreed that a bridge of pontoons should be constructed as expeditiously as possible, and that the whole army should go over.

The Allies did pass the Ebro accordingly, between one and seven in the morning of the 19th, and pursued their march by the left bank, in the afternoon. At three o'clock the vanguard of Stanhope, and at five the other divisions coming up, descried the walls of Zaragoza at but a short league from them, and the Spanish army ranged in order of battle with the city on its left. Between the two armies there was still

however a deep BARRANCA or ravine, once the scene
of a fierce encounter with the Moors, and still surnamed
BARBANCA DE LOS MUERTOS, the valley of the dead.
The day was too far spent and the troops too much
exhausted for the Allies to attack at once, especially
with this obstacle before them, but the men were eager
for a battle on the morrow which the commanders
resolved to try. Staremberg, who although timorous
in tactics was personally brave and fearless, may have
shared as a soldier, the ardour which as chief he disapproved.

Both armies continued all night under arms.
Next morning, the 20th of August, they began a cannonade at daybreak which was continued briskly on
both sides until noon. Meanwhile they drew out their
lines of battle. Stanhope commanded the left wing of
the Allies, which was formed of English, Dutch, and
Palatines. There were also eight squadrons of Portuguese who, wearing at this time red coats, were mistaken by the enemy, as Stanhope had hoped, for
English. It was in this quarter and opposite the Allies'
left wing that the enemies had brought up their best
cavalry, and massed their principal strength. The Allies' right wing consisted of Portuguese foot and a
part of the German, under Count Atalaya. Marshal
Staremberg took his station in the centre, as in the
opposite ranks did also the Marquis de Bay. As to
infantry the two armies were nearly equal, but it is allowed that the Spaniards were superior by nine
squadrons of horse. On the whole they have been
computed at twenty-five, and the Allies at twenty-three
thousand men.

On another point also the advantage was with the

Spaniards. They were well fed from the adjoining city. The Allies, on the contrary, had out-marched their scanty supplies; and were looking out in vain for a promised convoy of bread. As is noticed by one of the officers: "we lost many men this morning who pressed by hunger and thirst ventured to go and gather grapes in the vale between the two armies, and were shot by the enemy's advanced guard."[2] Yet the troops showed no symptom of faintness when at noon came the signal for battle. Marching with alacrity down the Barranca before them, and then up its opposite bank, they bore full upon the enemy.

On the right Count Atalaya soon prevailed. There the Spaniards, mostly new-raised troops, after making one charge were seized with sudden panic, and in great part threw down their arms and dispersed. But opposite to Stanhope stood the veteran regiments, the Walloons and Royal Guards. Their first line was broken by the impetuous onset of the English General, but they rallied in a moment and not only recovered their ground, but turning fiercely on the Portuguese cavalry, which formed the extreme left of the Allies, put it to the rout. The Portuguese fled at once from the field and were pursued by some of the Spanish squadrons till near a Carthusian convent in the rear of the Allies, where Charles, after riding through his lines in the morning, had retired for the rest of the day.

This unguarded pursuit however left open a gap in their line through which the English General pouring his cavalry retrieved the fate of the battle. The Walloons and Royal Guards stood firm for some time

---

[2] MS. narrative embodied in Tindal's History, vol. v. p. 292.

longer but at last were beaten back. Staremberg meanwhile had encountered the Spaniards in the centre with much courage and coolness, but they maintained their ground until the victory on both his wings enabled him to complete his own. With less than three hours fighting the day was everywhere decided. The veteran Spanish regiments left the field still preserving their martial array though grievously thinned in numbers. But great part of the other troops disbanded. King Philip with some attendants spurred away at once, in the direction of Madrid. The Marquis de Bay fled to Soria, where he endeavoured to rally the troops.

King Charles that same afternoon entered Zaragoza in triumph, and before the sun had set issued a proclamation restoring the ancient privileges or Fueros of the Crown of Aragon. At eleven that night, Colonel Harrison was despatched with the standards taken and the news of the battle to the Queen. He went by way of Genoa, and touched at the Duke of Marlborough's camp.

In this battle the Spaniards left upon the field all their colours, all their cannon, all their baggage. Of their army there were nearly four thousand prisoners and five thousand slain or wounded, while the loss of the Allies was only fifteen hundred. Among several accounts of the day we may notice especially that of General Carpenter, written as follows the same evening: "This business and that of Almenara is entirely owing to Mr. Stanhope, both for pressing in council and for the execution." And again: "All Her Majesty's troops did well and the officers, but no pen can do justice to Mr. Stanhope, having hectored the Court and Marshal into these marches and actions and then commanded himself the advanced body."[3] We have Marlborough's testimony also to the importance of this action. Thus he writes to Godolphin: "Before this you have heard by Colonel Harrison the particulars of the battle in Spain, which is so deciding that it must have given us peace, had not the French been heartened by our divisions in England."[4]

These divisions had indeed not only continued but augmented. The dismissal of Sunderland, so tamely borne by the Whigs, gave of course new spirit to the secret advisers of Anne. It was determined no longer to delay the dismissal of Godolphin also. For this the Treasurer unwarily afforded a pretext, having at a Council, the Queen being present, addressed to Her Majesty some peevish words. On the 8th of August in Old Style—the very day before the victory of Zaragoza—he received a note from his Sovereign which thus concluded: "The many unkind returns I have received since (from you), and especially what you said to me personally before the Lords, make it impossible for me to continue you any longer in my service. But I will give you a pension of 4,000*l.* a year; and I desire that, instead of bringing the Staff to me, you will break it, which I believe will be easier to us both."

The great office of Treasurer thus made vacant was not filled up; it was placed in Commission. A Peer of no significance in politics, Earl Poulett, was declared First Lord, but the seals of Chancellor of the Exchequer were given to Harley, who was henceforth regarded and with good reason as Prime Minister.

3 Letter to Robert Walpole, August 20, 1710, as published in Somerville's Queen Anne, p. 639.

4 Letter dated Sept. 18, 1710. Coxe's Transcripts, Brit. Mus.

One of his closest friends, Earl Rivers, was despatched at once on a special mission to the Court of Hanover. The main object was no doubt to reconcile the Elector and the Dowager Electress to the recent changes. But Godolphin suspected something more. As he writes to Marlborough, "I imagine the chief errand is to propose to the Elector the coming into your post another year."

CHAP.
XII.
1710.

The leading Whigs in the administration were at first, as Sunderland says, stunned by so great a blow. They continued to indulge a hope that the dismissal of Godolphin might not be followed by their own. In this hope some at least amongst them were confirmed by secret overtures from Harley, who expressed his desire to effect in some degree a combination of parties. Thus he induced the Duke of Newcastle to continue in the government as Lord Privy Seal, by bestowing on him a rich sinecure office—Chief Justice in Eyre north of Trent. But he could not prevail with Robert Walpole whose rising talents he discerned and whose aid he was anxious to secure. "You are worth half your party," he said.[5] He had interviews in like manner with Somers, Cowper, and Halifax, and pressed them to continue in office, assuring them that there was "a Whig game intended at bottom." Somers and Cowper both were firm against his overtures, and Halifax also after some wavering declined. Of Somers the Queen spoke with much commendation after he had left her service, saying to Lord Dartmouth that he was a man who had never deceived her[6] — a praise which, I think, she could not have bestowed as truly

5 Coxe's Walpole, vol. I. p. 32.
6 Lord Dartmouth's note to Burnet's History, vol. VI. p. 12.

on many other statesmen of that time. Cowper also stood high in the Queen's esteem, as is best shown by the fact that she put back the Great Seal "at least five times" into his hands when he offered to give it up to her Majesty.[7]

The Whig Ministers however did not in general resign: they waited to be turned out. Nor had they long to wait. Harley finding his private overtures to them rejected fell back wholly on the Tories. With that party he now made a General Election his leading object. About five weeks after the dismissal of Godolphin the Queen came to a Council, and called for a Proclamation dissolving the Parliament. Cowper who still held the Great Seal offered to speak, but the Queen rising up forbade all debate and ordered the Writs to be prepared. Thus on the 21st of September was the Parliament dissolved. The Writs were issued five days afterwards, the new Parliament being summoned to meet on the 25th of November.

At the same period, though by degrees, the new administration was appointed. The Great Seal was put into Commission, Harcourt being, in the first instance, restored to place as Attorney General. But before the next meeting of Parliament, he was named Lord Keeper, and finally Lord Chancellor. The Admiralty also remained in Commission, Sir John Leake, who had hitherto been a junior, becoming First Lord instead of Orford. Rochester became Lord President in the place of Somers. Buckingham became Lord Steward in the place of Devonshire. Ormond became Lord Lieutenant in the place of Wharton. But above all the post of Secretary of State,

7 Lord Cowper's Diary, Sept. 22, 1710, as printed for the Roxburgh Club.

left vacant by Boyle, was bestowed on the "all-accomplished St. John"—already eminent for speeches in the House of Commons, of which unhappily not one word has been preserved. But from this, his last accession to office, until the Queen's demise, we have his published correspondence—a worthy monument of his genius and a perfect model, it may be said, of style.[8]

Thus fell the great Whig administration of Queen Anne. Considering its high fame in history, it is remarkable for how short a period it endured. The changes in Godolphin's government, bringing it round from Tory to Whig, took place, as we have seen, by slow degrees; but the latter party can scarcely be thought to have gained an entire ascendency, until the resignation of Harley in the spring of 1708. According then to this computation, the Whigs were dominant for a period of but two years and a half. So far as regards the great battles of this war, the two parties, looking only to their tenure of power, are entitled to divide the credit between them. The Tories held office during Blenheim and Ramillies; the Whigs held office during Oudenarde and Malplaquet. But as regards the policy which led to these successes the praise, as I conceive, belongs almost wholly to the Whigs. It was that war-policy, aimed at the ambition of Louis the Fourteenth, which King William had pursued with more spirit than success—that policy which Somers and Somers' friends had consistently

---

[8] Correspondence, public and private, of Lord Viscount Bolingbroke (from the papers of his Under-Secretary of State, Thomas Hare), 2 vols. quarto, 1798. Mr. Pitt, as I have heard from my father, was fond of referring to this book.

CHAP.
XII.
——
1710. maintained—that policy brought at last to a triumphant issue by the genius of Marlborough and Eugene.

In a History by the author of the present work, published so far back as 1832, it was observed, "how much the course of a century has inverted the meaning of our party nicknames—how much a modern Tory resembles a Whig of Queen Anne's reign, and a Tory of Queen Anne's reign a modern Whig."[9] But this view of the subject was warmly controverted by Lord, then Mr., Macaulay. In a justly famous essay .he said: "We grant one-half of Lord Mahon's proposition; from the other half we altogether dissent. We allow that a modern Tory resembles in many things a Whig of Queen Anne's reign. . . . Society, we believe, is constantly advancing in knowledge. The tail is now where the head was some generations ago. But the head and tail still keep their distance. . . . The stag in the Treatise on the Bathos, who 'feared his hind legs would o'ertake the fore' was not more mistaken than Lord Mahon, if he thinks that he has really come up with the Whigs."[1]

It is worthy of note, however, that as time passed on, Lord Macaulay came on full consideration to adopt the very view which he here opposes. This appears from his second essay on Lord Chatham, published eleven years later. Ever fertile of most ingenious illustrations, he has now a serpent to allege in the place of a stag. For he writes as follows: "Dante tells us that he saw in Malebolge a strange

---

[9] War of the Succession in Spain, p. 349. Many instances of this singular counter-charge are adduced in the Appendix to the first volume of the History of England from the Peace of Utrecht (p. 424, Tauchnitz Ed.).

[1] Edinburgh Review of January 1833, p. 535, and since in the Collected Essays.

encounter between a human form and a serpent..... CHAP.
Then a wonderful metamorphosis began. Each creature
was transfigured into the likeness of its antagonist.....
Something like this was the transformation which,
during the reign of George the First, befell the two
English parties. Each gradually took the shape and
colour of its foe. . . . Whatever judgment the Whig
or Tory of that age might pronounce on transactions
long past, there can be no doubt that, as respected
the practical questions then pending, the Tory was a
reformer, and indeed an intemperate and indiscreet
reformer, while the Whig was conservative even to
bigotry."[2]

[2] Edinburgh Review, October 1844, p. 527, and Collected Essays. The
passage referred to in Dante is *Inf.* xxv. 100.

CHAPTER XIII.

CHAP.
XIII.
1710.

Now began the war of the Elections. Now was shown the angry spirit which the impeachment of Sacheverell had first excited. Handbills were sent round by the High Church party proclaiming both in prose and verse that their favourite institution was in danger.[1] Many took advantage of the cry even without sharing in the sentiment; and the result was, that in the contests the Tories commonly prevailed. They carried their candidates in the centres of popular election, and sometimes even in the strongholds of lordly influence. Thus St. John triumphantly observes in one of his letters, that the Duke of Somerset had been defeated not only in the county of Sussex but in the small town of Marlborough; that Lord Wharton, in like manner, had succumbed both in Buckinghamshire and in Appleby. St. John himself, who had not been in the last Parliament,[2] was returned for Berkshire. Harley, who through his brother had hitherto divided with Lord Coningsby the influence at Leominster, was now enabled to cast the Whig Lord from that borough.

No contest however, among the many of this time,

---

[1] Here is one of these as given in the Complete History of Europe, 1710, p. 589. It was meant especially for the Middlesex election :

"Join Churchmen, join, no longer separate,
Lest you repent it when it is too late.
Low Church is no Church."

[2] "Since H. St. John has resigned his place, his father refuses to choose him in Parliament"—that is for Wotton Basset. (H. Walpole to Stanhope, April 30, 1708 MS.).

appears to have stirred up so much interest as that at
Westminster. There the constituent body was large
and the franchise low. There many great merchants
had built houses; there many French Protestant pastors
—all of them of the Low Church creed—had found re-
fuge, and preached—as then no dominant body would
—the principles of toleration. There if anywhere the
Whigs were likely to hold their ground. They had
selected for candidates, first in his absence General
Stanhope, commended to popular favor by his recent
victories in Spain; and secondly a gentleman of note
in Herefordshire, Sir Henry Dutton Colt. These proved
to be the mob-favourites, which the Whigs were not at
that time, in other large towns. Swift as he drove out
with a friend has noted in his Journal to Stella: "October 5. In the way we met the electors for Parlia-
ment-men and the rabble came about our coach crying
A Colt! A Stanhope! et cetera. We were afraid of a
dead cat or our glasses broken and so were always of
their side."—But when from empty acclamations they
came to solid votes, it was found that the Whigs had
gained no advantage from all this shouting, and that
the High Church candidates—Cross and Medlicott—
were returned by large majorities.

Nor were the Ministry less successful with the
Scottish representative Peers. As St. John writes:
"The election of Peers is over for the northern part
of the island, and you will find by the list which is
published that we have every one. Our Parliament
will therefore be as entirely in the Queen's interest as
her most affectionate servants can desire."[3] It must
however have been some drawback to the delight of

3 To Mr. John Drummond, Nov. 17, 1710.

this northern triumph that, as the Duke of Queensberry declared to Lord Cowper, "none of the Scotch
Lords of Parliament except Annandale is able to live
here, without money from the Queen."[4]

The confidential diary of Swift, from which I just
now quoted, and which begins at this period, continues
thenceforth of the utmost interest and value. He was
also engaged in a graver composition—a "History of
the Four Last Years of the Queen." But there is very
great reason to doubt whether the work under that
name, which is commonly ascribed to him, was truly
his. Lord Macaulay more than once expressed to me
a strong conviction that it was not. It was published
for the first time long after Swift's decease, that is in
1758, and then by a hostile and anonymous editor;
and there are other circumstances of suspicion that
attend it. Be this as it may, it is certainly a mere
party effusion, which seems to me as unworthy of confidence upon the one side as for example Cunning-
ham's History upon the other.

While these things were passing in England the
campaign was concluded abroad. In the Netherlands
there is little to record after the fall of Bethune, beyond
the siege and the surrender of two small towns, Aire
and St. Venant. The latter made little defence, but
Aire—its garrison commanded by General de Guébriant
—held out most bravely till the 8th of November, having
caused to the Allies a loss of 7,000 men in killed and
wounded. Then Marlborough placing his troops in
winter-quarters repaired to the Hague. Cowper notes
in his diary this autumn: "Lord Sunderland showed
me a letter from Duke of Marlborough; he resolved to

4 Lord Cowper's Diary, December 21, 1710.

stand and be advised by his friends the Whigs." But
Cowper adds this cautious commentary: "Nota bene.
This was dated before the Elections of this Parliament
known. Query. What opinion after will Duke of Marlborough be of?"

In Spain there were greater events. The victory at
Zaragoza had laid Castille open and free to the Allies.
Philip indeed had returned to his capital but only to
leave it again in all haste for Valladolid, accompanied
by his Queen and Court and some thousands more of
his adherents. There was nothing to bar the way of
Staremberg and Stanhope except only the caution of
the former. In several councils of war held at Zaragoza in the days that followed the battle, the Marshal
maintained that, instead of advancing, the Austrian
Prince should rather remain in Aragon, seeking to
reduce Navarre on the one side and Valencia on the
other, and thus combining to himself the provinces in
the north and east of Spain. On the other hand the
cry of Stanhope was still "Forward!" He argued that
by pressing to Madrid, and calling the Anglo-Portuguese to join them from the Portugal frontier they
might probably establish Charles upon the throne.
After some sharp altercation and much demur, these,
the bolder counsels, prevailed.

But the difficulty for supplies was as usual in Spain
extreme. On the 26th of August, the day on which
the army was to commence its march to Madrid, Stanhope wrote as follows to Mr. Mead, its Paymaster at
Barcelona: "We have wanted bread for three days
since the battle, and are like to continue to want. If
we should want money too, I leave you to judge what
will become of us notwithstanding our victory. . . .

With all the endeavours I have used, I have not found credit in this town for a shilling; therefore our only dependence must be from Barcelona. If nothing should have come from Portugal or Italy, yet I hope that upon such an occasion as this, your Catalan merchants will open their purses and lend you what you will."

In the days that followed, the Allies continued their march through Castille by the route of Calatayud and Guadalaxara, often straitened for want of bread but never encountered by an enemy. From the camp at Siguenza the General wrote again to the Paymaster on the 13th of September. "I hope to be in a week at Madrid where, if we do not find credit, the Lord have mercy upon us, for we have not a shilling in the army. I therefore pray of you not to trust so absolutely to Providence, but to use your utmost endeavours to supply us."

It was, as he expected, on the 21st of September that Stanhope with the vanguard of cavalry came in sight of Madrid. The occupation of that capital by the English after the victory at Zaragoza may be compared to the similar event on the 12th of August 1812 after the victory at Salamanca. But there was this great variation between them. In the second case the English found the warmest greeting; in the first utter silence and cold averted looks. It is well described by General Napier how, as Wellington neared the gates, "the multitude who before that hour had never seen him came forth to hail his approach, not with feigned enthusiasm. . . . but with tears and every other sign of deep emotion they crowded around his horse, hung upon his stirrups, touched his clothes, or throwing themselves upon the earth blessed him aloud as the

friend of Spain."[5] How different the scene in 1710
as the Military Secretary of that day has portrayed it.
"About half a mile from the town Mr. Stanhope was
met by the magistracy.' After the usual compliments
the General sent them with an escort to the King.
We marched on the right of the town and encamped
in the walks of La Florida. General Stanhope went
from thence to the town-house, but the inhabitants
seemed very sorry to see us there, and not one showed
any expression of joy."[6]

Still less auspicious was the day when, shortly afterwards, Charles made his public entry with all the war-
like pomp he could command. There were a few cries
of VIVA! from children among whom money had been
thrown, but the people for the most part had shut themselves up in their houses. With a burst of anger the
Prince exclaimed that the city was a desert, and refusing to dwell in it, repaired to an adjacent country
house. Stanhope in his despatches observes, that not
one officer in the Duke of Anjou's service, nor any
other man of note, had come to join them, and that in
Castille they were masters of no more ground than
they encamped on. One source, however, of legitimate
triumph remained to the British army. For, as Stanhope writes to Craggs, "We have found at (the Church
of) Atocha all the colours which were taken at the battle
of Almanza."

It was hoped at this time, that the junction of the
Anglo-Portuguese would fully enable the Allies to overcome their difficulties. On that junction, said Stanhope, "would depend the fate of the campaign." At first

CHAP.
XIII.
1710.

---

5 Napier's Peninsular War, vol. v. p. 194.
6 Mr. Lenoir's Journal, Sept. 21, 1710.

there seemed every reason to expect it. Philip had called to his own camp, and for his own more immediate objects his body of troops from the Portugal frontier. At first then, and until Philip's forces moved down upon the Tagus, nothing interposed between the Portugal army and Madrid. There was the prospect also of that army being well commanded. The Earl of Galway had been recalled as soon as his Whig patrons had gone out of office in England, and in his place was named the Earl of Portmore, an officer of reputation. Although the tidings had not yet reached Madrid, it was believed that the new chief had already landed. Before the second week in October, Stanhope had sent off in succession five expresses, urging his advance. "I believe," thus he writes to Craggs, through life his intimate friend, "few men have taken so much pains as I am doing to get a Viceroy over himself;" since, after the junction, Lord Portmore as the senior officer would command in Stanhope's place.

In that event, however, it was Stanhope's wish to return on leave to England. He had already written to Lord Dartmouth to solicit that permission, if the prospects of the army should admit. Thus again to Craggs: "I am impatient to hear from you from England, where I think everybody is run mad, if half what I hear be true. But be it as it will, I pray you to get me home. If my Lord Portmore joins us, I shall have no longer any business here." And in another letter, "I am impatient to know whether you have got me leave. Without it you will easily believe that I shall not venture nor trust Mr. Harley with my head. I am the more desirous because my Lord Duke desires it; and he is not mistaken in believing that I am his faithful servant." To the Great Duke himself, at the same time, Stanhope wrote, "I can assure your Grace that I desire nothing with so much impatience as to be in England, for many reasons; but especially, that I may have an opportunity of making good what I have often promised, to be faithful to your Grace in all events." [7] Unhappily, however, Lord Portmore had delayed his departure from England, and had not yet arrived in Portugal. In his absence the command had fallen on the Conde de Villa Verde, who as a Grandee ranked in the first class but as a General in the very lowest. He was not to be urged forward even by the plainest considerations of public policy. The letters of Stanhope, the words of Mr. Lefevre the English Resident, assailed the Court of Lisbon equally in vain. From Madrid the Allies as we have seen sent out in succession five expresses; in return to them not one soldier came.

Nor was there any thing to cheer them in the tidings from Philip's camp. The enthusiasm of the Castillians had already in great measure revived his drooping cause. It had quickened his own sluggish though courageous temper. It had brought to his ranks numerous and zealous though but half-trained volunteers. By these and by the troops he drew from Galicia and Biscay as well as from the Portugal frontier he was enabled to muster an army equal to that which had fought at Zaragoza. A General of established reputation was still wanting. Philip had long been aware that his own service could not afford him any such, and he had earnestly pressed his grandfather that the Duke of Vendome might be permitted to come and command

CHAP.
XIII.
1710.

---

[7] Letters dated October 4, November 6 and 18, 1710 (MS.).

the Spanish troops. Louis however had steadily re-fused so long as the negotiations at Gertruydenberg were pending, and while there was yet the prospect that he might be called upon wholly to renounce as well as disavow the Bourbon cause in Spain. But as the hope of peace receded the reason of refusal ceased; and Vendome himself, conscious that he had been censured for remissness in his campaign with the Duke of Burgundy, was eager to retrieve his reputation and signalise his prowess in another sphere.

On reaching head-quarters at Valladolid the new chief took at once a bold and vigorous measure. The chief danger as he saw was in the long deferred but still possible junction of the Portugal army with Charles's. To anticipate this Vendome set his own army in motion, and crossing the mountain chain of Guadarrama took post upon the Tagus at the bridge of Almaraz. Here, at the head before long of four and twenty thousand men, he greatly out-numbered either force of the Allies and effectually prevented any future combination between them.

Nor was this his only enterprise. He had detached some light cavalry to harass the Allies at Madrid. And as Stanhope in consequence complains, "the enemies have had two bodies of horse continually hovering within a day's march of us, and have made our com-munication with Aragon impracticable otherwise than by sending of strong parties thither, which we have been obliged to do to get up some money."

Still however, in spite of these discouragements Stanhope proposed, and he carried through, a measure of great energy. "We are come to a bold resolution, which is to winter in the heart of Castille. To this end we are fortifying Toledo, where will be the left of our quarters. We shall put the Tagus before us, and stretch our right to the mountains of Aragon, by which we shall have communication, though troublesome, with Catalonia."[8]

CHAP.
XIII.
1710.

In pursuance of this resolution the Allied chiefs fixed their head-quarters at Ciempozuelos, a village five hours march to the south of Madrid, while they sent forward a strong division under Count Atalaya to hold and intrench Toledo. Madrid itself was relinquished though as it were kept in view. As the troops marched from the gates they had the mortification to hear behind them a joyful peal resounding from all the innumerable church bells of the city.

Scarcely moreover had the Allies taken post at Ciempozuelos before ill news came pouring in upon them from divers quarters. First they had accounts that the Portuguese had been so far disheartened by Vendome's advance, that they had relinquished all idea of further operations even upon their own frontier, and had withdrawn at once to winter-quarters. As Stanhope wrote to the Secretary of State in England: "I cannot help repeating to your Lordship that Her Majesty's troops in Portugal are of no manner of service, nor ever will be of any so long as a Portuguese General shall govern the operations of their army."

Nearly at the same time, the tidings came from Catalonia that the province was exposed to some danger from the Duke de Noailles, who had been concerting measures with the Duke de Vendome and threatened an invasion from the Roussillon side. Charles eagerly laid hold of this plea for his own departure, and set off

<hr>

[8] To Lord Dartmouth, Nov. 6, 1710 (MS.).

CHAP.
XIII.
1710. from Ciempozuelos with an escort of 2,000 cavalry. As Stanhope explains it: "The King has this day left this army, so that we shall have one difficulty less to struggle with, I mean his impatience to rejoin his Queen, which has made him for some time very uneasy, and pressing to break up."[9]

Charles's General was almost as unquiet as Charles himself. On the very day after the Prince's exit Staremberg gave in a paper of several articles to the other chiefs. "Whether" says Stanhope "it arises from a dissatisfaction of this Court or of the several Generals here, or whether only from the motive therein alleged, the want of health, I will not determine . . . ; but if one may give credit to his protestations he is fully determined to leave this country so soon as the army shall be settled in quarters. And I am so much persuaded that he is in earnest that I think no time ought to be lost in fixing upon another General for the next year. He will be very little regretted by the troops, and yet to do him justice I believe it will not be easy to substitute one in his room; for which reason I have endeavoured and will endeavour to keep him here, but as I have already told your Lordship he seems as far as I can judge to be determined."[1]

Other cares and more pressing were at hand. Inferior as were the Allies already to Vendome in the essential arm of cavalry, it was no light thing that two thousand of the number should depart as Charles's escort. That event and the defection of the Portuguese induced them to reconsider their plans. Nor was there much time to lose, since a speedy advance might be

---

[9] To Lord Dartmouth, Nov. 18, 1710 (MS.).
[1] To the same, Nov. 20, 1710 (MS.).

expected from Vendome. Stanhope still desired to abide by the former resolution and to winter in Castille. But in the Council of War all the other chiefs were against him. They urged that, cut off from their supplies, they could scarcely hope to maintain themselves against a superior force in a most unfriendly country, and a most inclement season. Stanhope could insist no longer; and it was determined to fall back to the borders of Aragon and there take up winter quarters.

As the first step in this design the Allied chiefs moved their encampment from Ciempozuelos to Chinchon on the other side of the Henares, while Stanhope rode off with some cavalry to bring back the troops from Toledo. Having arrived with these at Chinchon the retreat of the whole army commenced. But so scanty were the supplies and so hostile the inhabitants that the soldiers could only hope to subsist by marching in separate bodies and sweeping over a wide extent of country. Staremberg led the Germans and Dutch in the centre; Atalaya the Catalans and Portuguese on the right; and Stanhope the English on the left, which, as nearest to the enemy, was the post of principal danger.

Vendome also was in motion. Accompanied by Philip he had led his army in the first place from the bridge of Almaraz to Talavera. There they met deputies from Madrid announcing that the city was freed from the invaders and impatient for His Majesty's return. The King and Duke accordingly pressed onward, and finding no enemy before them entered the city amidst loud acclamations on the 3rd of December

—the same day on which the Allies were commencing their retreat from Chinchon.

But though the Allies marched fast Vendome marched faster still. In his former campaigns he had often been accused of sloth and sluggishness. His late hours of rising—on some days indeed he would not rise at all—his gluttonous indulgence at meals, and his gross addiction to the worst of vices, had cost his countrymen some severe disasters. Now on the contrary, roused by the occasion, and eager to vindicate his fame, he showed almost incredible diligence. While the infantry straight from Talavera marched over the Henares by the Guadalaxara bridge, Vendome, still in company with Philip, coming from Madrid to another point on that river then in flood, plunged in and swam across at the head of the cavalry. From the opposite bank they still pressed forward with the light troops, horse and foot, leaving the rest to follow; and thus they overtook the left wing of the Allies.

That left wing under Stanhope consisted of eight battalions and as many squadrons; all of them English except only one battalion of Portuguese, and even that commanded by English officers. Thinned as were both battalions and squadrons by this toilsome campaign the total numbers did not exceed 5,500 men. It had been agreed with Staremberg that he and Stanhope should proceed in parallel lines. Stanhope was to march in four days from Chinchon to Brihuega and there halt to give his troops some rest and to bake for them some bread, while Staremberg did the like at Cifuentes, the two places being about five hours march from each other. Brihuega is a town of great antiquity; the Roman Centobriga, built on the river Tajuna and with

high uplands around it on every side but one. For its CHAP.
defence it had only a decaying Moorish wall.[2]

In pursuance of this plan Stanhope had entered
Brihuega late at night on the 6th of December. Next
day he employed himself in collecting corn and in
baking loaves. So adverse to him was the disposition
in all Castille that neither at Brihuega nor through his
four days' march did he receive the slightest intimation
of the enemy's advance. It was therefore with surprise
that, on the morning of the 8th, he observed some of
their horse on the brow of the neighbouring hills. His
surprise increased when, early in the afternoon, there
appeared some infantry also. "Till that time" he
writes "nobody with me, nor I believe did the Marshal
imagine that they had any foot within some days' march
of us. And our misfortune is owing to the incredible
diligence which their army made; for having, as we
have since learnt, decamped from Talavera on the
1st of December they arrived before Brihuega the 8th,
which is forty-five long leagues."[3]

In face of a force so superior to his own Stanhope
could not attempt to march out of Brihuega and seek
a junction with Staremberg. He despatched one of his
aides-de-camp full speed to apprise the Marshal of his
danger, gave a becoming answer to a summons of
surrender which was sent him by Vendome, and prepared for a resolute defence until succour should arrive.

[2] Some account of the affair at Brihuega, as also of *Milord Preterbourg*
(Peterborough), and of *El General Estanop* (Stanhope), is given in a history of
the neighbouring townlet of Orche, called on the titlepage *Ilustre y leal Villa*
and also strangely enough *Señora de su misma*. The volume was printed at
Madrid in 1748, the author's name *Fray Juan Talamanco*. It was shown me
by my friend Mr. Ford, and is, I believe, extremely rare.

[3] To Lord Dartmouth from Valladolid, January 2, 1711.

All that night his men were most actively employed in barricading the gates and making loopholes for musketry in the houses.

Before sunset there had already come up 6,000 of the enemies' cavalry and 3,000 of their foot. Vendome sent the Marquis of Valdecañas with one division to seize the bridge over the Tajuna, which was outside the town; and he completed his investment of the latter. Towards midnight he was joined by several more bodies of his troops with twelve pieces of the battering train. These he at once disposed in due order, and at day-break of the 9th of December they began to play. Two breaches were soon made in the old Moorish wall. Through these the Spaniards poured in. But the English had cast up intrenchments behind the breaches, as also barricades across the streets, and they continued to defend themselves with the utmost intrepidity. Several times were the assailants driven back in disarray.

After some hours of sharp conflict a short pause ensued. But at three in the afternoon Vendome having sent a second summons, which was rejected like the former, gave orders for a general assault. Besides playing field-pieces from the hills which were so close as to command most of the streets, and besides renewing the onset in the two breaches, he sprung a mine under one of the gates. Some of his men moreover found means to break passages through the wall into houses which adjoined it; and there they established themselves in force before they were perceived. The English however with unabated spirit still fought on. Still on every point they beat back their assailants. How many an anxious look must they meanwhile have cast to the opposite heights on which they expected every moment to see Staremberg and his army appear! Hour after hour passed and no sign of such succour came. Still worse was the rumour now rife among themselves, that their own ammunition had begun to fail.

Even then the resistance of these stout soldiers did not cease. "Even with bayonets"—so writes Stanhope to Lord Dartmouth—"the enemy were more than once driven out by some of our troops who had spent their shot; and when no other remedy was left, the town was preserved some time by putting fire to the houses which they had possessed, and where many of them were destroyed . . .; and when things were reduced to the last extremity, that the enemy had a considerable body of men in the town and that in our whole garrison we had not five hundred men who had any ammunition left, I thought myself obliged in conscience to save so many brave men who had done good service to the Queen and will I hope live to do so again. So about seven of the clock I beat the chamade and obtained the capitulation of which I send your Lordship the copy."

In this capitulation the enemy had been willing to grant most honourable terms; and on these terms then did Stanhope and his gallant little army become prisoners of war. Their defence of Brihuega had cost them 600 men in killed and wounded, while that of the Spaniards was acknowledged by themselves as double, and may even have amounted to 1,500 which was Stanhope's computation.

The delay of Staremberg on this occasion is not easy to explain or excuse. The aide-de-camp sent to him by Stanhope in the afternoon of the 8th must have reached him in the course of that night. Had Staremberg, next morning, set in movement the troops under his own immediate orders, he might have been in sight of Brihuega before noon. It is most probable that he forbore from marching until he could call in his right wing. It is certain at all events that it was only on the forenoon of the 10th that his vanguard appeared. As he heard no sound of firing and received no answer to his signals he rightly concluded that Stanhope had already surrendered. Under these circumstances he desired to avoid a general engagement, but the impetuosity of Vendome forced it on. Staremberg finding that he could not resume his retreat unmolested drew off his troops to the neighbouring plain of Villa Viciosa, and disposed them to the best advantage, his left behind a steep ravine, and his right with squadrons and battalions interlaced. From the loss of Stanhope the superiority of numbers was greatly against the Allies. They had but thirteen thousand men to oppose to twenty, but on the other hand they held the stronger position and they would encounter an enemy exhausted by many days' long marches and by one day's hard fight.

Vendome however would not postpone the onset beyond that afternoon. By his advice Philip put himself at the head of the Royal Guards, Spanish and Walloon, and with them rode fiercely up against the left wing of the Allies. So bold was the charge and so inspiriting the presence of the Sovereign that he threw it into utter confusion. The Allies in this quarter lost their baggage, which some of the Spaniards turned aside to plunder; and three of their best chiefs, the Dutch Generals Belcastel and St. Amant, and the Palatine General Frankenberg were slain. But the veteran skill of Staremberg retrieved the day. Bringing up some of his best troops by a movement in flank, he made a counter-charge upon the centre and left wing of the enemy. There the Spanish infantry, in great part weary and foot-sore, could offer no steady or sustained resistance. On this point therefore he was enabled to break their first and beat back their second line. Vendome and Philip at these tidings relinquished their success upon the right and hastened back to the endangered centre; but there found the rout so general that they looked upon the whole battle as lost, and issued orders for retreat in the direction of Torrija.

At this critical conjuncture one of Vendome's best officers, the Marquis de Valdecañas, putting himself at the head of the reserves and combining with them some of the Walloon cavalry, succeeded in rallying his countrymen and arresting the progress of his foe. Thus the conflict was resumed, and waged with obstinate valour until closed by the early coming of the winter night. Both chiefs—Staremberg as well as Vendome—had signalised themselves by their courage and conduct, both at the close maintained a strong position, and both, it may be said, equally divided the honors of the day. The killed and wounded in each army amounted to nearly the same number—namely from three to four thousand; and while Staremberg might boast the capture of some cannon, Vendome might boast the capture of some standards. Therefore although the victory was claimed in the most confident terms by both commanders, and although services of thanksgiving for it were offered up alike in the churches of Madrid and in those of Barcelona, the battle was in truth undecided.[4]

4 Of this battle there is a very fair account in a letter written by Philip to

But if even the discomfiture of Vendome had been more complete, Staremberg was not in a condition to profit by it. During the night he spiked his own and the Spanish cannon for want of means of transport, and before daybreak resumed his retreat from Castille. On his way, though not pursued by Vendome, he was harassed in his hasty marches by frequent attacks of irregular horse; he sustained a further loss of several hundred men; and finding that he could make no stand in Aragon fell back to Barcelona. He brought back to Charles an army reduced to 7,000 men—a grievous contrast to his numbers when the campaign began. Gloomy was the retrospect but no less gloomy the view before him. He learnt that the Duke of Noailles had already invaded the province and invested the important city of Gerona, which Staremberg had no means of effectually relieving. Vendome on the other hand, as though entirely victorious, had advanced to Zaragoza, where Philip established his Court and was rejoined by his Queen.

The news of Brihuega and of Villa Viciosa, but the former more especially, diffused of course great joy at Madrid and through all the people of Castille. How welcome the thought that the English HIJOS DE LUTERO (sons of Luther), were now captives—the same English whom they had so recently beheld as conquerors! Nor did a holy legend fail to spring up in that congenial soil. It was alleged that the Allies at Toledo (who, by the way however, were mostly Portuguese) had there committed divers acts of sacrilege and profane-

his Queen and published in the appendix to the Mémoires de Berwick, vol. II. p. 361 ; and another not quite so even-handed from Staremberg to Charles in the Complete History of Europe, 1710, p. 617.

ness in the churches, wholly disregarding the authority CHAP.
of St. Leocadia, the patron Saint of that city. But XIII.
St. Leocadia had soon avenged herself. She had compelled the intruders to capitulate on the 9th of December—the very day held sacred to her worship in
the Church's calendar. Thus writes of it a zealous
Spaniard, the historian of those times, the Marquis de
San Phelipe, "Heretics may laugh, but misdeeds are
not forgotten, and there is no such thing as chance in
the decrees of Providence."[5]

It might in like manner have beseemed the sanctity
of Leocadia had she also inflicted some penalty upon
the French Marshal for the breach of faith which
ensued. The capitulation of Brihuega, as he signed it,
stipulated that the officers and men who laid down
their arms should not be separated from each other
but be conveyed to some towns near the coast, there
to remain until they were exchanged. By order of
Vendome, on the contrary, the officers were quartered
at Valladolid and other inland cities, and the men dispersed in villages, and there exposed to various acts of
ill-treatment and indignity, as to which the earnest remonstrances of Stanhope could obtain but a tardy and
partial redress.

Before I leave the events of this year in Spain I
may observe that, strangely chequered as they were
with good and evil fortune, they appear to have strongly
impressed the imagination of the Spaniards. This is
shown not merely nor so much by the legend of Leocadia already mentioned, but above all by the multitude of popular ballads and broadsides which this year
produced among them, while scarce any, as I believe,

5 *Comentarios de la Guerra de España*, tom. II. p. 51.

are to be found for a long period either before or since. All these ballads are on the Castillian side, and love to remind their readers that the Allies were in great part heretics. Luther and the Devil are often brought into play. Staremberg is commonly mentioned by his Christian name of Guido, as being no doubt more metrical; Stanhope appears as Estanope; and Queen Anne as Doña Ana; and there are frequent attempts at a jingle on these rhymes.[6]

In England the new Parliament having met as summoned on the 25th of November, the Commons in

---

[6] Here is one sample:

> *Quien nuestras leyes profana?*—ANA.
> *Quien nuestro cuchillo ha sido?*—GUIDO.
> *Y de la Fè quien su tope?*—ESTANOPE.

Another of these conceits is in the *Soneto à la entrada del Señor Archiduque en Madrid y à las tropas auxiliares de Demonios.* Here the point seems to be that every line is to conclude with the same syllable *te.* Thus:

> *El Señor Archiduque de repen-*
> *A reynar se nos viene à nuestra Cor-*
> *A su lado trayendo por consor-*
> *Herege Estanope, con su gen-*   } TE
> *Entra, gobierna, y manda diligen-*
> *Consejos forma, ofrece passapor-* &c.

But the most spirited perhaps of these numerous effusions is an imaginary *Carta de Estarember à Estanop,* with Estanop's reply—

> *Digo es esta la conquista*
> *Del Señor Carlos Tercero?*
> *Mas le durò à Sancho Pança*
> *Su imaginado Govierno.*
>
> *Querias hazer Serrallo*
> *Para passar este invierno*
> *Para tener conveniencias*
> *De un obispo de Lutero?*

Several of these pieces are bound together in a book entitled *Papeles varios,* now at the British Museum; and a volume with many others was purchased by me at the sale of Lord Stuart de Rothesay's library in June, 1855.

their very first act manifested the colour which they derived from the recent Elections. They chose for Speaker without a contest William Bromley, one of the members for the University of Oxford, and one of the foremost men in the High Tory ranks. On the 27th the Queen in person delivered the opening Speech. "My Lords and Gentlemen" she said "I shall in the plainest words tell you my intentions. . . . I am resolved to support and encourage the Church of England as by law established; to preserve the British Constitution according to the Union; and to maintain the Indulgence by law allowed to scrupulous consciences. And that all these may be transmitted to posterity, I shall employ none but such as are heartily for the Protestant Succession in the House of Hanover; the interest of which Family no person can be more truly concerned for than myself." To these expressions on Home policy there were added some others on Foreign, declaring that to carry on the war in all its parts, but particularly in Spain, with the utmost vigour, was the likeliest means with God's blessing to procure a safe and honourable peace, for us and all our Allies.

These sentiments, held to indicate the policy of the new Prince Minister, appear to have given general satisfaction. There was only some demur that the word "Indulgence" had been substituted for the better known word "Toleration." Loyal Addresses in answer were voted without opposition in both Houses; and Harley might indulge the prospect of a long and prosperous sway.

On one point only did the Opposition that day attempt to raise its banner, and that but very feebly.

Lord Scarborough in the House of Peers moved a vote of thanks to Marlborough, for his services in the last campaign. This was opposed by the Duke of Argyle, since in truth the last campaign had not been marked by any considerable exploit; but the Ministers had no desire to press the debate upon that issue, and on a whisper from one of them to the Duke of Devonshire the question was allowed to drop until the General's return. As St. John wrote next day to his friend Mr. Drummond: "One would imagine that Scarborough had been hired by somebody that wishes Lord Marlborough ill to take so unconcerted and so ridiculous a measure."

The Queen and her Ministers were at this time the less inclined to show the Duke any special sign of favor as being grievously harassed by the angry passions of the Duchess. To such lengths did she carry her resentment at this very juncture, that she declared her intention to publish the Queen's letters to herself, written in the utmost unreserve during her many years of Court favor. Anne more than once desired that her "scribbles," as she termed them, should be returned to her, but the Duchess declined to comply with this surely not unfair request. St. John in the same letter to Mr. Drummond, which was just now quoted, observes that the new Ministers are very willing to act cordially with Marlborough "the great man" but only on certain conditions which St. John goes on to explain: "If he comes home and disengages himself from the Whigs, and if he puts a stop to the rage and fury of his wife."

There was now another cause of difference. Three General officers serving with the army in Flanders, by name Meredith, Honeywood and Macartney, carried CHAP. XIII. their attachment to Marlborough so far that at a con- 1710. vivial entertainment, not satisfied with drinking his health, they drank also "Damnation and confusion to the new Ministry, and to those who had any hand in turning out the old."[7]   Such an insult could scarcely pass unpunished.   On being apprised of it, the Secretary at War wrote to inform the three gentlemen that the Queen had no further occasion for their services. They were allowed as an act of grace to dispose of their commissions; still however Marlborough was deeply chagrined.   Nor was the Duke less displeased at another incident of the same period.   His especial favourite General Cadogan was recalled from the post of Envoy to the States both at Brussels and at the Hague; and in his stead was appointed another officer, the Earl of Orrery, whom the Duke did not love.[8]

Marlborough himself having landed at Solebay reached London in the afternoon on the 28th of December.   As he passed through the city he was loudly cheered by the people.   There were shouts: "God bless the Duke of Marlborough!   No Popery!   No wooden shoes!"—the last a frequent taunt in that century against the SABOTS of the French.   Fearing that the Queen might be offended at these outcries, Marlborough went in the first instance to Montague House, and waiting till the multitude had dispersed, proceeded in a common hackney coach, so as to shun observation, to wait upon Her Majesty at St. James's.   His reception was civil but cold.   The Queen said: "I am de-

---

[7] Tindal's Hist. vol. v. p. 337.   We are also told of their " contemptuous gestures against Harley."   (Coxe's Marlborough, vol. v. p. 361.)

[8] "Against whom" says Coxe in the same passage "he had particular objections."   What these were is not stated.

sirous you should continue to serve me and will answer for the conduct of all my Ministers towards you." But she added "I must request you would not suffer any Vote of Thanks to you to be moved in Parliament this year because my Ministers will certainly oppose it." The Duke made no rejoinder to this last request but said in reply to the former: "I shall always be ready to serve your Majesty if what has recently passed should not incapacitate me." He added that he was neither covetous nor ambitious, which the Queen afterwards repeated with a bitter comment of her own to St. John.

On the following days the General received visits of compliment from all the Ministers except Harley who sent him a message to desire that their first meeting might occur as if by accident at the Council or the Court. It seems that Marlborough had come back to England in almost the very frame of mind that St. John had desired. St. John gave an account of his visit to Swift almost immediately after it took place. "The Duke" he said was lamenting his former wrong steps in joining with the Whigs.[9] This may be deemed not far from an overture to rejoin his old friends the Tories. To Dartmouth he talked in nearly the same strain. "I hope" he said "you will do me good offices with the Queen. I know she has an entire confidence in you and I am sincerely glad of it." Words surely of no slight significance as coming from the father-in-law of Sunderland whom Dartmouth had displaced. But further still and yet more surprising Marlborough went on to complain of the conduct of his wife. "She has acted strangely" he said "but there

9 Journal to Stella, Dec. 31, 1710.

is no help for that; and a man must bear with a good CHAP. XIII.

1710.

deal to be quiet at home."[1]

Peace in Europe may be purchased too dearly—such was at the time the very just feeling of Marlborough and his friends. Perhaps the same remark might be applied to "quiet at home." But even in the more difficult domestic sphere Marlborough in some degree prevailed. Within the first days of the new year he had wrought so far with the Duchess as to bring a conciliatory message from her also. "Lady Marlborough offers, if they will let her keep her employments, never to come into the Queen's presence."[2]

Here then was perhaps an opening. Here then it might be possible in a cordial spirit to welcome Marlborough as an old friend back again into the Tory ranks. Such a course was commended to the Ministers both by policy and patriotism—by policy as detaching from the opposite party its pillar and mainstay—by patriotism as enabling them to leave at the head of the army, not in half-hearted adherence but in full and thorough concert of measures, the man who beyond all possible comparison could command that army best. It would have bound him to exert according to their wishes his great influence with the Continental Powers and brought the Allies more readily to moderate terms of peace. The Queen was indeed much incensed and with good reason against the Duchess. But Her Majesty might have been prevailed upon to leave the Duchess in possession of her Court-places, or of one or two of them, provided Her Grace would untertake never again by right of office to intrude herself into Her Majesty's presence.

[1] Note by Lord Dartmouth to Burnet's History, vol. VI. p. 33.
[2] Journal to Stella, January 12, 1711.

Much, very much, might depend upon this feminine question, since the Duke had announced his positive determination of resigning if the Duchess were dismissed.

A reconciliation with Marlborough—if sought by himself—was therefore I conceive both the interest and the duty of the Ministers. It was just what the Tories should have wished for—it was just what the Whigs apprehended. Such, as we may gather from his private Diary, was Swift's opinion. "I think" he adds "our friends press a little too hard on the Duke of Marlborough." To that opinion it is probable that St. John also inclined. But Harley could not resist the pleasure of humbling the great chief who had humbled him; and the Ministers as a body were hurried onward by the mean spite of their chief. It was resolved to keep no measures with the Duke and to proceed to extremities with the Duchess.

The scene in Parliament may be first considered. Lord Peterborough had now been appointed to a secret mission at the Court of Vienna, the object being partly to satisfy that restless spirit, and partly to promote a better understanding between the Emperor and the Duke of Savoy; and he was on the very point of setting out, his servants indeed already at Greenwich ready to embark. But in the first days of January, the Queen having sent a Message to the House of Peers relative to the ill news from Spain, their Lordships resolved to investigate the former miscarriages in that country resulting in the battle of Almanza. For this inquiry the presence of Peterborough was desired, and the Queen was addressed that he might be directed to postpone his journey. Galway had already

come back from Portugal. There ensued a long train
of recrimination between the two Earls, and three
sharp debates in which many other Peers took part.
Marlborough did his best for Galway. "It is some-
what strange" he said "that Generals who have acted
to the best of their understandings and lost their limbs
in the service should be examined like offenders about
insignificant things." But not the least regard was
shown to the Duke's opinion. Finally, as desired by
the Government, there was a Vote of Thanks to Lord
Peterborough for his "great and eminent services;"
and there was a Vote of Censure on Lord Galway for
having given the right to the Portuguese out of their
own country. There was also another Vote of Censure on the late Ministers for having, as was alleged,
contributed to the disappointment at Toulon by urging
at the same time an offensive war in Spain. In this
last Censure Marlborough himself was plainly involved and he was one of the Peers who signed a
Protest against it.

Still more mortifying to him was the scene at Court.
The Queen had given a peremptory order for the Duchess
of Marlborough to send back her Gold Key in token
of her resignation of her offices. The Duchess endeavoured through several channels to soften the Royal
displeasure but in vain. At last, on the 17th of January,
the Duke obtained an audience for that object. He
began by presenting a letter from his consort couched
in terms of great humility. Anne after reading it said
only "I cannot change my resolution." Marlborough
then addressed Her Majesty in the most moving terms,
entreating that the Duchess might still be left in possession of her offices, or that at the very least a longer

interval of time should be allowed her. He threw himself down upon his knees and continued with passionate eagerness to urge his pleas for place. The Queen answered as before, that she would have the Gold Key and that within two days.

Finding the Queen inexorable Marlborough rose from kis knees and resuming his composure adverted to another matter which he said was very painful to him— the dismissal of the three officers in Flanders. But the Queen broke off the conversation abruptly by exclaiming, "I will talk of no other business till I have the Key." The Duke would yet have lingered, but the audience had already lasted an hour; and so with a heavy heart he took his leave.

With a heart still heavier perhaps he next appeared before his consort and told her that the Queen expected the Gold Key. The Duchess with great passion took the Key from her side, and threw it into the middle of the room bidding him take it up and carry it to whom he pleased.[3] That very evening then Marlborough returned to the palace to deliver the Key into the Queen's own hands. Nothing further of any moment then passed between them. The Duchess however was not withheld by her own vehement anger from taking a step which I have elsewhere and by anticipation related. She sent in to the Queen an account of the sums which she would have received during the last nine years had she at their outset accepted Her Majesty's offer of an additional pension from the Privy Purse. The Queen with great gene-

---

[3] All the rest of the transaction is derived from the Duchess's own narratives in Coxe's Life (vol. v. p. 410-7). But this last point of her violent demeanour rests on the authority of Lord Dartmouth, who had it from "one very intimate in the family" (note on Burnet's History, vol. vi. p. 32).

rosity—far greater perhaps than the occasion required —directed the whole of this money to be paid her.

Of the three great offices held by the Duchess of Marlborough two—as Mistress of the Robes and Groom of the Stole—were conferred on Her Grace of Somerset, while Mrs. Masham received the Privy Purse. Shortly afterwards the Duchess had also to relinquish for the use of her successors her apartments at St. James's Palace. She could only console herself by giving orders to tear down and carry away the brass locks from the doors and the marble chimney-pieces from the walls. It is gratifying to find that Marlborough disapproved this spoliation and wrote from the Continent to forbid its progress. As it was it had well nigh exhausted the patience of the Queen, who threatened to stop the monthly payments for the works at Blenheim. "I will build no house for the Duke of Marlborough" she said "when the Duchess has pulled mine to pieces."

It was free to the Duke, upon the Duchess's dismissal from office, to carry out the determination which he had expressed in that event, and to throw up his command. Meanwhile however he had received several letters from his friends abroad, and above all from Heinsius and Eugene, strongly deprecating his retirement as likely at that juncture to dissolve the Grand Alliance and ruin the common cause. Godolphin and others of his friends in England concurred in those representations. It is certain that for the great General of the age to continue at the head of the army in spite of many mortifications was a course to be fully justified by love of country and devotion to the public service. It is certain also that to relinquish a post of vast power and no less vast emoluments is a course that seems very far less inviting when no longer viewed as contingent or uncertain but as close at hand and immediately impending. Under the influence of these motives, or of some of them, Marlborough signified to the Ministers that he was willing to retract his resolution and to serve in the next campaign. In answer he was assured that he should be well supported and his army be well supplied. But no wonder that he was impatient to quit the scene of his mortifications. So early as the 18th of February we find him set out from London for the Hague.

The Ministers were not solely intent on the prosecution of the war. They had also on foot an overture of their own for peace. There seems no good reason why such an overture might not be made openly and frankly and in concert at least with Holland. It would be time enough to separate from our Allies if during the negotiations their demands should be found excessive or unjust. But a dark and tortuous course was at all times the most consonant to the character of Harley. For his instrument on this occasion he selected a priest named Gaultier, who had been Chaplain to Marshal Tallard during his embassy to England. Since then he had continued to reside in London, from whence he was able to send at intervals secret intelligence to the Court of France. There also he became well known to the Countess of Jersey, herself a Roman Catholic, and to her husband, who was in secret a warm friend of the Pretender. The interest of that person was almost as dear both to Gaultier and to Torcy as that of Louis the Fourteenth, or in truth it was the same. For the greater security of their intelligence they had

agreed, besides other cant names for the English Min- CHAP.
isters, to designate in their letters the young Prince as XIII.
Montgoulin and Queen Anne as Madame Protose. 1711.
They also, as was usual with the Jacobite intriguers
down to a much later time, frequently adopted as a
blind the language of trade.

Here are some extracts from this most secret correspondence in the autumn of 1710: "Are you aware"
writes Gaultier to Torcy "that Madame Protose has a
very tender feeling for M. de Montgoulin, and looks
upon him as though her own child? Mr. Rolland (Earl
of Jersey) assures me that all the changes she is now
effecting are made partly for the love of him; and that
Messieurs Morand (Duke of Shrewsbury), Vivant (Duke
of Buckingham), and Vanderberg (Mr. Harley) are
working for him only, with the view of restoring what
was formerly taken from him, and making good the
wares which had been confiscated."

And again, three days later: "I must refer to what
I have already had the honor of communicating to you
in regard to M. de Montgoulin. Our new merchants
have a very great consideration for him; and it seems
to me that if he had the same way of thinking as they
have, there would be no difficulty of giving him back
what belongs to him, that is, after the decease of
Protose." It is easy to perceive what in this place
Gaultier desires to indicate by "the same way of
thinking." He refers to the Roman Catholic religion
held by the young Prince, which was held, and justly,
as the main obstacle in the way of another Restoration.

A few weeks later Gaultier has still more explicit
tidings to announce: "Two days back M. Rolland
(Earl of Jersey) gave me of himself occasion to speak

to him openly respecting M. de Montgoulin.   I found him most fully disposed to do that person service; and he told me that he had already begun, with two or three of his partners, to frame a plan that cannot fail of success to prosper the affairs of the aforesaid Montgoulin.   As soon as this plan is perfected it will be placed in my hands, but meanwhile it is desired to learn what amount of confidence you have in me, and how far you wish my friend and myself to discuss this question together.   We agreed that I should write to you about this to-day, and that you would let him know your sentiments upon it by the same channel as before."[4]

It is painful to trace in this correspondence how party spirit may prevail over love of country.   We find the Earl of Jersey, Peer of the Realm and sworn Counsellor of the Queen, sending advice to the Ministers of a Sovereign with whom Her Majesty was at war, and pointing out by what means the successes of her Generals might be most effectually arrested.   We find him, as his conversation is reported by Gaultier, lamenting the recent victory of Almenara as likely to impede the conclusion of a peace upon the basis that Philip should continue to hold the throne of Spain: "Surely" added Jersey "it would be good policy in you to press the Archduke closely and without loss of time, and to confine him if possible within the walls of Barcelona. And then, why not attempt to detach the Duke of Savoy from the Grand Alliance, considering his causes of complaint against the Court of Vienna?"[5]

---

[4] Letters from London (originals in French) of October 3 and 7, and December 28, 1710, all New Style. (Archives des Affaires Etrangères.)

[5] Letter dated September 5, 1710, N. S.

Such being the terms of confidential intercourse on which Gaultier stood with Jersey, it is no wonder that the Earl should recommend him as a man of trust to Harley. He was now directed to go to Paris on a secret mission, though for greater security with only verbal instructions delivered to him by Lord Jersey. He was to state in confidence to the French Ministers the desire of the English for peace, and the suggestion that Louis might himself propose to renew the negotiation in Holland.

In pursuance of these instructions, Gaultier landed at Nieuport on the 15th of January, and under the name of Delorme made his way to Versailles. There he had an interview with M. de Torcy, whom he greatly surprised by the sudden prospect of a peace—"a thing," says Torcy in his Memoirs, "most necessary to us, and most anxiously wished for, but of which at that time we had not the smallest expectation."—"Asking us," he adds, "whether we wished for peace was like asking a sick man whether he wishes to recover." Gaultier added that so far from seeking to entangle the French Minister by any written declarations, he desired on his return to England to take with him no credential beyond a short note of compliment.[6]

It is not hard to imagine how highly pleased with these overtures were both Torcy and his Royal Master. But they were far too politic to show their joy in unmeasured terms. It was resolved, on full deliberation,

CHAP.
XIII.
1711.

---

[6] "Donnez-moi, dit-il, une lettre pour Milord Jersey : écrivez-lui simplement que vous avez été bien aise d'apprendre de moi qu'il était en bonne santé. . . . Cette lettre seule sera mon passeport et mon pouvoir." (Mémoires de Torcy, vol. III. p. 21.)

14*

to make answer that the King was justly offended at the inveterate spirit shown by the Dutch in the late negotiation, and that it would not be consistent with his dignity to renew it by again applying to them. The King however would most cheerfully accept the mediation of England. He would lay before the English Ministers the concessions he was willing to make, and leave it to them whenever they thought fit to impart his offers to the Dutch.

With this answer as verbally given Gaultier took his departure. After an interval he reappeared at Versailles bringing with him the assent of Harley and his colleagues to the mode of negotiation proposed, but desiring the utmost secrecy to be observed.

CHAPTER XIV.

WHILE thus a peace was mysteriously preparing, CHAP.
the House of Commons showed great readiness in vot- XIV.
ing the large Supplies which were required for the 1711.
war, and which amounted this year to no less than
6,000,000*l*.   To assist in obtaining this sum there
were two Bills passed to raise 3,500,000*l*. by two Lot-
teries, to be paid back in thirty-two years; and for a
fund to answer this Duties were laid on hops, candles,
cards and dice, and on the postage of letters.   There
was also proposed a Duty on leather, but against this
on a division a majority of Members declared.   Still
the Ministers did not give up their point.   They brought
forward a motion for the same amount of Duty upon
skins and tanned hides, and this was agreed to by the
House, although in fact still leather otherwise expressed.   So much may depend on a name![1]

There was another scheme of the High Tories, now
forming the majority, by which they hoped both to fill
the Exchequer and to distress the Whigs.   This was a
further resumption of King William's grants, appoint-
ing in the first instance a Commission of Inquiry.   A
Bill for that object passed through its stages in the
Commons, but was finally rejected by the Lords.

A different subject which at this time engaged the
attention of both the Houses related to the Palatines.
These poor emigrants, chiefly Lutherans, had during

[1] Parl. Hist. vol. VI. p. 999.

the last two years come over from the Continent in considerable numbers. The Queen had afforded them her bounty; and the Whig Ministers had generously striven to establish them to their advantage; about eight hundred families being sent to Ireland and many more to the North American plantations, while others were supplied with funds at home. But these charities, being bestowed at a season of distress when bread had greatly risen in price, excited much displeasure among the lower ranks in England. There was a cry that we supported strangers while our own people were starving. There was also a cry from other persons higher in station though scarcely so in sense, that this was only part of a subtle design against the Church of England, the true object of the immigration being to increase the numbers and the strength of the Protestant dissenters. So strong were these feelings that Bishop Burnet does not hesitate to ascribe to them a considerable share in the ferment that rose upon Sacheverell's trial.

The friends of the Church as they called themselves, having now the ascendency in the House of Commons, were not slow in re-echoing the Anti-emigrant cry. After some inquiry before a Select Committee they passed two vehement Resolutions. First "that the inviting and bringing over the poor Palatines of all religions at the public expense was an extravagant and unreasonable charge to the kingdom, and a scandalous misapplication of the public money, tending to the increase and oppression of the poor of this kingdom, and of dangerous consequence to the Constitution in Church and State." And secondly, "that whoever advised the bringing over the poor Palatines into this kingdom was an enemy to the Queen and kingdom." It was desired to apply this last Resolution, in a specific manner, to the Earl of Sunderland, there being produced a letter on the subject addressed by him as Secretary of State to the Board of Trade. On further reflection however that intention was at last let fall. But the House eagerly carried through a Bill to repeal the Act for the general naturalization of all Protestants, which had passed two years before. Far different was the feeling of the Lords. When the Bill came up to their House it was rejected, even at its first reading, to the great joy of all the foreign Protestants.

While thus the two Houses were engaged in public business, the life of the Prime Minister was exposed to sudden danger. There was a certain French emigrant who called himself the Marquis de Guiscard, and who had several times been consulted by Marlborough and Godolphin on their projects of descent in Languedoc and Picardy. Finding his counsels neglected and his pension reduced by Harley he was provoked to a signal act of treachery. He wrote some secret letters to Paris offering to make his peace and disclosing whatever he knew. But these letters being by good fortune intercepted, a Warrant for High Treason was issued against him by Secretary St. John; and on the 8th of March he was apprehended in St. James's Park. Being conveyed to the Cockpit and hopeless of a pardon he indulged only the hope of revenge, and observing in the room where he waited a penknife on a standish, he contrived to take it up and secrete it, unperceived by the messengers who watched him. Being next brought before the Lords of the Council he was shown his letters from Paris and convicted by his own hand-writing. Then wholly desperate he desired, it was thought, to kill the Secretary of State who had signed the Warrant and produced the letters, but as St. John sat out of his reach he suddenly stooped down over Harley, and with a cry J'EN VEUX DONC A TOI, drew out the penknife and stabbed him in the breast. The slender blade broke in the gash about half an inch from the handle, which Guiscard not perceiving redoubled the blow. When St. John saw the Prime Minister fall to the floor he cried out "The villain has killed Mr. Harley," and drawing his sword, as did also the Duke of Newcastle and some more, they dealt Guiscard several wounds. Other Lords of the Council with greater prudence secured themselves with chairs from the rage of the assassin; and others more prudent still ran out of the room to call for help. Messengers and door-keepers rushed in pell-mell, and one of the former, Wilcox by name, a very strong man, secured Guiscard at last by grappling with him and bringing him to the ground, Guiscard sustaining in his fall a heavy bruise in the back.

Harley, it is acknowledged, showed great firmness and magnanimity. As St. John wrote at the time, "I who have always admired him never did it so much. The suddenness of the blow, the sharpness of the wound, the confusion which followed, could neither change his countenance nor alter his voice." When the surgeon came to dress his wound he calmly desired to be told if it were mortal, that he might have time to settle his family affairs. And when after the examination the surgeon assured him that the wound was not

dangerous, he was just as little elated beyond his former CHAP.
composure. [2]

Guiscard meanwhile was conveyed a close prisoner to Newgate where at first he sullenly refused a surgeon's aid. He was twice examined by a Committee of the Privy Council but made no disclosures, and in all probability had none to make. On the 17th he died of his wounds, or rather of his bruise, which had turned to a gangrene.

The wound of Harley though slight in itself brought on a fever which confined him for some time to his chamber. Indeed, as his enemies alleged, he took care for the sake of popular effect to remain in the surgeon's hands as long as possible. But, as it seems to me, no such artifice was needed. Even the first tidings of the outrage called forth the strongest expressions of sympathy. The two Houses combined in a joint Address to the Queen stating their concern at this "barbarous and villanous attempt;" insisting on the fact that Guiscard was "a French Papist;" and in conclusion urging Her Majesty "to give such directions as in your great wisdom shall seem most proper for causing Papists to be removed from the cities of London and Westminster." Accordingly the Queen did issue a Proclamation "strictly to put in execution the laws against Papists." The two Houses on their part proceeded to pass a Bill making an attempt on the life of a Privy Councillor in the execution of his office to be felony without benefit of Clergy.

Harley as a party chief was beyond all doubt a gainer by his wound. Many of his followers, since he became

---

[2] Bolingbroke's Correspondence, vol. I. p. 63. Complete History of Europe, 1711, p. 126.

Prime Minister, had begun to see or to suspect his real unfitness for the chief part in affairs—how dubious he was in his views and how dilatory in his conduct. Some already looked to the rising genius of St. John; many more relied on the veteran merit of the Queen's uncle the Earl of Rochester. At this period the most thorough-going of the Tories in the House of Commons were wont to meet in what was termed the October Club, and there the Earl of Rochester had become a favourite toast. But all this was changed by the penknife of Guiscard. Once again was Harley proclaimed on all sides as the hero, nay the martyr, of his cause. Once again did the Tories not only applaud his actual eleva-tion, but aspire for him to those higher honors that had come in view. Meanwhile, as the party now in full ascendant, they were steadily pursuing their favourite aim of adding strength to both the landed interest and the Established Church. As regards the former there was carried through the two Houses, even before the attack on Harley, a Bill making a qualification in land essential to a seat in Parliament; 300*l.* a year for a Burgess and 600*l.* for a Knight of the Shire. Scotland was excepted on the ground and the estates were much smaller in that country. "The design of this Bill" says Bishop Burnet "was to exclude courtiers, military men, and merchants from sitting in the House of Commons, in hopes that this being settled the land interest would be the prevailing consideration in all their consultations." But whatever the value of the object it has not been at all promoted by the Act. Nominal and fictitious quali-fications were constantly granted, so that men engaged in trade or otherwise unconnected with land have at all times found an easy entrance to the House. Yet in spite of its hollow security this law has continued on the Statute Book for nearly a century and a half, not having been repealed till 1858.[3]

As regards the Established Religion the want of new churches in the growing suburbs of London had for some time past engaged the thoughts of Convocation. An Address upon the subject from its Upper House was presented to the Queen by the Archbishop of Canterbury; while Dr. Atterbury, as Prolocutor of the Lower House, waited with a similar petition on the Speaker. The result was a Message from the Queen to the House of Commons, which was brought down by Secretary St. John, and which warmly recommended the promotion of "so good and pious a work." The Commons showed equal zeal. As they declared in their reply: "Neither the long expensive war in which we are engaged, nor the pressure of heavy debts under which we labour, shall hinder us from granting to Your Majesty whatever is·necessary to accomplish so excellent a design." Resolutions were passed accordingly for building fifty new churches within the Bills of Mortality, computing 4,750 souls to each church; and for the expenses assigning that part of the Duty on Coals which had defrayed the reconstruction of St. Paul's.

St. John on the 20th of April brought down another Message from the Queen, referring to an event of grave concern which had just been announced from Germany. The Emperor Joseph was not yet thirty-three years of age. He had a strong constitution, and might expect a long life. But he was struck down by a malady so frequently fatal in that age, the small pox, which in this same month carried off the Dauphin, only son of

3 Compare the Acts 9 Anne c. 5 and 21 & 22 Vict. c. 26.

Louis the Fourteenth. Joseph expired at Vienna on the 17th of April New Style, leaving no male issue behind him. Thus his next heir was his brother, acknowledged by the Allies as King Charles the Third. It was obvious what new complications might arise from this untoward event. The balance of power and the liberties of Europe, endangered by the reign of the Bourbons at Madrid, might be no less in peril if the monarchy of Charles the Fifth were revived, and the Crown of the Empire once again united with the Crown of Spain.

The immediate object however was not to guard against this future contingency, but rather to cement the Grand Alliance and combine to one end the High Allies. "Her Majesty"—so said the Queen in her Message to the Commons—"is desirous to let you know that immediately on the first news of the Emperor's sickness she came to a resolution to support the interest of the House of Austria in this conjuncture, and to use her utmost endeavours to get the King of Spain made Emperor, in which the States General have likewise concurred with Her Majesty." The Queen further expressed her hope that she might be able to bring this war to a happy conclusion by a safe and honourable peace. And St. John adds in a private letter written the same day—"We persuade ourselves here that there is no doubt to be made of King Charles's being elected Emperor; but the satisfying the Duke of Savoy on his pretensions to Spain seems to be the knot of the whole affair."

On the 26th Harley reappeared in the House of Commons, for the first time since his illness. Then by previous direction of the House, the Speaker addressed him in a speech of florid compliment and congratulation, and Harley made a suitable reply. On the 2nd of May following he brought forward his scheme of finance. He proposed to satisfy all the outstanding Debts and Deficiencies, which amounted in the Navy alone to upwards of five millions, and on the whole to nearly ten millions sterling, by allowing proprietors of these Debts and Deficiencies a yearly interest of six per cent. redeemable by Parliament, and incorporating them to carry on the trade to the South Seas. This project was far more specious than solid, as ere long was proved by the event; nevertheless at the time it was received with great applause. And the charges then beginning to be raised against the late administration for irregularity and mismanagement in the public accounts, served, even while the inquiry upon them was pending, to swell the triumph of Harley.

By another favor of Fortune to this most successful Minister, it so chanced that, on the very day when he brought forward his scheme of finance, there died suddenly his principal rival in his party's favor, Laurence Hyde Earl of Rochester. The elevation of Harley had been even previously resolved upon; it was now but little delayed. On the 24th of the month came forth the Patent which made him Earl of Oxford. It was the revival of an ancient and illustrious title, borne by twenty Earls in succession, of the race of De Vere.[4] The last having died but nine years before it was deemed probable that from so long a lineage a remote descendant might yet appear and be able to

---

4 A very interesting sketch of this the noblest of the English noble families is given by Lord Macaulay (Hist. vol. III. p. 140, Tauchnitz Ed.). The Earldom, created in 1137, became extinct in 1702.

establish his claim. To provide for such a contingency a second title, also eminent in former ages, was conferred on Harley; and his title ran Earl of Oxford and Earl Mortimer.

But this was not all. On the 29th of May—selected as the anniversary of King Charles's Restoration—Oxford was raised to the further dignity of Lord Treasurer. He went in due form to take the oaths first in the Court of Chancery and then in the Court of Exchequer, on which occasion he was addressed by Lord Keeper Harcourt in a true Lord Chamberlain style: "My Lord Oxford, the Queen who does everything with the greatest wisdom, has given a proof of it in the honors she has lately conferred on you, which are exactly suited to your deserts and qualifications." To a bystander it might well seem wonderful what a train of accidents—some of them at first sight most unpromising—had led to this vast rise of a very commonplace politician. As Swift puts it: "This man has grown by persecutions, turnings out, and stabbing. What waiting and crowding and bowing will there be at his Levee!"[5]

Besides the Earl of Rochester, there died at this time another of the Ministers the Duke of Newcastle, from a fall of his horse at Welbeck. The Duke of Buckingham succeeded Rochester as Lord President, and the Earl of Jersey was designed in Newcastle's place to hold the Privy Seal. But Jersey expired in a fit of apoplexy on the very day for which the appointment had been fixed. "I never remember" says Swift "so many persons of quality to have died in so short a time."

5 Journal to Stella, May 22, 1711.

Under the circumstances of this sudden mortality, CHAP. XIV. the Privy Seal thus left vacant was conferred on 1711. Dr. John Robinson, Bishop of Bristol. It was the last time in our annals that a Bishop has been called upon to fill a political office. Even in the reign of Queen Anne this nomination is said to have excited great surprise; and it was regarded as a proof how thoroughly the Church had acquired the ascendant.

There were other appointments also. The Duke of Argyle, at this time closely banded with the Tories, had been earlier in the year sent as General and Ambassador to Spain instead of Stanhope, who was still detained a prisoner. Lord Raby, lately Minister at Berlin, was chosen to succeed Lord Townshend at the Hague, and was moreover promoted to the rank of Earl of Strafford. Another Earldom was granted to Lord Dartmouth. Earl Poulett, the nominal chief of the Treasury while yet in commission, was made Lord Steward in the place of Buckingham. Meanwhile the Session had been protracted to the unusual period of the 12th of June, the chief employment of the House of Commons being to discover grounds of charge against the late Lord Treasurer. Auditor Harley, a brother of the new one, took the Chair of a second Committee upon the public accounts, which pursued its inquiries in a spirit of party rancour, and with a view to represent irregularities of form as flagrant depredations, or abuses of trust. It summed up its accusations by reporting that, of the monies granted by Parliament for the public service up to Christmas 1710, no less than thirty-five millions remained unaccounted for, as to great part of which no accounts had ever been so much as laid before the Auditor.

For Flanders Marlborough had formed his plans in concert with Eugene. These chiefs, as in the last preceding years, were to be confronted by Villars, who had with great care and labour constructed a new series of defensive lines in the direction of Arras and Cambray. Early in the spring Marlborough was prepared to quit the Hague and to join the head-quarters at Tournay, there to be speedily joined by his German colleague. But the unexpected death of the Emperor entirely disconcerted his schemes. Eugene was detained at Vienna, as Marshal of the Empire and as guardian of the rights of Charles. When at last, after a month's delay, Eugene did reach the camp of the Allies, it was only to receive within a very few days a peremptory order of recall.

To explain this order it must here be noted, that a Diet had been convened at Frankfort for the election of an Emperor, and that to secure this election was now the paramount and ruling object of the House of Austria. Under such circumstances the movement of some French troops on the frontiers of Alsace excited apprehension. It was feared that there might be a design, either to intimidate the Electors or interrupt the election. The Ministers at Vienna therefore sent most positive injunctions to Eugene, bidding him withdraw a main part of his army from Flanders to the Rhine, there to assume the command and to cover Frankfort and indeed any part of the Empire from attack.

Marlborough heard these tidings with a heavy heart seeing how ill they boded for his own success in the campaign. But there was no choice. The two great chiefs and friends took leave of each other on the 14th of June; the last time they ever met in the field. Eugene repaired in the first instance to the Hague, to soothe the alarms of the Dutch; while Marlborough, still desirous to try the issue of a battle even with diminished numbers, took post on the plains of Lens. Villars was however far too closely bound by his instructions to hazard an engagement at this time. But he was on the watch to avail himself of any favourable opening for a slighter blow; and thus one day he surprised a British detachment at Arleux. Here he seems to have disregarded the courtesy, or rather the humanity, of modern welfare. For as in a letter hitherto unpublished Marlborough tells it to Godolphin: "I was so out of humour that I did not write to you by the last post. The Marshal de Villars took in our post at Arleux 400 men, who were stripped naked. Notwithstanding his superiority, I hope yet this campaign to return him some of his men, as naked as they came into this world."[6]

Over-confidence was, amidst many merits, another and main fault of Villars. So much elated was he at this period, that in a letter to the King of France afterwards published, he boasted that the lines constructed by him had brought his adversary to a NON PLUS ULTRA. In truth however Marlborough was intent on a wide scheme of aggression. He had planned some masterly manœuvres by which, deceiving the French Marshal and pressing through the French lines, he might in this campaign invest and reduce first Bouchain and secondly Le Quesnoy—take up his winter-quarters within the enemy's lines—and next spring, in conjunction with Eugene, march forward into the heart of

[6] Letter dated July 27, 1711. Coxe's Transcripts, Brit. Mus.

France. On this the "grand project," as it was termed at the time, the Duke was now in close correspondence with Oxford and St. John. He appears after a short interval to have stifled his resentment at the dismissal of the Duchess. He may even have resumed his wish to join the Tories. When he set out from England it is stated by St. John that "he made us parting protestations of reconciliation and inviolable friendship." St. John, though mistrusting his motives, gave him fair words in return. "General Lumley will have been able to tell your Grace how sincerely I wish you established on that bottom which alone suits the merit and the character of a man like you. . . . I hope never again to see the time when I shall be obliged to embark in a separate interest from you."[7]

We turn with pleasure from Marlborough in the Cabinet to Marlborough in the field. Having by skilful movements drawn the attention of Villars to another quarter he suddenly, late on the 4th August, sent forth a vanguard under Cadogan and Hompesch, which marching all night seized a point left undefended in the enemy's lines; so that Marlborough following at the head of his whole army became possessed of this formidable barrier ere the French could interpose. Hence, throwing some pontoon bridges across the Scheldt he passed that river and disclosed his real object by commencing the investment of Bouchain. Prince Eugene, writing to the Duke to congratulate him on these brilliant manœuvres, drily observes in reference to Villars's letter, "Your Highness has penetrated into the NON PLUS ULTRA."[8]

<hr>

[7] Bolingbroke's Correspondence, vol. i. p. 79, 81, 87.
[8] Coxe's Marlborough, vol. vi. p. 66.

The reduction of Bouchain was indeed an enterprize requiring no little skill and patience, with a watchful enemy in the field and with a resolute garrison in the place. To complete the circumvallation, it was found necessary to construct an entrenched camp on either side of the Scheldt. "If"—so writes Marlborough to Godolphin—"we can succeed in this siege we shall have the honor of having done it in the face of an army many thousand men stronger than we are." A different passage from his correspondence at this period shows by retrospect the vigilance and the success of his command in former years. "The Comte d'Arbach, a Lieutenant-General of the Dutch, was taken at their last forage; he is the first Lieutenant-General that has been taken of this army during the war."

There is yet another transaction of this time tending greatly to the honor of Marlborough. He gave a signal proof of his reverence for men of genius and virtue in the case of Fenelon, the Archbishop of Cambray and—a still higher distinction—the author of Télémaque. The estates of the See being exposed to plunder by the presence of a hostile army, the Duke ordered a detachment of foot to guard the magazines of corn at Cateau Cambresis, and subsequently sent them to Cambray with an escort of dragoons. How praiseworthy the contrast with the cruelty of the French chief to the prisoners at Arleux!

Meanwhile, in spite of many obstacles, Marlborough was warmly pressing the siege of Bouchain. It cost him far more time than he could have wished. The batteries however began to play on the 30th of August, and on the 11th of September the troops of the garrison were dislodged from two bastions on the right and left of the lower town. Next morning they beat a parley, and after some demurs agreed to a capitulation by which they remained prisoners of war. They were still about 3,000 strong.

The next step as planned by Marlborough would have been to invest Le Quesnoy. But from divers circumstances he found it impossible to proceed any further with his "grand project." There was lukewarmness in England arising from the prospect of a speedy and separate peace; there was resentment among the Dutch produced by the same cause; there was on the part of Austria the tardiness, or rather the entire absence, of its promised aid. As regards the last indeed the Court of St. James's had for many months bitterly complained. Even at the beginning of this year St. John wrote: "We are almost tired of an ally who expects every thing and does nothing."[9]

In this manner shortly stated it happened that the Great Duke could neither proceed against Le Quesnoy, nor take up his winter-quarters in France. The achievements of this campaign were confined to the reduction of Bouchain. Twenty-four years later as Bolingbroke was reviewing these transactions in the celebrated Letters on the Study of History, which he addressed to Lord Cornbury, we find him urge that fact as an argument against the prosecution of the war. "The conquest of Bouchain being in fact the only one the Confederates made in 1712, Bouchain may be said properly and truly to have cost our nation very near seven millions sterling, for your Lordship will find, I

9 To Mr. Drummond, January 12, 1711.

believe, that the charge of the war for that year amounted to no less."

In Catalonia the Duke de Noailles had prevailed so far by his sudden invasion of the province and investment of Gerona that the city yielded to his arms before the close of January, the troops of the garrison however not to remain prisoners of war. But with the secret hope of a separate peace the Court of Versailles resolved to run no further risk on this side and to restrain the ardour both of Noailles and Vendome. As regards the Allies their cause seemed to be revived by the arrival of some English regiments and of Argyle to command in Stanhope's place. Still Charles was by no means able to cope with his opponents in the open field; and the death of his brother gave a wholly new current to his hopes. Henceforth he looked to Vienna far more than to Madrid; nor was it long ere he embarked for Genoa, thence to proceed by land to his hereditary states, leaving however his Queen at Barcelona as a-pledge to the Catalans of his promised return. Meanwhile his partisans at Frankfort had not been idle; and on the 12th of October, after the usual ceremonies, he was in due form elected Emperor of Germany and King of the Romans by the title of Charles the Sixth.

War was waged also in a distant quarter of the globe. An expedition to reduce Quebec, which had been planned during the late administration, was carried out by the present with little vigour or success. Eearly in the year five regiments, were withdrawn from the army in Flanders, much to Marlborough's chagrin, and with some other troops, about 5,000 in all, entrusted to Brigadier Hill, brother of the favourite. They embarked in transports with a strong squadron of ships of war commanded by Sir Hovenden Walker, and towards the middle of August entered the mouth of the St. Lawrence. Within a few days however they were assailed by a violent tempest and driven among rocks, where eight transports perished with several hundred men. Sir Hovenden at once sailed back to Spanish River, and there in conjunction with the General he held a Council of War. At this it was resolved unanimously that, since the fleet and forces were victualled for ten weeks only, and could not at that stormy season depend upon New England for supplies, they should return home without any further attempt to achieve their object.

The secret negotiation with France was still continued. Towards the close of April De Torcy sent back Gaultier to London with an offer to treat comprised in six articles. It was by no means clear or explicit in its language. It promised real securities to the English trade in Spain in the Indies, and in the Mediterranean; a sufficient Barrier and freedom of commerce to the Dutch; and a reasonable satisfaction to the Allies of England and Holland. It cautiously referred to the sovereignty of Spain as no longer in question since King Philip's late successes, but it added that in consequence of those successes new expedients might be found to regulate the succession of that monarchy, to the contentment of all the parties engaged in the present war.

Vague and unsatisfactory as these terms appear they were with little delay transmitted by St. John to Lord Raby at the Hague. There went with them an ostensible and also a secret letter.[1] Lord Raby was directed to show the inclosure in the strictest confidence to Pensionary Heinsius and the other Dutch Ministers and to obtain their opinion upon it. And St. John added, "Though there is an air of complaisance through the whole paper shown to us, and the contrary to those among whom you reside, yet this can have no ill consequence so long as the Queen and States take care to understand each other." St. John's public letter further stated, "The Duke of Marlborough has no communication from hence of this affair; I suppose he will have none from the Hague."

The answer of the Dutch Ministers, Heinsius and Buys, was couched in most general terms; they expressed their wish for peace, but desired more explicit proposals. Their secret object was that these proposals might be made directly to themselves. Pettekum—"the peace-broker," as in one of his letters St. John calls him—wrote to France at the suggestion of Heinsius to say, that if the King would renew the negotiations in Holland he would certainly be satisfied with the conduct of the Dutch. This overture was at once declined by Louis in compliance with the wish of the English Ministers. It was to London that he looked henceforward and not to the Hague.

Oxford and St. John on their part were resuming their negotiations with Le Grand Monarque. For the sake of secrecy they resolved to employ no person of rank. They sent over to confer with Torcy their personal friend Matthew Prior, a man of quick talents, and not in poetry alone. He had been, before the

---

[1] Bolingbroke's Correspondence, vol. I. p. 106.

war, Secretary of Embassy at Paris and was well versed in French affairs.

The credentials of Prior were signed by the Queen's own hand, but consisted of no more than a few lines giving him powers only to state her claims and to bring back the replies. Repairing to Fontainebleau, where the Court then resided, Prior had several secret interviews with Torcy. His first inquiry was whether the King had authority to stipulate for Spain as well as France. Being assured that Philip had sent full powers for that purpose, he intimated that England no longer insisted on wresting the Spanish Crown from the House of Bourbon, provided full securities were taken that it should never in any case be united with the French. Prior next proceeded to bring forward divers demands of his Royal Mistress on her own part or for her Allies; for England, among other things, the cession of Gibraltar, Minorca, and Newfoundland, the demolition of the works at Dunkirk, four towns for trade in South America, and large commercial advantages; the latter to be allowed to the Dutch also, with a Barrier for them of fortified towns in the Low Countries, and for the House of Austria a similar Barrier on the Rhine.

In considering these terms Louis felt especial difficulty on the point of the commercial advantages, which he feared might prove ruinous to his own subjects as well as to those of Spain. Yet he was unwilling by any direct refusal to estrange his good friends—for so he began to think them—at the Court of St. James's. He therefore took advantage of the fact that the powers of Prior were so strictly limited. He desired, he said, to transfer the seat of the negotiation to London by

sending over, at the same time that Prior returned, a
person in his own confidence, who should have full
authority to sign the Preliminary Articles. For this
purpose he selected Mesnager who, though a merchant
by profession, had shown himself a skilful negotiator
in the Gertruydenberg negotiations.

In England meanwhile the secret was closely kept.
Even Swift, familiar as he was with the chief Ministers,
was not entrusted with it. So late as the 24th of
August there is the following entry in his journal:
"Prior has been out of town these two months, nobody knows where, and is lately returned. People confidently affirm he has been in France, and I half believe it. They say he was sent by the Ministry and
for some overtures toward a peace. The Secretary (St.
John) pretends he knows nothing of it."—Even this
half knowledge of the public might have been avoided
but for an untoward accident. Prior had landed at
Deal from a small vessel and under a feigned name,
but being taken for a smuggler he was seized by
the custom-house officers and obliged to produce his
pass, nor was he released until orders from London
came.

Mesnager on his arrival was well received by the
English Ministers, but found considerable difficulties in
the way of his negotiation. While yielding most of the
points demanded, he was instructed to insist especially
that the Electors of Bavaria and Cologne should be
reinstated in their rank and territories, and that, to
compensate the King of France for the demolition of
Dunkirk, the cities of Lille and Tournay should be
restored to him. After some weeks of contestation,
and another reference to Louis, it was agreed that

these last points should be postponed to the final treaty. Then, on the 27th of September, Mesnager on the part of France signed eight Preliminary Articles of peace with England. By these Louis bound himself to acknowledge Anne as Queen of Great Britain as also the succession to her Crown as by law established. A new treaty of commerce was to be framed. Dunkirk was to be demolished, some fair equivalent being first determined. Gibraltar and Port Mahon were to remain in the hands of the English. Newfoundland also was to be ceded with some fishing rights reserved. The ASIENTO—by which Spanish word signifying only "compact" was meant in fact the slave-trade as the most excellent of all possible treaties—would be granted by Spain to the English instead of the French, some places in America to be assigned "for the refreshment and sale of their negroes."

The Preliminaries being signed, and a peace in some measure secured, several acts of courtesy ensued. Marshal Tallard, who had been detained a prisoner ever since the battle of Blenheim, was permitted to return on his parole to France. Monsieur Mesnager, before he went back, was presented to the Queen at Windsor and graciously received. She said to him: "It is a good work; pray God prosper you in it. I am sure I long for peace; I hate this dreadful work of blood."[2]

But besides the Preliminaries of Peace with England, there was another document signed by Mesnager on the 27th of September. This was a different set of Preliminaries drawn out in seven articles, and designed mainly for communication to the Dutch. Indeed St.

---

[2] Compare the Mémoires de Torcy, vol. III. p. 87, and a note to Burnet's History, vol. VI. p. 77.

John writing to the Queen the same day goes so far as
to call this "the paper for Holland."   From it were
omitted, to give no ground of jealousy, the clauses which
especially favoured England; and above all the intended
cession of Gibraltar and Mahon.   On the other hand
there were inserted new stipulations which most concerned the other Allies; as the promise of measures to
hinder that the Crowns of France and Spain should
ever be united on the head of the same Prince; a
Barrier for the Dutch; and another to be formed for
the Empire and the Austrian Family.

Armed with this document the Earl of Strafford, who
had come over to England to be married, was within a
few days sent back to his post at the Hague.   He was
further directed to show to the Ministers of Holland a
list, transmitted by the King of France, of four towns,
at any one of which the King was willing that the conferences should be held.   "We have refused" writes
St. John "to let the general treaty be carried on in
our own country; and we are ready to send our plenipotentiaries to such of these four towns as may be most
agreeable to the Dutch States."[3]

These proposals, however skilfully varnished, proved
to be most unwelcome at the Hague.   The ruling
Dutchmen demurred to any negotiation thus conducted,
and sent over Buys to urge their remonstrances in
London. Buys was courteously received both by Queen
and Ministers, but could not make the least impression.
St. John said drily, that as England bore by very far
the largest share in the burthen of the war, England
was entitled to take the leading part in the conclusion
of the peace. With great reluctance the States were at

[3] Correspondence, vol. i. p. 249.

last obliged to allow, in practice at least, the truth of St. John's words. They consented to negotiate in the manner that England had proposed; and for the place selected Utrecht the first town named in the French list. There it was settled that the conferences should begin in the first days of January next.

On the Austrian side the resentment at the course of England was even greater, or at least more publicly shown. Count de Gallas, the Imperial Minister in London, received from St. John a copy of the paper in seven articles already transmitted to Holland. The communication was designed in the first instance as private, but De Gallas in his wrath sent it to the newspapers. "It has been rendered as public as the Daily Courant can make it"—so St. John writes. The Count was not content with this single indiscretion. He reviled the English Government in unmeasured terms, not sparing even the Queen herself, and declaring that her Ministers must be fools or worse. Further still it appeared that he was taking an active part in promoting the pamphlets and lampoons which began to swarm against the project of a peace.

It was thought necessary by some decisive step to assert the Royal dignity. On Sunday the 28th of October, Sir Clement Cottrel, Master of the Ceremonies, was ordered to go to the Count de Gallas and forbid him the Court in Her Majesty's name; adding that she no longer looked upon him as a public Minister, nor would receive any further application from him. At the same time, Mr. Watkins the Secretary of Embassy at the Hague, was directed to proceed to Frankfort, where the newly elected Emperor was expected to arrive in order to be crowned. Mr. Watkins was to deliver to

His Majesty a letter in the Queen's own hand, announcing her displeasure with the Count de Gallas and her desire to receive another Austrian Minister.

The pamphlets and lampoons which have been already mentioned grew more and more in numbers and gave much annoyance to the Ministry. There was no lack of good writers to put forth other tracts in answer or retaliation—with arguments as keen or with ribaldry as coarse. But besides these the Government of that day relied on what the Covenanters would have called "the arm of flesh." So early as the 17th of October we find St. John report to the Queen: "I have discovered the author of another scandalous libel, who will be in custody this afternoon; he will make the thirteenth I have seized and the fifteenth I have found out."

Nor did these libellers confine themselves to prose. As Swift notes a few days later, "The Whig party are furious against a peace; and every day some ballad comes out reflecting on the Ministry on that account." Five years afterwards these effusions received a compliment they little deserve; they were collected and published in a dreary volume entitled "Pills to purge State Melancholy."

It was in the very midst of this political crisis that Marlborough returned to England. He set out from the Hague in company with Baron Bothmar, the Hanoverian Envoy to St. James's; and they landed at Greenwich on the 17th of November. This was the anniversary of Queen Elizabeth's accession to the Crown; when some tumults were apprehended. The apprentices and others of that class in London had been wont for many years to celebrate the day as a triumph to the Protestant cause; marching in nightly procession, and burning at a bonfire effigies of the Devil, the Pope, and the Pretender. This year, as a side-blow to the Tory Ministers—the friends of France as they were called—it was desired to enhance the usual solemnities; and there were it was said Whig subscriptions for that object. An account of the pageant as intended was soon afterwards published. Nothing could well be more offensive to the Roman Catholics in England. We find among the Items for instance: "Two Jack-puddings sprinkling Holy Water"—"Twelve streamer-bearers with different devices, representing Sandals, Ropes, Beads, Bald-pates, and pregnant Nuns"—"After these four fat Friars in their habits, Streamers carried over their heads, with these words EAT AND PRAY"—"The Pope under a magnificent canopy, with a silver fringe, accompanied by the Chevalier de St. George on the left, and his counsellor the Devil on his right."[4]

But the Ministers were on the alert. In the night of the 16th they sent to seize the effigies prepared, which were deposited in an empty house in Angel Court, Drury Lane. These being carried to the office of the Secretary of State Lord Dartmouth and there secured, the intended procession was nipped in the bud. Next day moreover the Trained Bands were called out and regular troops disposed in different places, so that the alarming anniversary passed off in perfect quietness. The result was only an increased exasperation between the political parties. The Tories declared that their

4 Complete History of Europe, 1711, p. 402. As to the alleged Whig subscriptions, the Journal to Stella fixes the amount at 1,000l., and names one subscriber, Dr. Garth. The Tory papers of the day accuse the Kit-Cat Club, and give these as the initials of subscribers: G. G. G., S. S. S., W. H. M., by which are meant Godolphin, Grafton, Garth, Somers, Sunderland, Somerset, Walpole, Halifax, and his brother Montague.

adversaries had planned this pageant to profit by the confusion which might ensue and overthrow the government. On the other hands the Whigs exclaimed that these fears were merely feigned as an excuse for rigorous and re-actionary measures.

Marlborough with his customary prudence stayed at Greenwich the whole night of the 17th, lest if in London he might be accused of countenancing any tumult that arose. Finding all quiet he passed through the City next morning and went to Hampton Court to pay his respects to the Queen. His wish was at this time to remain neutral, or nearly neutral, in the affair of the Peace—to remonstrate in private with Her Majesty on the course proposed—but to take no public part against it. It was his object, according to Coxe, to obtain from the Queen the warrants for continuing the works at Blenheim.[5] But he soon perceived that his neutrality would not be possible. The Peace would be assailed as soon as Parliament met, and above all in the House of Lords; and he must then declare himself—Content or Not Content.

Under these circumstances the Great Duke took counsel in secret with his friends and former colleagues of the Whig party; and they confided to him a plan which they had formed to defeat the Ministry and themselves return to power. —The majority against them in the Commons was very large. In the Lords on the other hand there was no great preponderance on the side of the Government; and a small band of Tories if won over would suffice to turn the scale. Such a band was now directed by Lord Nottingham.

5 On Marlborough's views at this time compare Bolingbroke's Correspondence, vol. 1. p. 298, with Coxe's Life, vol. vi. p. 130.

That veteran chief, so conspicuous in former years, had been passed over in all the recent nominations. There was indeed a rumour that he would be appointed Lord President at the death of Rochester. But Lord Oxford was it seems determined not to place him again in office from a dread of his extreme views and overbearing temper. "Mr. Harley would think his power at an end, if that person were taken in"—so writes a well-informed bystander.[6]

Much incensed at this neglect Lord Nottingham, as the period of the Session drew near, made overtures for an union with the Whigs. They, seeing that a majority could thus and thus only be secured, welcomed him with readiness. A coalition was formed on terms not altogether to the credit of the Whigs, as involving on their part some sacrifice of principle. It was agreed by them to support Nottingham's favourite measure, the Occasional Conformity Bill, which in former years they had so sharply and so successfully opposed. Nottingham, on the other hand, though at the outset he had desired only a defensive war, thought it open to him after the victories achieved to join his new allies in resisting the conclusion of a Peace, except upon the basis that Spain and the Indies should be wrested from the House of Bourbon.

Besides their compact with the Earl of Nottingham, the Whigs had also been tampering with some men in eminent posts, and above all with the Duke of Somerset, then in high favor with the Queen and her Master of the Horse. The promised aid of that very variable

---

[6] Letter from Mr. Maynwaring to the Duchess of Marlborough, May 4, 1711. According to Lord Dartmouth moreover "the Queen would not hear of Lord Nottingham." (Note to Burnet's Hist. vol. VI. p. 9.)

nobleman was of especial value to them, considering the confidential offices held by the Duchess, in close attendance on the Royal Person. On the whole they were and with good reason confident of victory, and had already begun to plan a new administration, in which Somers was to be chief and Walpole leader of the Commons. Apprised of this favourable prospect and himself far from approving the Preliminaries, Marlborough resolved to cast in his lot with his old friends. He broke from the Ministry, and there was henceforth open war between them. The Ministry on their part, though not as yet fully informed of the designs against themselves, prepared with spirit for the coming strife. Hoping, with a little more time, to gain over or convince several of the Peers, they prorogued the Parliament for another fortnight, and fixed its meeting finally for the 7th of December. As St. John writes at this crisis to the Hague, "Friday next the Peace will be attacked in Parliament indirectly. I am glad of it, for I hate a distant danger which hovers over my head; we must receive their fire and rout them once for all."[7]

The interval was actively employed by the Opposition also. They had used and were using their best endeavours to proclaim and manifest the discontent of the High Allies. From Milan, on his way to Frankfort, Charles had written to the States General at the Hague declaring that he utterly rejected the Preliminaries as well for the present and the future, and would by no means allow any ambassador of his to take part in the conferences. This letter, by the care of the statesmen out of power, was published in the London papers. From Frankfort the Emperor further intimated, that, to

---

[7] To the Earl of Strafford, Dec. 4, 1711.

give full effect to his remonstrances, he desired to send Prince Eugene to England—an announcement very far from welcome to the English Ministers. But the main blow dealt upon them at this time was in the name of Hanover. Baron Bothmar, the Elector's Envoy at St. James's, who was acting in close concert with Marlborough, drew up a Memorial expressing in vehement terms the objections of his master to the Preliminary Articles; and Marlborough took care that this Memorial should be both presented and published, at the most critical moment for the Ministry—only a few days before the Meeting of Parliament. The Duke had calculated that a great Parliamentary effect might ensue from the strong protest at that juncture of the Heir Presumptive.

The long-expected day, the 7th of December, came at last. In her Speech from the Throne, the Queen informed the Houses that both place and time were appointed for opening the treaty of a General Peace, "notwithstanding" she added "the arts of those who delight in war"—an indirect reflection, as it was then considered, on Marlborough and the Whigs. The Speech having been concluded, and the Royal robes laid aside, the Queen returned to the House "incognito," partly to hear the debates, and partly in the hope, as was supposed, that its asperities might be allayed by her presence. If such were her hope it most signally failed. No sooner had the Address in answer to the Royal Speech been in due form moved and seconded than up rose Nottingham. In bitter terms he inveighed against the Articles signed by Mesnager, declaring that hostilities ought to be carried on with the utmost vigour until the objects of the Grand Alliance had been fully attained. "Although" he said "I have a numerous family, I would readily contribute half my income to such a war rather than acquiesce in such a Peace;" and he ended by moving a Clause to the Address, representing to the Queen, as the opinion of the House, "that no Peace could be safe or honourable to Great Britain or Europe if Spain and the West Indies were allotted to any branch of the House of Bourbon."

There followed a long and very warm contest. Nottingham was supported by Wharton, Sunderland, Cowper, Bishop Burnet, and the whole strength of the Whigh party, while on the other hand, so far as we can gather, he was but feebly opposed by the office-holders. They were damped no doubt by the sudden defection of one of their own number, the Duke of Shrewsbury. But the main incident of this debate related to the Duke of Marlborough. Lord Anglesey, who had come post from Ireland in company with the Duke of Ormond, and had travelled the last thirty miles that morning, descanted—perhaps in some heat from his journey—on the blessings of peace, which he added might have been enjoyed soon after the battle of Ramillies, but for some persons whose interest it was to prolong the war. Then with much emotion the Great Duke rose. First bowing to the place where Her Majesty sat he said, "I appeal to the Queen whether, while I had the honor to serve Her Majesty as General and Plenipotentiary, I did not constantly inform her and her Council of all the proposals of peace that were made, and desire instructions for my conduct on that subject. I can declare with a safe conscience, in the presence of Her Majesty, of this illustrious assembly, and of that Supreme Being who is infinitely above all

16*

the powers upon earth, and before whom in the ordinary course of nature I must soon appear to give an
account of my actions, that I ever was desirous of a
safe, honourable, and lasting peace; and was always very
far from any design of prolonging the war for my own
private advantage, as my enemies have most falsely
insinuated. . . . But at the same time I must take the
liberty to declare, that I can by no means give into
the measures that have been lately taken to enter into
a 'negotiation of peace with France upon the foot of
the seven Preliminary Articles, since I am of the same
opinion with the rest of the Allies, that the safety and
liberty of Europe will be in imminent danger if Spain
and the West Indies are left to the House of Bourbon."

In the division which ensued the hopes of the Whig
leaders were most fully confirmed, since the clause of
Nottingham was carried by 62 votes against 54. It is
true that in the Commons the same evening a like
amendment, being moved by Robert Walpole, was rejected by an overwhelming majority, 232 against 106.
Yet still the fact remained, that one branch at least of
the Legislature would certainly demur to peace on the
terms proposed. And there was still another more
secret cause of apprehension. Next day, in strict confidence, Mrs. Masham whispered it to Swift: "I begin
to fear," she said, "Her Majesty is changed. For
yesterday when she was going from the House where
she sat to hear the debate, the Duke of Shrewsbury,
Lord Chamberlain, asked her whether he or the Great
Chamberlain Lindsey ought to lead her out. She answered short, 'Neither of you;' and gave her hand to
the Duke of Somerset, who was louder than any in the
House for the clause against peace."

At this crisis the best friends of Oxford and St. John lost all hope of their continuance in power. "Here" writes Swift "are the first steps towards the ruin of an excellent Ministry, for I look upon them as certainly ruined." And again: "At the Secretary's office I met Prior, who told me he gave all for gone, and was of opinion the whole Ministry would give up their places next week. Lewis thinks they will not till spring when the Session is over; both of them entirely despair."[8] Oxford himself maintained a resolute tone. He spoke on the subject to Gaultier, now again in London; and, as Gaultier reports to Torcy, "My Lord Treasurer bids me assure you that you may rely in the most positive manner upon his firmness; that he will write to you in eight or ten days; and that you shall see the full effect of his promises and of his determination."

Flushed with his great victory, Nottingham lost no time in introducing his dearly cherished bantling, the Occasional Conformity Bill, with only some very slight modifications to satisfy in show at least his new allies. It enacted that if any officer civil or military, or any magistrate of a Corporation, obliged by the Acts of Charles the Second to receive the Sacrament, should during his continuance in office attend any Conventicle, or religious meeting of Dissenters, such person should forfeit 40*l.* to be recovered by the prosecutor; and every person so convicted should be disabled to hold his office, and incapable of any employment in Eng-

CHAP.
XIV.
1711.

---

[8] Journal to Stella, December 15, 1711. Of the latter politician Swift says in one of his lighter pieces:

> "This Lewis is a *cunning shaver*,
> And very much in Harley's favor."

land. This intolerant Bill, carried through the House of Lords by the active assistance of the Whigs, was received with enthusiasm by the Tory majority in the House of Commons, and was quickly passed into law, continuing as such for more than seven years.

In another transaction of this time the same reckless spirit appeared. The Whigs, as then possessing the ascendant in the House of Lords, viewed with much jealousy the possible admission through British peerage patents of more Scottish Peers—a class of men whom they regarded, and not without some reason at that period, as wholly subservient to the Crown. It came to an issue by the recent creation of the Duke of Hamilton to be Duke of Brandon in England. The question being put—and a consultation of the Judges first refused—whether Scottish Peers created Peers of Great Britain have a right to sit in the House, it was carried in the negative by the narrow majority of 57 against 52. Even at the time of this decision by the Lords, the Duke of Queensberry was sitting among them by virtue of a British peerage granted since the Union; and there was scarce even a shred of law to cover the manifest party-object of the vote. It remained in force however for upwards of seventy years. At length in 1782 the question of the disability of Scottish Peers to receive patents of peerage in Great Britain being raised anew on a petition from the Duke of Hamilton and Brandon, was referred to the Judges, who decided unanimously that no such disability had been created by the Act of Union. The Lords thereupon revoked their former decision.[9]

9 See a passage in Sir Thomas May's interesting and valuable work, Constitutional History of England since the Accession of George the Third, vol. 1. p. 239. Also the Lords Journals, June 6, 1782.

On the 22d of December the House of Commons adjourned for the Christmas holidays until the 14th of January. But the newly formed majority in the Lords were so eager in controlling the hostile Ministry, that they would scarce allow themselves any holiday at all, adjourning only from the same day in December till January the 2nd. Before they separated they gave other tokens of their power. To gratify the House of Hanover, the Duke of Devonshire brought in a Bill giving to the Electoral Prince as Duke of Cambridge the precedence of all Peers. To embarrass the negotiations at Utrecht, Lord Nottingham carried an Address that Her Majesty might instruct her plenipotentiaries to consult with the Ministers of the other Allies in Holland, and concert the necessary measures to preserve a strict union amongst them all. In vain did the Lord Treasurer assert that this had been done. Nottingham persevered with his Address, and the Ministers only prevailed so far as to insert in it the words, "in case Her Majesty had not already given such orders."

While these things passed in Parliament, since the first vote on the 7th of December the Ministers had been most anxiously reviewing their position and determining their course. They soon found that there was not, as at first they feared, any change of purpose in the Queen. As St. John wrote to Strafford on the 15th, "the only difficulty she laboured under, besides a little natural slowness, was the habit which she has with the Duchess of Somerset, and the apprehension of not finding somebody to fill a place so near her person, whom she could like." In fact there was now the same difficulty about the Duchess of Somerset as in former days there had been about the Duchess of Marlborough. But in politics the Queen had no doubts. She was willing to support the Church party, as she deemed it, by even the most violent stretch of her prerogative. On this knowledge the Ministers acted.

Their first step was to strike down Marlborough. For this purpose they used a weapon which had been for some time in their hands, and which it might be in their power to withhold or draw forth as they pleased. The Commission of Public Accounts as appointed by themselves, consisted of some ardent Tories, with Lockhart of Carnwath as its Chairman; and among the documents laid before it there was one that bore hard on the Great Duke. It was the deposition of Sir Solomon Medina, a wealthy Jew and the contractor for bread to the army in Flanders. Sir Solomon stated that from 1707 to 1711 he had paid to the Duke of Marlborough for his Grace's own use on the several contracts for the army a sum of 332,000 guilders— that on each contract he had presented Mr. Cardonnel, secretary to the Duke, with a gratuity of 500 ducats— and that moreover he had paid to Mr. Sweet, deputy paymaster at Amsterdam, the farther allowance of one per cent. on all the monies he received. As regards the payments to the Duke, it further appeared that the same had been made by the previous contractor M. Machado. From these facts the Commissioners computed, that in ten years, the Duke of Marlborough had received from the bread-contractors and applied to his own use a sum equivalent in English money to upwards of 63,000l. It was probably to the substance or main facts of Medina's deposition that St. John desired to refer, so far back as the January preceding, when writing in confidence to Drummond he says of the Duke, "We shall do what we can to support him in the command ,of the army without betraying our Mistress; and unless he is infatuated he will help us in this design, for you must know that the moment he leaves the service and loses the protection of the Court, such scenes will open as no victories can varnish over."[1] In November, Marlborough being then at the Hague, the Commissioners had sent him this deposition in a private form. Writing in reply the Duke admitted that he had received the sums in question, but observed first, that in receiving them he had followed the precedent of every former General or Commander in Chief in the Low Countries, both before the Revolution and since; and secondly, that he had applied the money so received to public uses, in obtaining secret intelligence of the enemy's designs. The Commissioners however did not deem this answer satisfactory. In the Report which they now proceeded to draw up, they denied that the sums of which Marlborough had acknowledged the receipts were either legal or warrantable perquisites; and they asserted that on the strictest inquiry they could not find proof that any English General, either in the Low Countries or elsewhere, had ever received the like.

But the Commissioners did not stop here. They brought into account also a deduction of two and a half per cent. from the pay of the foreign troops subsidised by England, which sum was paid to Marlborough under a warrant from the Queen in the first

---

[1] Bolingbroke's Correspondence, vol. 1. p. 50.

year of her reign, and designed, as the warrant states, for "extraordinary contingent expences." Lockhart and his colleagues—I had almost said accomplices—took little heed of that warrant or those services. They reckoned that even excluding from the calculation the foreign auxiliaries employed in Spain, Portugal, or Italy, Marlborough must have received and applied to his own use the sum of 177,000*l.*; which sum they declared to be public money for which the Duke as receiver was accountable.

The Report of the Commissioners was presented to the House of Commons on the 21st of December, but the deposition of Sir Solomon was deferred till the 22nd, the very day of the adjournment, so that in Parliament at least no present answer could be made. Thus the popular impression was increased. On the 30th Swift notes in his journal, "The Duke of Marlborough was at Court to-day and nobody hardly took notice of him." The courtiers showed that admirable prescience which has been observed of certain other creatures, and which enables them in sufficient time to leave a falling house. In this case the fall was not long delayed. On the 31st the Queen appeared at the Council, and ordered this entry to be made in the Council-books: "Being informed that an information against the Duke of Marlborough was laid before the House of Commons by the Commissioners of the Public Accounts, Her Majesty thought fit to dismiss him from all his employments that the matter might have an impartial examination." Her Majesty wrote with her own hand to the Duke announcing to him his dismissal, and further complaining of "the treatment she had met with." The Duke's answer, conveyed to the Queen

through his daughter Lady Sunderland, was couched CHAP
in terms of great dignity and moderation. XIV.

1711.

So bold a stroke required another still bolder to
sustain it. The same Gazette of the 31st of December
which announced that the Queen had dismissed the
Duke of Marlborough from all his employments, made
known also the creation of twelve new Peers. By this
COUP D'ETAT it was intended to overrule or rather to
invert the majority in the Upper Chamber, and to secure
from opposition a Peace on the terms proposed. It is
the only time in our annals that a stretch of the prerogative in this direction has been actually effected,
though not the only time that it has been threatened
and intended. In 1712 it seems to have excited less
emotion than might at present be supposed. The
Whigs were already so indignant at some late transactions that their wrath would scarce admit any further
increase; and the Tories were so far wrought upon by
the injuries which they deemed themselves to have
sustained, as to consider almost any measures justifiable,
so that it kept their party in power.

To form this phalanx of new Peers the Ministers
proceeded as follows. First they called up by Writ the
eldest sons of two Earls, Northampton and Ailesbury.
Next in the same spirit they conferred a barony on the
eldest son of a Peer less high in rank than the pre-
ceding, Lord Paget, and another barony on the eldest
son of a Scottish Peer the Earl of Kinnoul. Viscount
Windsor in the Irish peerage obtained the title of Lord
Mountjoy in the English. Two Baronets, Sir Thomas
Mansell and Sir Thomas Willoughby, became respectively
Lord Mansell and Lord Middleton. Sir Thomas Trevor,
Chief Justice of the Common Pleas, became Lord

Trevor, and George Granville, of Stow in Cornwall, Lord Lansdowne. Thomas Foley was created Lord Foley, Allan Bathurst, Lord Bathurst, and Samuel Masham, husband of the favourite, Lord Masham.

In this last case, the Queen might be supposed to have gratified her own predilection. But such was not the fact. Lord Dartmouth tells us that he was the person sent to suggest to her that Mrs. Masham's husband should be one of the new Peers. Her Majesty, it was found, by no means relished the proposal. "I never had any design," she said, "to make a great lady of her, and I should lose a useful servant about my person; for it would give offence to have a Peeress lie upon the floor and do several other inferior offices." At last however the Queen relented, but only upon condition that her new Ladyship should remain a dresser.[2]

Masham in fact was only a makeshift. The person first designed for a peerage in his place was Sir Miles Wharton, a country gentleman of old descent. But Sir Miles with noble spirit declined the offer. "This looks," he said, "like serving a turn. Peers used to be made for services which they have done, but I should be made for services that I am to do."

On the 2nd of January, when the House of Lords met again, the twelve new Peers came to take the oaths. "It was apprehended," so Swift writes, "the Whigs would have raised some difficulties, but nothing happened." Nor is it easy to see how in point of strict law any objection could be made. Immediately after the oaths there was a Message delivered from the Queen to the effect, that having matters of great importance

---

[2] Lord Dartmouth's note to Burnet's History, vol. VI. p. 36.

to communicate to both Houses of Parliament, she
desired the Lords to adjourn immediately to the 14th,
the same day to which the Commons had adjourned
themselves. So unusual a measure as a Message of
Adjournment to one House only gave rise to a keen
debate, and the adjournment was carried by a majority
of no more than thirteen, including the twelve new
Peers. On this occasion, seeing their number the same
as of a petty Jury, Lord Wharton sarcastically asked
them whether they would vote singly or by their fore-
man.

CHAPTER XV.

It was just after this crisis of affairs, that is, on the 6th of January, that Prince Eugene arrived in London. His presence a few weeks before might perhaps have produced a strong effect, but, like most other measures of the House of Austria at this period, it was delayed too long. He found Marlborough, whom he desired to befriend, already discarded; he found the majority in the House of Lords on which he reckoned already overwhelmed. The Government had much disapproved and endeavoured to prevent his coming; but when he came, he was received, outwardly at least, with every token of attention and respect. At his first audience of Her Majesty, when he delivered a letter from the Emperor, there were present Oxford and St. John only. Anne, who during the last few months had suffered renewed and increasing attacks of gout, said to him in answer: "I am sorry that the state of my health will not allow me to speak with your Highness as often as I wish, but"—and here she pointed to the two Ministers— "I have ordered these gentlemen to receive your proposals whenever you think fit." At a subsequent audience she made the Prince the present of a sword richly set with diamonds to the value of 4,500*l.*

Eugene soon found however that he made no progress. He could neither alter the intended terms of peace, nor avert the coming Congress. All his movements, all his conversations, were jealousy watched.

Nor did his high character shield him. He was ex- CHAP.
posed in secret to calumnious charges brought to the XV.
notice of the Government, in part by a Jesuit spy and 1712.
intriguer named Plunket, and in part by anonymous
accusers. He was said to be conspiring with Marlborough and the Whig chiefs to raise an insurrection
in the streets—fire the City—and seize the person of
the Queen. Even the midnight brawls of some drunken
revellers of this period, who called themselves Mohocks,
were held forth as signs and tokens of this pretended.
plot.[1] The Ministers did not discountenance these
shameful rumours so fully as they might; they went so
far as to examine Plunket before the Cabinet Council,
and on the Queen's birthday to double the customary
guards. At last, after some weeks' stay, Eugene perceiving that his presence did not promote his objects
and served only to embitter his opponents, took his
leave, and went back much chagrined to the Hague.

On the 14th of January the Queen was suffering
from gout and unable, as she had intended, to make
her Speech to Parliament. On the 17th, her illness
still continuing, she sent her communication as a
Message to both Houses. It was mainly to announce
that the Congress was now on the point of opening;
and that Her Majesty's plenipotentiaries had already
arrived at Utrecht. These were the Bishop of Bristol,
Lord Privy Seal, and the Earl of Strafford. France had
sent the Maréchal d'Huxelles, the Abbé de Polignac,
and M. Mesnager; while M. Buys was the principal
negotiator on the part of Holland, and the Marquis de
Borgo on the part of Savoy. It had been hoped that

---

[1] For Plunket see especially Macpherson's State Papers, vol. ii. p. 451;
and for the Mohocks the Spectators of March 27 and April 8, 1712.

business would commence in mid January, but some time was consumed in visits of ceremony and regulations of form, so that the first conference was not held until the 29th of the month.[2]

Some particulars of the Court at this period are supplied by Abbé Gaultier. "Every time that the post comes in from Holland the Queen never fails to ask for the 'Gazette de Paris,' and she delights in reading the articles headed 'Londres.' Therefore your friends here request you to give directions that henceforth there may be nothing in those articles that could displease this Princess. And if your Excellency could now induce the King to write to her, such a step on the part of His Majesty would engage her very far in our interest, and our affairs would proceed much the faster. Montgoulin might take the same opportunity to declare his sentiments to Madame Protose, and assure her that he will always follow with pleasure the advice or the injunctions which may be given him in her name."[3] It appears that Louis the Fourteenth did write accordingly; that Anne was much pleased with his letter; and that she entrusted Gaultier with her reply.

James also complied with the suggestion of Gaultier. Here is his letter to the Queen. "In the present situation of affairs it is impossible for me, dear sister, to be any longer silent, and not to put you in mind of the honor and preservation of your family; and to as-

---

[2] The Bishop of Bristol is the last English Prelate employed on a diplomatic mission. His attire and attendance at the first meeting of the Congress are described as follows. "The Lord Privy Seal appeared in a black velvet gown adorned with gold loops with a long train borne up by two pages in ash-coloured coats laced with silver orris and waistcoats of green velvet." (Complete History of Europe, 1712, p. 64.)

[3] Letter to Torcy, of January 27, 1712, N.S. (Archives des Affaires Etrangères).

sure you at the same time of my eternal acknowledg-
ment and gratitude if you use your most efficacious
endeavours towards both. Give me leave to say, that
your own goodnature makes me already promise it to
myself; and with that persuasion I shall always be ready
to agree to whatever you shall think most convenient
for my interest, which after all is inseparable from
yours: being fully resolved to make use of no other
means but those you judge most conducing to our
mutual happiness and to the general welfare of our
country. Your most entirely affectionate brother." This
letter, derived from a draft in the Pretender's own
hand-writing, has been already published in the Stuart
collections.[4] There seems little doubt that it was
through some channel safely conveyed to the Queen;
but there is no proof that, even indirectly, it received
any notice in return. The risk would indeed have been
extreme. Nor is it at all certain what were in truth
the Queen's wishes at this time. Her attachment to
the Church of England, and her apprehension of another such King as James the Second, might more than
balance her feeling for a brother, whom, since his
cradle, she had never seen.

The Queen in her Message of the 17th had given
a satisfactory promise: "You may depend on Her
Majesty communicating to her Parliament the terms of
peace before the same shall be concluded." Meanwhile the Session was in progress. In the Lords the
opponents of the Ministry, damped by the late creations, made but little show. The Duke of Devonshire
however was proceeding with his Bill to give precedence to the Prince of Hanover. But the Lord Trea-

4 Macpherson's Original Papers, vol. II. p. 295, ed. 1775.

surer, being determined to outbid him, introduced another Bill giving precedence to the whole Electoral family as to the children and nephews of the Crown. Devonshire upon this withdrew his measure, and Oxford's was so warmly pressed, that it passed through both Houses in two days. The Act was then despatched to Hanover by Thomas Harley, first cousin of the Treasurer, who hoped to ingratiate himself at that Court both by the message and the messenger.

In the Commons a course of blind vengeance against the members of the late administration seemed to be the prevailing wish of the new majority. Robert Walpole was too conspicuous a man to be passed by. The Commissioners of Public Accounts had brought a charge against him of illicit gains derived from some forage contracts in Scotland, while he was Secretary at War. Walpole spoke ably and powerfully in his own vindication, but he spoke to hearers already for the most part determined to condemn him. It was voted that he was guilty of notorious corruption—that he should be sent to the Tower—that he should be expelled the House. The two last Resolutions were however carried by so far reduced majorities—only 12 in the one case and only 22 in the other—as to indicate in the clearest manner how strong were in truth the grounds of his defence.

Marlborough's case came next. It led to a long and vehement debate, sustained with much ability on the one side by Secretary St. John, Sir William Wyndham, and Sir Thomas Hanmer; on the other by Sir Peter King, Sir Richard Onslow, and Mr. Pulteney. Sir John Germaine, who had been aide-de-camp to Prince Waldeck in 1689, gave evidence at the Bar in

the Duke's behalf. He deposed that the allowances CHAP.
made to His Grace by the contractors for bread were XV.
customary perquisites of the commander-in-chief in 1712.
Flanders, and as such had been always paid to Prince
Waldeck. It was by the skilful application of these
sums that Marlborough had been enabled to obtain the
early and exact intelligence which was one of the
secrets of his great successes. As regards the deduction of two and a half per cent. from the pay of
the foreign troops, it was shown by the signatures of
the foreign Princes to have been a voluntary gift on
their part, and this gift had been confirmed by a
warrant from the Queen. The other deduction of one
per cent. allowed to Mr. Sweet as Paymaster was not
for Marlborough's profit but his own, and was made
without Marlborough's knowledge. Yet in spite of
these grounds for Marlborough's exculpation, the majority of the Commons, inflamed by party zeal against
their leading opponent, declared by 265 votes against
155 the payments made to Marlborough by the bread
contractors to have been unwarrantable and illegal.
By a second Resolution, carried without a division, it
was also affirmed that the two and a half deducted
from the foreign troops was public money and ought
to be accounted for. It was further ordered that these
Resolutions should be laid before the Queen.

From the great man the Commons passed to the
great man's Secretary. It appearing from the Report
of Commissioners that Mr. Cardonnel had received an
annual gratuity of 500 gold ducats from the bread
contractors, he was expelled the House. As to Mr.
Sweet, it was voted that the one per cent. received by
him was public money and ought to be accounted for.

Dismissed in this manner from the service of his Sovereign, and assailed by the violence of an overbearing faction, Marlborough showed the same composure, the same admirable serenity of temper which had so often marked his conduct in the field. He would not plead before the Commons, whom he did not acknowledge as his judges. But he caused to be drawn up in his own name a statement of his case on all the points arraigned, and this statement was subsequently published. It is a well-written and convincing paper. Not only does the Duke give a full answer to the charges, but he shows with how little fairness they were urged. Thus, on the yearly sums from the bread contractors, he declares that this perquisite or payment had been always allowed to the General or Commander-in-Chief in the Low Countries both before and ever since the Revolution, and had been constantly applied by him to the procuring intelligence and other secret service. And he adds: "The Commissioners may have observed very rightly that, by the strictest inquiry they could make, they cannot find that any English General ever received this perquisite. But I presume to say the reason is, that there was never any other English General besides myself who was commander-in-chief in the Low Countries."

In the same spirit the Commons proceeded to consider the Barrier Treaty which they desired to be laid before them. Deeming its stipulations far too favourable to the Dutch they passed an intemperate vote that Lord Townshend, who had negotiated and signed the Treaty, and all those who advised its ratification, "are enemies to the Queen and kingdom."

It is worthy of note, and it ought to be a warning

to all those who might be tempted to similar excesses
of party violence, how slight, or rather how null, was
the moral effect that they produced. No one appears
to have thought the worse on that account of any of
the persons so solemnly found Guilty. Walpole for
example, who disdaining to make any submission remained a prisoner in the Tower until the close of the
Session, received in his captivity visits of compliment
and friendship from men of the highest note in England, such as Lord Somers and Lord Godolphin. The
vote which declared him notoriously corrupt was so
well understood as the mere fruit of Tory rancour,
that it did not form the smallest objection or obstacle
in his path, as he rose to the highest dignities in the
next ensuing reign.

In this Session there was passed an Act to protect
the members of the Episcopal Church in Scotland,
from disturbance and interruption in their public service.
It provided that they might be free to worship after
their own manner, and that the Sheriff of the county
should be bound to secure them from the insults of the
rabble. Simple as the object seems, it excited great
resentment among the Scottish Presbyterians; and the
General Assembly declared itself astonished and afflicted
at this monstrous measure.[5]

From London we pass back to Utrecht. There
the French plenipotentiaries, gave in a Project of
Treaty which greatly surprised those who as yet knew
only the seven Preliminary Articles signed by Mesnager,
and sent to Holland the year before. By this project

---

5 Act 10 Anne c. 7, and Burton's History of Scotland, vol. II. p. 43. The
Bishop of Derry, addressing the House of Lords upon the Irish Church Bill,
June 14, 1869, made skilful use of this Scottish incident.

Louis claimed both Lille and Tournay as an equivalent for the demolition of Dunkirk. To complete his own barrier in the Low Countries he demanded Aire and St. Venant, Bethune and Douay. The Queen's title was not to be acknowledged until the peace was signed. The Electors of Cologne and of Bavaria were to be re-established in their dominions. There was to be a mutual restoration of conquests between France and Savoy. Philip was to continue King of Spain and the Indies, but measures were to be concerted to hinder the Crowns of Spain and France from ever being united on the same head.

This project being made known to the Dutch Ministers was by their connivance published in the Dutch Gazettes, and through these found its way to England. There it stirred up no little indignation. Not the Whigs only but even many of the Tories exclaimed against it, declaring that such terms on the part of France were arrogant and insupportable after so many defeats. Lord Halifax seized the favourable moment, and on the 15th of February moved an Address to the Queen against this project, in the House of Lords. Oxford, seeing how strong the current ran in that direction, did not venture to divide, and so the motion passed. As Swift writes on this occasion to excuse the mishap, "The House of Lords is too strong in Whigs notwithstanding the new creations."

The Ministers, although a little disconcerted, trusted partly to the effect of time in cooling the first resentments, and partly to the persuasions of Abbé Gaultier, whom they despatched to Paris with a representation to his master, that the Queen had gone as far as was possible for her, and that if Louis desired peace he

must moderate his claims. But meanwhile the course CHAP.
of events at Versailles tended to raise other difficulties XV.
on the side of Spain. A grievous epidemic, the most 1712.
malignant form of measles, swept away the flower of
the Royal Family, and spread desolation around the
hearth of the aged King. First on the 12th of February
died Marie Adelaide of Savoy, the young and charm-
ing Dauphiness better known by the title of Burgundy,
which she bore till a few months back. Nine days
later she was followed by her husband, the worthy
pupil of Fénélon and the rising hope of France. They
left two sons, the Dukes of Brittany and Anjou; the
former only five and the last only two years of age.
Both fell ill of the same malady which had proved
fatal to their parents, and the eldest expired on the
8th of March. Thus had three Dauphins of France
gone to the grave in one year. The survivor, then
become the heir-apparent, grew up to long life as
Louis the Fifteenth, but was still a sickly infant whose
life was for a time despaired of. Yet in the order of
birth this one frail child was now the only bar between
Philip of Spain and the throne of France. Under
these altered circumstances it was doubtful whether
Philip would consent to forego his eventual claim.
There was much delay in his answer; there was plainly
much hesitation in his mind; and until that essential
point could be cleared up the entire treaty languished,
and the conferences at Utrecht were suspended.

The Ministers in England had from the first protested, that if unable to conclude a peace on the
terms which they desired they would be found willing
and ready to prosecute the war. Already was the
Duke of Ormond named General in Flanders in suc-

cession to the Duke of Marlborough; and in the course of April he joined his colleague Prince Eugene at Tournay. They had under their command a formidable army exceeding in its numbers 120,000 men, while Villars who confronted them had but 100,000; and these, from the necessities of the kingdom, ill appointed and ill supplied. With such superiority on the side of the Allies it was the desire of Eugene to resume the "grand project" of Marlborough—invest at the same time both Le Quesnoy and Landrecies—overwhelm the French army—and march onwards into the heart of France. "I do not hesitate in declaring to you"—so he wrote a few weeks afterwards—"that it was entirely in our power to force the enemy to risk a battle to their disadvantage or repass the Somme."[6] Ormond, on his part, a man of honourable character though slender capacity, was ambitious of military fame, and like a good soldier told Eugene that he was ready to join in the attack.

Louis the Fourteenth had been at the outset almost overpowered by the anguish of his domestic losses; above all, the untimely death of the Dauphiness, the favourite and frolicsome companion of himself and Madame de Maintenon in their cheerless old age. No sooner could he again apply to business, than he bent his mind to frame some plan of renunciation for King Philip which should satisfy the Court of St. James's. In the course of April came an explicit letter on this subject from Torcy to St. John. It was now proposed, that in the Treaty of Peace the contracting parties should still stipulate most expressly that the Crown of France should never, under any circumstances, be

6 Letter to Marlborough, Camp at Hayn, June 9, 1712.

united to the Crown of Spain. Should the King of
Spain become, by order of succession, the heir to
France, he was to make an immediate option between
the two. If he chose Spain, the Crown of France was
to pass to the next male heir; and, in the far more
probable case of his preferring France, he was not to
be permitted to leave Spain to any son or descendant
of his own. On the contrary, that throne should then
immediately devolve on some foreign Prince, to be
named in the Treaty of Peace, and such as could
cause no umbrage or jealousy to any of the contracting parties. The King of Portugal, wholly unconnected
with the House of Bourbon, was suggested as a person
for whom this stipulation might be fitly made; and it
was proposed that, to this stipulation, all the Powers
of Europe should be Guarantees.

This project found no favor. It made no way with
the English Ministers. St. John answered Torcy by
a masterly despatch in the French language. "In
either," he said, "of the cases which you put, what
security can Europe have that the option which you
promise will be really made? All the Powers you say
should be Guarantees to this engagement; and no
doubt such Guarantees might form a Grand Alliance
to carry on war against the Prince who attempted to
violate the conditions of the Treaty. But surely we
ought to seek the means of averting, rather than the
means of sustaining, a new war. No expedient will
give any real security unless the Prince, who is now
in possession of Spain, will make his option at this
very hour, and unless his option so made be an article
in the Treaty of Peace."[7]

<hr>

[7] The despatch of Torcy to St. John, April 8, N.S., and the answer of

Only a few days from the date of this despatch, Gaultier, who had been both at Paris and at Utrecht, reappeared in London. He had several interviews with each of the two leading Ministers, and was, ere long, able to announce a counter-project they had formed. This had at all events the merit of novelty. It proposed that if Philip were unwilling to resign in due form his eventual claim to the Crown of France, he should immediately relinquish Spain and the Indies, to which the Duke of Savoy should succeed. On the other hand, Philip should at once step into the dominions of the Duke of Savoy, adding to them the Duchy of Mantua as also the island of Sicily, with the title of King. He would then, with the assent of the Great Powers, retain his claim on France, and, in the event of his ever succeeding to that Crown, would annex to it the Savoy dominions.

Of this scheme of the English Ministers it might certainly be said that it treated dominions much like a pack of cards, and dealt them round with no regard to the good will or repugnance of the nations most concerned. It was not ill-framed, however, to meet the perplexities of Sovereigns at this time; and as such it was transmitted by Gaultier on the 1st of May. A special courier bore it posthaste to Versailles, and Oxford bade Gaultier write to Torcy that a favourable answer was expected, if possible, by the 10th of the same month; in which case, he added, there might ensue a suspension of arms. Gaultier took the same opportunity to warn Torcy of the growing dissensions in the English Ministry. "Whenever," he said, "you

St. John, April 6, O. S. 1712, are both published in the Bolingbroke Correspondence, vol. i. p. 448-456.

write to our Lord Treasurer take care in your letter to make no mention of 'M. de Saint Jean,' because the Treasurer does not love him, nor place any confidence in him. In the same manner the last-named person is never to know that you correspond with the Treasurer. He is not to be told that the King has written to the Queen, or the Queen to the King."

Gaultier thus concludes: "I entreat you, Monseigneur, if the transmigration of King Philip to Turin be possible, at present to make every effort with the King to consent to it. I have a thousand reasons for pressing you not to defer the business to another time; for if the Queen, whose health is not good, were to die, we should be here in the greatest confusion in the world. It would then be impossible for our Ministers to make peace; they would have, on the contrary, to take new measures to continue the war."

It was not till the night of the 9th that the courier sent to Versailles came back to London, bringing with him in a letter from Torcy a full compliance with the terms proposed. Louis undertook to lay before his grandson for decision the two alternatives; either a public and immediate renouncement of his claim, to be inserted in the Treaty of Peace, or else a transmigration, as Gaultier termed it, to Turin. It would be necessary to await the return of the messenger despatched with these offers to Madrid, but, meanwhile, Louis positively pledged himself to conclude the Peace, either on one basis or the other.

Next morning then, the 10th of May, the very day that the Treasurer had asked, there was read to the Queen in his presence and in St. John's, this letter from Torcy. So well pleased was Her Majesty, as

Gaultier relates it, that she directed St. John, as Secretary of State, to take immediate measures for the suspension of hostilities. That same afternoon then, St. John sent by special express to the Duke of Ormond, what were subsequently called "the restraining orders." Here follow his own words: "Her Majesty, my Lord, has reason to believe that we shall come to an agreement upon the great article of the union of the two monarchies, as soon as a courier sent from Versailles to Madrid can return. It is therefore the Queen's positive command to your Grace, that you avoid engaging in any siege, or hazarding a battle till you have further orders from Her Majesty. I am at the same time directed to let your Grace know, that the Queen would have you disguise the receipt of this order; and Her Majesty thinks that you cannot want pretences for conducting yourself so as to answer her ends, without owning that which might at present have an ill effect if it was publicly known. . . I had almost forgot to tell your Grace, that communication is given of this order to the Court of France; so that if the Maréchal de Villars takes in any private way notice of it to you, your Grace will answer accordingly."

The tortuous character of these instructions stands in no need of comment. England with such Ministers showed herself far more careful of France—there being still open war between them—than of Holland to which she was bound by the closest ties. She was to manifest ill will to her Allies and reserve her friendship for her foes. The spirit of the army was to be depressed and the fame of the country tarnished. Ormond, mortified as he might be, had as a soldier no alternative but to obey. He entered into a secret correspondence with

Villars, and apprised him that the troops under his own CHAP.
command would henceforth refrain from all offensive XV.
operations. It was impossible, however, to conceal the 1712.
fact from his colleague. When Eugene warmly pressed
him to join in an attack of the French camp as he had
recently agreed to do, he could only give an evasive
answer and at last a point-blank refusal. In this manner the true nature of his orders came to be apparent.
Foiled in this first object, Eugene next proposed to
invest Le Quesnoy, while Ormond should assist in or
cover the siege, and Ormond feeling that he could
carry his resistance no further, though against his instructions, complied.

Expostulations and complaints came as may be
supposed thick and fast to England, and the Opposition was of course not slow to profit by them. The
matter was discussed in both Houses on the 28th of
May. In the Commons William Pulteney, a young
orator of rising fame, moved that the General in
Flanders might have instructions to prosecute the war
with the utmost vigour; but he was defeated by a vast
majority—203 votes against 73—and the House agreed
to a Resolution for putting an entire confidence in the
Queen. With the Peers Lord Halifax, as on the last
occasion, took the lead. Wharton and Cowper joined
him and warmly denounced the restraining orders.
The Lord Treasurer said in reply, "that though the
Duke of Ormond might have refused to hazard a
general action, yet he could be positive he would not
decline joining with the Allies in a siege, orders having been sent him for that purpose."

Marlborough rose next. "I am at a loss" he said
"how to reconcile to the rules of war the orders not

to hazard a battle but to engage in a siege; since it is impossible to make a siege without either hazarding a battle in case the enemy attempts to relieve the place, or else shamefully raising the siege." But there was yet another objection to Oxford's answer besides that which Marlborough so forcibly stated. It was in truth no more than an ignominious after-thought, since the original instructions of the 10th of May forbade, as we have seen, a siege quite as distinctly as a battle. It was only by a subsequent despatch that St. John gave his sanction to the course which Ormond had already adopted by taking part in the investment of Le Quesnoy.

Being further pressed, the Treasurer in a second speech declared that in a few days the Queen, according to her promise, would lay before her Parliament the conditions that were contemplated. Some Lords had expressed their apprehensions of a separate peace. "Nothing of that nature" cried Oxford "was ever designed. Such a peace would be so base, so knavish, and so villanous a thing that every servant of the Queen must answer for it with his head to the nation." It is even alleged that he added, "The Allies know of our proceedings and are satisfied with them."[8]

So positive an assurance from the leading Minister was deemed satisfactory by the great majority of the Peers. Halifax seeing their temper desired to avoid a division, but it was forced on, and the Government prevailed by 68 votes against 40. A Protest against this decision, couched in very strong language, was

---

[8] Lockhart of Carnwath was present at this debate and has given an account of it (Commentaries, &c., vol. I. p. 387), not agreeing on all points with that in the Parl. History, vol. VI. p. 1135.

signed by 27, including the name of Marlborough—a
Protest afterwards expunged by order of the House,
and marked only by asterisks in the Journals.

CHAP.
XV.
1712.

There was yet another incident that day, which
proved only ridiculous to one of the parties, but which
might have been of serious concern to one or both.
Earl Poulett was so ill bred and so unjust as to use
these words in the course of the discussion: "No one
can doubt the Duke of Ormond's bravery, but he does
not resemble a certain General who led troops to the
slaughter to cause a great number of officers to be
knocked on the head in a battle or against stone walls,
in order to fill his pockets by disposing of their commissions." This dastardly taunt received no notice at
the time from the great man at whom it glanced. But
on the rising of the House the Duke sent Lord Mohun
to Lord Poulett with an invitation, according to the
language of the time, "to take the air in the country."
The Earl, inquiring innocently whether this was meant
as a challenge, received for answer that the message
required no explanation. Lord Mohun added "I shall
accompany the Duke of Marlborough, and your Lordship would do well to provide a second."

At this summons, which he does not seem to have
anticipated, the impetuous courage, which no doubt
was vibrating through Lord Poulett's frame, may perhaps have shown itself by some tremor in his limbs.
Certain it is that on returning home he could not
wholly conceal his emotion from his wife. A hint
was promptly conveyed to Lord Dartmouth as Secretary
of State, who at once placed Lord Poulett under arrest,
and conveyed to Marlborough an order from the
Queen to proceed no further in this business. Nay

CHAP.
XV.
1712.

more, by the subsequent aid of the Lord Treasurer, the two parties were brought in appearance at least, to a reconciliation.

The double victory of the Ministers in both Houses of Parliament was felt by them as a great triumph, and emboldened them in their ulterior measures. Their chief source of anxiety and distrust was now on the side of Hanover. As St. John had complained in confidence a little while before: "The Elector had till this winter behaved himself so that Whig and Tory equally courted him, and had equal expectations from him. He has now placed himself at the head of a party, and that too, whatever he is made to believe, by great degrees the least at this time, and whenever we have got rid of our war likely to be still weaker. The landed interest will then rise, and the monied interest, which is the great support of Whiggism, must of course decline." [9]

Meanwhile there had come from Madrid the expected messenger. Philip on full deliberation had determined to accept the first of the two alternatives submitted to him. He would make a full renunciation of his eventual claim to the Crown of France; that renunciation to be confirmed in the most solemn manner by the French Parliaments and by the Spanish Cortes. It was also agreed that, in case the posterity of Philip failed, the Crown of Spain should devolve not on any other French Prince but on the Duke of Savoy, who had likewise an hereditary claim to that succession as descended from a daughter of Philip the Second. Moreover the Court of Versailles undertook that the Pretender, so constant a source of jealousy to the

[9] To the Earl of Strafford, March 7, 1712.

English Parliament and people, should at once quit the French dominions as though of his own free choice, and retire to Switzerland or Lorraine. And as a further pledge of its good faith the Court of Versailles consented, even before proceeding with the treaty, to admit an English garrison into the town and citadel of Dunkirk.

The negotiation with France and Spain being in such a state of forwardness, the Queen went down to the House of Peers on the 6th of June, and delivered an elaborate speech to fulfil, as she said, her promise of communicating to her Parliament the terms of Peace before it was concluded. "The assuring" she said "of the Protestant Succession as by law established to the House of Hanover being what I have nearest at heart, particular care is taken not only to have that acknowledged in the strongest terms, but to have an additional security by the removal of that person out of the dominions of France who has pretended to disturb this settlement. Her Majesty proceeded to explain the measures taken to prevent the Crowns of France and Spain from ever being united on the same head. "The nature of this proposal is such" she added "that it executes itself." France was willing to give up its portion of the island of St. Kitts, with Newfoundland, Nova Scotia, and other territory in North America. Spain would yield to us the fortress of Gibraltar, the whole island of Minorca, and the monopoly in the trade of negroes for thirty years. "I have not"—thus Her Majesty proceeded—"taken upon me to determine the interests of our confederates; these must be adjusted in the Congress at Utrecht, where my best endeavours shall be employed, as they have hitherto been, to procure to every one of them all justice and reasonable satisfaction. In the meantime I think it proper to acquaint you that France offers to make the Rhine the barrier to the Empire, to yield Brisach, the fort of Kehl, and Landau, and to raze all the fortresses both on the other side of the Rhine and in that river. The Spanish·Low Countries may go to His Imperial Majesty; the kingdoms of Naples and Sardinia, the Duchy of Milan, and the places belonging to Spain on the coast of Tuscany may likewise be yielded to the Emperor by the treaty of peace. As to the kingdom of Sicily, though there remains no dispute concerning the cession of it by the Duke of Anjou, yet the disposition thereof is not yet determined. . The interests of the States General with respect to commerce are agreed to as they have been demanded by their own Ministers, with the exception only of some very few species of merchandise; and the entire Barrier as demanded by the States in 1709 from France, except two or three places at most. . . . The difference between the Barrier demanded for the Duke of Savoy in 1709 and the offers now made by France is very inconsiderable; but that Prince having so signally distinguished himself in the service of the common cause, I am endeavouring to procure for him still further advantages."

Such then were the principal terms which Anne announced. And in conclusion Her Majesty said: "Nothing on my part will be neglected to bring the Peace to a happy and speedy issue; and I depend on your entire confidence in me and your cheerful concurrence with me."

To bring this disposition to a trial Addresses of

confidence and concurrence were moved at once in both the Houses. In the Commons it was carried nem. con. In the Lords there was a keen debate in which Marlborough spoke with no little acrimony. "The measures" he said "pursued in England for a year past are directly contrary to Her Majesty's engagements with the Allies, have sullied the triumphs and glories of her reign, and will render the English name odious to all other nations." Godolphin, though suffering from illness, spoke on the same side, as did also Wharton, Nottingham, and Cowper. They moved a clause in addition to the Address, that Her Majesty's Allies should be invited to join her in a mutual guarantee. Against this the Lord Treasurer contended, that such a scheme would subject the Queen and the whole treaty to the pleasure of the Allies, who might prove backward and intractable; and that since England had borne the greatest share of the burthen of the war, it was reasonable that the Queen should be the principal arbiter of the Peace. These considerations appear to have prevailed with the Lords, who rejected the amendment by 81 votes against 36, and passed the Address in its first form. But a Protest, designed as a popular argument against the terms of the treaty, was signed by 24 Peers, Marlborough and Godolphin included. Like the former Protest it was expunged from the Journals by direction of the House, but it was put into print, and circulated in great numbers through the country, notwithstanding an Order of the Queen in Council, which was immediately levelled against it, offering a reward for the discovery of all persons concerned in the dissemination of this "malicious and scandalous paper."

18*

The Commons of that day were fully determined not to be left behind in the race of tyranny; and to show the same zeal as either the Lords House or the Privy Council, in suppressing the publications of their political opponents. With this view they fell upon a volume of Sermons, just then sent forth in print by a most estimable prelate, Bishop Fleetwood of St. Asaph. These Sermons, four in number, were of old date, as preached on the deaths of Queen Mary and of the Duke of Gloucester, on the death of William, and on the accession of Anne. But they had a new Preface, in which the terms of peace proposed were earnestly lamented and condemned.[1] Sir Peter King, Sir Joseph Jekyll, and Mr. Lechmere stood forth in defence of the Bishop in the Commons; but the House heeded them not, and by a majority of 119 to 53 resolved that "the said Preface is malicious and factious," and that it "be burnt by the hands of the common hangman upon Thursday next (June the 12th) at twelve of the clock in Palace Yard, Westminster."

Fortified by this spirit in both the Houses the Ministers, immediately upon the Queen's speech of the 6th of June and the Addresses in reply, concluded an armistice with France, limited however to the space of two months and to the sphere of the Low Countries only. Orders were sent accordingly to Ormond to separate his army from Eugene's, and refraining from further warfare fall back and take quiet possession of Dunkirk. But Eugene and the Dutch Deputies anticipating a course of this kind had to some extent

---

[1] An eloquent passage from this Preface is cited in the History of England from the Peace of Utrecht, vol. i. p. 5, Tauchnitz Ed. See also the Spectator, No. 384. This last was before the vote of the Commons.

provided against it. They had addressed themselves
in secret to the chiefs of the auxiliary troops in British
pay, and had so successfully wrought upon their military ardour as to make them engage, that if Ormond
should depart they would remain even against his
orders, and look elsewhere for their pay. When therefore the Duke did announce to his colleague the cessation of arms and broke up from his camp at Cateau
Cambresis, he had the mortification to be followed
only by the 12,000 men to which the English force
was now reduced, together with four battalions of
Holstein and one regiment of dragoons from Liege.
Nor did his disappointments end here. As he marched
back the Dutch governors of Bouchain, Tournay, and
Douay closed their gates against him; and Ormond
thereupon, as if in reprisal, took possession of Ghent
and Bruges in the name of the Queen. He was now
at hand and ready to throw also an English garrison
into Dunkirk, but the King of France declaring that
the question had been altered by the stubbornness of
the British stipendiaries, appeared to hesitate, and
delayed for some time the surrender of that fortress.

Even after the separation from Ormond, the army
of Eugene was still in its numbers slightly superior to
the French. The Prince might still hope to prevail in
the campaign. But this separation between gallant
soldiers who had so long fought beneath the same
banners, and had achieved so many triumphs shoulder
to shoulder, was felt as a deep grief by all. A common Serjeant in the British ranks who was present
has, in homely but impressive language, described the
scene: "As they marched off that day both sides
looked very dejectfully on each other, neither being

permitted to speak to the other to prevent reflections that might thereby arise."[2]

Some strong reasons there were certainly to urge for such a course. As St. John said in one of his despatches to Ormond, "the Queen cannot think with patience of sacrificing men, when there is a fair prospect of attaining her purpose another way." But even allowing the utmost weight to these considerations, we may still deplore the crooked policy which estranged us from our old Allies. We may acknowledge that this secession of the English troops with the enemy before them was painful and humiliating, to all among them who thought of their former exploits achieved on the same plains.

The Session of Parliament, which had been protracted to a most unusual length, was closed by adjournment on the 21st of June and by prorogation on the 8th of July. Immediately upon the last event St. John was raised to the peerage—a reward which had been for some months past intended for him, but delayed to enable him to carry through the business of the Session in the House of Commons. There was an Earldom of Bolingbroke in his family, which had become extinct only a year before, and it was this that St. John desired to revive. But Oxford, to mark his own supremacy in the Cabinet, insisted with the Queen that St. John should receive no higher rank than that of Viscount; and Viscount Bolingbroke he was made accordingly. To mark this supremacy in another manner also, Oxford a few weeks later received from the Queen—or to speak more truly gave himself—the Order of the Garter. He was now at the very summit of honors.

<hr>

[2] Narrative of Serjeant Milner, p. 356, as cited by Coxe.

Early in August the new Viscount set out for France, to settle if he could by his presence the points in the negotiation that were still depending. He took with him both Prior and Gaultier. There were great marks of honor shown him on his way from Calais; and at Paris he was welcomed in a manner beseeming both his splendid talents and his eminent post. At nine o'clock one Sunday morning, he was presented to the King at Fontainebleau and most graciously received. During his stay of about one fortnight at Paris, he appears to have divided his time most impartially, between business and pleasure. He brought to a decision several controverted questions in the terms of peace; and he paid court—and not without success—to the beautiful Countess de Parabère.[3] It was agreed between Bolingbroke and Torcy, that Sicily should at the peace be ceded to the Duke of Savoy, who might then with the assent of all the Powers take the title of King. It was agreed that this Prince and his family should be named in succession to the Crown of Spain and the Indies, failing the descendants of Philip. It was further agreed, after many and warm attempts on the part of Torcy to extort a contrary decision, that England should stand free of any pledge or promise to obtain the restoration of the Elector of Bavaria.

The conditions of a treaty being thus far adjusted, Bolingbroke and Torcy signed a suspension of arms for four months, a term afterwards prolonged, and which was not, like the former, confined to the armies

---

[3] Madame de Parabère afterwards became the favourite mistress of the Regent Duke of Orleans. His mother the Dowager Duchess calls her "la Sultane Reine," and adds a minute description of her charms. (Corresp. vol. 1. p. 239, ed. Brunet). I have seen only one portrait of her, an exquisite miniature, now in the collection of Earl Beauchamp at Madresfield Court.

in the Netherlands but extending to all parts of the world, both by land and sea. From this moment it may be said that in effect peace was re-established between the two nations, although minor matters, some unexpectedly arising, impeded its conclusion for months to come.

In these negotiations with France and Spain, the case of the Catalans, betrayed by the English Ministers, and left unaided to the vengeance of Castille, forms, among many dark blots, perhaps the darkest in the political career of Bolingbroke. But I shall say nothing further of it at this place, since—together with its results extending far beyond the Peace of Utrecht—it is fully detailed elsewhere.[4]

The departure of the Pretender from France, so positively promised, had been accidentally delayed. Both he and his sister, the Princess Louisa, had fallen ill of the small pox. The young Princess died, early in May, to the great grief of her family; and the Prince only regained his strength by slow degrees. On this plea, and even beyond his convalescence, he still lingered in the French capital, or near it. Bolingbroke always declared that he had no communication with him during his stay at Paris, and saw him only once, which was at the Opera at a great distance across the house.[5] At length, on the 7th of September, James, being warmly pressed by Torcy, did commence his journey, but he proceeded only to Chalons-sur-Marne, still within the French dominions.

When Bolingbroke set out from Paris, on his re-

---

[4] History of England from the Peace of Utrecht, vol. I. p. 71-74 (Tauchn. Ed.), and for the siege of Barcelona the War of the Succession in Spain, p. 372-390.
[5] Swift's Works, vol. XVI. p. 297.

turn to England, he had left Prior with a letter of cre- CHAP.
dence as Chargé d'Affaires. We find that accomplished XV.
man—the poet, the wit, the politician—even from his 1712.
outset in the closest intimacy with the leading Ministers.
As he reports it to his chief, "I have a thousand compliments to make you. Every night I sup with M. de
Torcy 'en famille.' Madame drinks two healths I have
taught her 'à Harré et à Robin.'[6] Madame de Parabère
is very proud of her good fortune."

It was however by no means designed that a man
of humble birth and station such as Prior should continue to represent the Queen in France. A man of the
highest rank had been selected as Ambassador on either
side.   The French Court named the Duke d'Aumont,
and the English Court named the Duke of Hamilton.
But the last never proceeded to his post, for having
unhappily engaged in a private quarrel on the subject
of a lawsuit, he was slain in a duel by Lord Mohun,
who also fell.[7] Thus does Bolingbroke describe the
tragical event: "My Lord Mohun had on Thursday
given very brutal language to the Duke of Hamilton
at the chambers of a Master in Chancery; the latter
replied in no provoking manner, and intended to pass
it over as the effect of wine; but the next day Mohun
sent him a challenge by MacCarthy—that is, he who
gave the affront demanded satisfaction of the person
who received it.   They fought, received three or four
wounds each, and both died on the spot, or a few

6 Henry Viscount Bolingbroke and Robert Earl of Oxford.   Bolingbroke's
Correspondence, vol. II. p. 33.

7 Of this nobleman, who was completely, in French phrase, a *ferrailleur*,
a character is to be found in Swift's Works (vol. x. p. 307).   But Sir Walter
Scott as editor has misprinted the name, changing Lord Mohun to Lord Mahon.
I hope that I may be allowed to disclaim the honor of this relationship.

minutes after."[8] In the place of Hamilton as Ambassador, the Duke of Ormond was at first suggested, but finally the Duke of Shrewsbury was sent.

Meanwhile the campaign was in progress. Prince Eugene had pressed the siege of Le Quesnoy, and on the 3rd of July forced the town to surrender, the garrison to remain prisoners of war. Next he invested Landrecies as he had formerly proposed, being eager, it would seem, to prove to the world that the secession of the English had not altered his plans and would not affect his successes. On the other hand Marshal Villars more justly estimated the loss sustained by the Allies in an army even though a very small one, of excellent troops which carried with them the renown and influence of the English name. He found also that he could gather to himself reinforcements from the garrisons of other French towns which, since the armistice, were no longer exposed to danger. Watching his opportunity with consummate skill he suddenly fell upon Denain. There Eugene had stationed a force of about 8,000 men, in great part Dutch, and commanded by the Earl of Albemarle; his object being to cover the lines which he had formed and to secure the passage of the convoys to his camp at Landrecies. Lord Albemarle, taken by surprise on the afternoon of the 24th of July, was put to the rout. The French chief slew or scattered the greater part of the force at Denain and took prisoners no less than 3,000; among these Albemarle and the Princes of Anhalt and Nassau-Siegen. To add to the poignancy of their defeat it had for one of its witnesses Eugene himself, who was approaching rapidly on the other bank of the Scheldt, but who was

---

[8] Bolingbroke to Argyle, November 19, 1712.

stopped short by the redoubt of the Denain bridge
which the French had seized.

This triumph of the French, the first which they had achieved in the Low Countries for a period of many years, made of course on that account the stronger impression. It wrought especially upon the Dutch. The Ministers of that Republic had hitherto inclined to carry on the war even without the aid of England. They now saw that victory had departed from them at the same time with the British standards; and they felt that if they could not avert a peace at Utrecht, it would be wisest for them to take part in it.

The recent ascendency of Villars was moreover maintained by him through the rest of the campaign. Not only did he compel Eugene to raise the siege of Landrecies; not only did he reduce the small posts of Marchiennes, Mortaigne, and St. Amand, but he proceeded to invest Douay. That fortress, after a fruitless effort of Eugene to relieve it, yielded to his arms, and Villars found himself henceforward superior in numbers and master of the field. He was enabled to besiege and recover both Le Quesnoy, the conquest of Eugene in this very campaign, and Bouchain, the conquest of Marlborough in the last; and in this manner with great lustre to himself he concluded the operations of the year.

In Spain as in France we find in the course of this year diplomacy succeed to warfare. We find the British troops withdrawn from Catalonia; we find Lord Lexington sent ambassador to the Court of Madrid. The principal event in that country was the death of a great commander. The Duke of Vendome, prone to every form of self-indulgence, desired to avail himself of the lull in military operations, and hearing the sea-fish at the village of Vinaros highly renowned went thither, unattended by any of his officers, to pass some days in strict seclusion, and to gorge himself at will. Ere long he was seized with a surfeit, and other unexpected symptoms arising, he was quickly at the point of death. Then his domestics, some of them bound to him by the basest ties, fled and left him, first plundering what they could. It is said that in piteous tones he pleaded, and pleaded perhaps in vain, that the coverlet might not be drawn from his bed before he had expired. Expire he did, thus forsaken and bereft, on the 10th of June. "In this ignominious manner" adds St. Simon "died the most haughty and arrogant of mankind."[9]

In the autumn of this year there was made to Gaultier an important overture respecting the Pretender, which he imparted in a secret letter to Torcy. "My Lord Bolingbroke," he writes, "desires to begin in right earnest some measures for the interest of Montgoulin; and for that object he presses to know who are those among the Whigs who, about eighteen months ago, offered Montgoulin to do him service if he would wholly confide in them, and follow their counsels in all that they advised. I would ask your Excellency to forward this letter to him after you have read it, if you see no objection. They assure me here that they have no kind of communication with him except only through your channel. I have told those who have spoken to me of him since my return of the assurances which you have given him on the part of your Master, that his removal from France would not prevent his being

<hr>

[9] Mémoires, vol. x. p. 315.

thought of when there should be an opportunity, always
saving, however, the rights of Protose. As far as I
could see, this resolution was deemed quite satisfactory.
Be careful, if you please, that Mr. Prior should learn
nothing of all this; for, as it appears to me, Lord
Bolingbroke desires to keep it secret from him."[1]

In September of this year an eminent man was withdrawn from the political scene in England. There died
the Earl Godolphin. His malady was the stone; and
he had retired for rest and quiet to the house of the
Duke of Marlborough near St. Alban's, where he closed
his eventful and on the whole most prosperous career.
It is worthy of note that his most confidential papers
—the private letters to him of his Sovereign and of his
colleagues—were brought to sale by auction and dispersed only a few months before the period at which
the Preface of my present History is dated. The correspondence of Queen Anne especially—as the public
was then enabled to peruse it—displays great violence
in her likings and dislikings, but at the same time great
rectitude of purpose. Thus, on September 12, 1707,
she writes: "Whoever of the Whigs thinks I am to be
hectored or frighted into a compliance, though I am a
woman, is mightily mistaken in me. I thank God I
have a soul above that, and am too much concerned
for my reputation to do anything to forfeit it." In a
postscript Anne desires that Godolphin "will not let
this be seen by anybody, no, not by my unkind friend;"
by which she means the Duchess of Marlborough. In
another letter, without date of year, the Queen desires
his Lordship to look into the case of some Cinque
Port officers, whom the Earl of Westmoreland as Lord

CHAP.
XV.
1712.

---

[1] Letter dated October 12, 1712, N. S. (Archives des Affaires Etrangères).

Warden desired to dismiss, especially "one Mr. Herbert, who is Deputy-Governor of Dover Castle, and the Mayor of the town is intended to succeed him. . . . As for the Deputy-Governor," continues Her Majesty, "I never heard any character of him; but if what the Prince was told some time ago, of the Mayor of Dover ordering the bells to be rung upon a report of the Prince's laying down his post of Lord High Admiral be true, I cannot think he is a fit person to succeed Mr. Herbert or anybody else." And she adds, "Let me know the truth. For God's sake tell me your mind freely, for I would not err in any thing. Whenever I do, it will be my misfortune, but shall never be my fault; and, as long as I live, it shall be my endeavour to make my country and my friends easy; and though those that come after me may be more capable of so great a trust as it has pleased God to put into my poor hands, I am sure they can never discharge it more faithfully than her that is sincerely your humble servant, A. R."[2]

To Marlborough, the loss of Godolphin was indeed a great one, more especially at this the crisis of his later fortunes. The Duke stood henceforward almost alone in politics, little relied on or consulted by either party and in some doubt apparently as to his future course. Under such circumstances he deemed it politic to withdraw for a time from England. It was not without difficulty that he obtained a passport for the purpose. Thus does Gaultier explain the case to Torcy: "My Lord Bolingbroke bids me write to you to-day,

---

[2] The Godolphin MSS. came up for auction by Messrs. Sotheby in April, 1869. Some of the most valuable were secured for the British Museum. But there has been a wide dispersion. Of the two letters of Queen Anne here quoted one was bought by a gentleman in Eaton Square and the other by a gentleman at Aberdeen.

and let you know from him that the Duke of Marl- CHAP.
borough has asked permission from the Queen to quit XV.
the kingdom and to travel in Italy, and that, after a 1712.
good deal of contest and consideration, Her Majesty
has given him leave. He is to pass by Ostend, Bruges,
Ghent, Brussels, and Liege to his principality (of Mindelheim), thence through the Tyrol to Venice, and finally
to Naples, where he is to sojourn as long as he pleases.
Such is the route which has been traced out for him
without permission to pass anywhere else. My Lord
Bolingbroke adds, that you need feel no uneasiness as
to this journey of the Duke, since it is no longer in his
power to do harm to any one."[3]

An abstract or summary of the passport so obtained
has been printed in Coxe's biography; it is quite general
in its terms, and states no limits to His Grace's route
or residence; so that the restrictions enjoined were
verbal only. It would appear also that, in the Cabinet,
the grant of this passport was forwarded by Oxford
and opposed by Bolingbroke.[4]

Marlborough accordingly embarked in the course of
November and landed at Ostend. But when once upon
the Continent he did not feel himself bound to adhere
to the conditions under which the passport had been
granted. From Aix-la-Chapelle he turned aside to
Maestricht, where he was rejoined by his Duchess in
the month of February following. After a short visit 1713.
to the principality of Mindelheim so gloriously gained,
he fixed his residence with Her Grace first at Frankfort
and then at Antwerp, within easy reach of England.

3 Letter dated November 11, 1712, N.S. (Archives des Affaires Étran-
gères).
4 Coxe's Marlborough, vol. VI. p. 221.

The New Year found the Treaty of Peace by no means concluded—a matter of just surprise, since, as we have seen, an agreement had been long since arrived at on the principal points at issue between France and England. This delay was due in part to the smaller Princes who, after much wavering, wished to be included, and who were by no means moderate in their pretensions; and in part to some insidious attempts of the French Ministers to avail themselves of the discord among the members of the Grand Alliance, and obtain on several points more favourable terms than those they had recently accepted. And as the affairs of the Peace so did those of the Pretender languish. The one indeed could only proceed in subordination and subsequently to the other. But the fault was also in part the Pretender's own.

In the first place James had persisted in remaining on French territory to the great discomposure of his English friends. We find Gaultier, on the 31st of January New Style, write as follows on the subject to Torcy: "It is absolutely necessary that the Chevalier de St. George should think of leaving the dominions of the King as soon as possible. I have orders from the Treasurer, and also from my Lord Bolingbroke, to let you know this very day that the Queen can never venture to sign the Peace so long as he continues in France. My Lord Bolingbroke told me this morning that he ought not to hesitate to go at once to Switzerland, if there continues to be any difficulty with the Emperor as to his safe-conduct to Lorraine."

But there were other points also on which James's conduct was complained of. Thus Gaultier goes on to say in the same letter, "Let Montgoulin know, if you

please, that, in spite of the fine promises he made me, CHAP.
he has sent to this country—or, at least, there have XV.
been sent in his name—day by day, a number of priests, 1713.
who spoil his business and cause him to be hated by
all those to whom they speak of him. He ought to be
very careful, and to send for some Protestants from
hence to be about his person. It is too early as yet
to think of his case; let him wait, and he shall be apprised when the right time comes. You may be sure
that every measure taken in his favor shall pass through
your hands as we had agreed."

Thus pressed in the strongest manner, both from
London and Versailles, the Chevalier did at last decide. He appears to have left Chalons on the 20th of
February,[5] and he betook himself to Bar, in Lorraine.
Even before this intelligence reached England the
Abbé asked the advice of his confidential friends as to
where—whether at Bar or at Berne—James had best
fix his residence in the next ensuing months. Here is
the answer as reported to Torcy. "It matters little
where the Chevalier may pass the winter, provided
only he departs from France and does not go to any
place where the Duke of Marlborough could meet him."
It would seem then that in England at this juncture
the secret advisers of Gaultier suspected Marlborough
of a design to make terms with the Pretender—terms,
of course, on his own account, and not at all to their
advantage.

As put in parallel with the Treasurer, the Secretary
was at this time considered more especially the friend
of France. We find Gaultier in his letters descant on
"our incomparable Lord Bolingbroke, LE PHÉNIX DES

5 See a note in Macpherson's Original Papers, vol. II. p. 384.

ANGLAIS." It is therefore only just to the memory of a statesman, whose conduct on most points is not to be defended, to observe that, in this last conjuncture, Bolingbroke acted as became an English Minister. He hazarded his personal favor at the Court of Versailles rather than wink at its intrigues or submit to its dictation. So early as the 3rd of January he had expressed to the Earl of Strafford at the Hague his earnest desire of ending "this tedious, intricate, and so much traversed negotiation." But finding the French still chaffer on small points and shadowy distinctions, as though on purpose to gain time, and seeking to derive advantage from the variety of views expressed at Utrecht, Bolingbroke, on the 17th of February, addressed a despatch to the Duke of Shrewsbury as ambassador at Paris—a despatch both haughty in its language and peremptory in its terms.[6]

In this despatch, of no common significance, Shrewsbury was directed to ask an immediate conference with the Ministers of France, and above all with M. de Torcy. He was to state to them that the Queen would endure no further suspense, nor consent much longer to postpone the meeting of her Parliament. At this meeting, the result of the negotiations, one way or the other, ought to be, and it should be, explicitly declared. And, added Bolingbroke, "the fruit which the Queen expects from this full communication of her intentions is either by these means to hasten the conclusion of the General Peace between Her Majesty and the Crowns of France and Spain, or else at the worst to prevent at this season of the year and the approach of spring any surprise on either side."

[6] See Bolingbroke's Correspondence, vol. II. p. 170 and 256.

With great ability and clearness Bolingbroke next proceeded to discuss the divers small articles not yet determined, and to declare the Queen's ultimatum upon each. There was a question as to the limits of the right of fishing on the coast of Nova Scotia, and the Queen insisted that the distance should be fixed at thirty leagues. The Queen persisted also in refusing the liberty claimed for the French subjects in the places to be ceded to sell their BONA IMMOBILIA. In regard to another privilege claimed for them, namely, the use of their own, the Roman Catholic, religion, the Queen would grant it only with this proviso, "as far as is consistent with the laws and policy of Great Britain." In the treaty with Portugal, the Queen refused to allow the claim of France for an equal right to the navigation of the Amazon river. As regards the Elector of Bavaria, Anne was willing that he should retain the sovereignty of Luxemburg until he had a satisfaction made to him on account of his claims in Germany, but he was not to be himself the judge of that satisfaction. As regards the Barrier of Holland, the French had agreed, after a long struggle, to yield the town and territory of Tournay, but they desired, and might be permitted, to retain the small posts of St. Amand and Mortaigne. On the other hand they must give up all claim to the fortress and the several dependencies of Ypres. Only as to Bailleul a discretion was allowed to the Duke of Shrewsbury.

The effect of this firmness was decisive. Torcy and his colleagues saw, with some alarm, that the much-desired Peace might slip from them if its terms were strained too far. They agreed almost at once to every-thing demanded, and Torcy, with all the gaiety and good humour of his countrymen, even when baffled in an object, protested that he had been all along as eager to conclude as they could be in England. Instructions were sent accordingly to Utrecht, and there were no further delays beyond what the slow forms of diplomacy in that age required. With this prospect Bolingbroke could also look with cheerfulness on the conduct of home affairs. Thus he wrote again to Shrewsbury on the 3rd of March: "I think the Whigs seem to give up the success of this Session. Their principal heroes are gone the circuit: Nottingham is pelted from all quarters. I cannot help saying in the fulness of my soul to your Grace, that if we do not establish ourselves and the true interests of our country it is the Queen's and Treasurer's fault. The clamour of Jacobitism seems to be the only resource of our enemies; and I am sorry to tell you that the Duke of Argyle gives too affectedly into that poor artifice." For Argyle, who had of a sudden joined the Tories, was now with his usual versatility veering back to the Whigs.

The difficulties, great and small, of the negotiation having been in this manner surmounted, the treaties were signed at Utrecht on the 31st of March according to the style of England, the 11th of April according to the style of the southern Continental nations. There was signed a Treaty of Peace and next a Treaty of Commerce between France and England. There were signed on the same day separate Treaties for the States of Holland, the King of Portugal, the King of Prussia, and the Duke of Savoy. The Treaty between England and Spain was in formal conclusion for some weeks further postponed; and the Emperor's Peace with

France re-establishing the two Electors was not signed until next year at Rastadt, on the 6th of March, between Villars and Eugene.

It is the earlier day however—the 31st of March in English style—which forms the point of departure for those Histories of England which profess to commence at the Peace of Utrecht.

CHAP.
XV.
1713.

CHAPTER XVI.

THE AGE OF ANNE.

CHAP.
XVI.
———
THE
AGE OF
ANNE.

As the Ancients might boast of their Augustan age; as in England men point with pride to the age of Elizabeth, in Italy to the age of Leo the Tenth, and in France to the age of Louis the Fourteenth, so again among the English a halo has gathered round the age of Anne. Succeeding as she did a Dutch and to be succeeded by a German King, she holds in our Literature an especial and an English place; and thus full many works of genius and renown, though they may have been commenced under William or continued under George, are taken by the world to be centered in her reign.

Certainly it was an illustrious period, a period not easily paralleled elsewhere, that could combine the victories of Marlborough with the researches of Newton—the statesmanship of Somers with the knight-errantry of Peterborough—the publication of Clarendon's History with the composition of Burnet's—the eloquence of Bolingbroke in Parliament and of Atterbury in the pulpit, with the writings in prose and verse of Swift and Addison, of Pope and Prior. It is also deserving of note how frequent was the intercourse and how familiar the friendship in those days between the leaders of political parties and the men in the front rank of intellectual eminence. Since Queen Anne

there has not been found in England the same amount
of intimacy between them, or any thing like the same
amount.   If this were only to say that the men who
were Ministers, or who desired to be so, sought out or
consorted with those persons who they thought could
assist them in their objects as negotiators, as pamphlet-
eers, or as party writers, the fact would scarce be
worthy the remark.   Even thus however it is not always that a Secretary of State and a Chargé d'Affaires
would, as Bolingbroke at St. James's and Matthew
Prior at Paris, drop the "My Lord" and "Sir" in all
letters not strictly official, and prefer to write to each
other as "Harry to Matt" and "Matt to Harry."   But
the case went much further than this.

Somers and Halifax especially on one side, Bolingbroke and Oxford on the other, being themselves accomplished in literature, loved the society of men of
letters for its own sake, and although there might not
be the smallest prospect of any political advantage accruing from it.   Nay more, they would sometimes on
personal grounds help forward or promote an adherent
or at least a well wisher of the opposite side.   With
men of genius of whatever rank they lived not on the
footing of chiefs or patrons but on equal terms as
friends.   All state or ostentation was avoided.   Thus
when Harley was created Earl of Oxford he would not
for some time allow Swift to call him by his new title,
and whenever Swift did so Oxford gave a jesting nickname in return.   Thus also one day at Court, when
Oxford as Lord Treasurer was in state attire and held
the White Staff in his hand, he walked up through the
crowd of courtiers to Swift, and asked to be made
known to Dr. Parnell who was standing by.   "I value

CHAP. myself" says Swift "upon making the Ministry desire
XVI.   to be acquainted with Parnell and not Parnell with the
THE   Ministry."[1]   Indeed there was perhaps no man of his
AGE OF
ANNE. time more genial, more truly at home with men of
genius, more thoroughly enjoying their converse and
desirous of their friendship, than this the last of the
Lord Treasurers of England. They were not ungrateful; and through their means it has happened that,
while Harley is but little to be valued or honored as a
statesman, he shines in History with a lustre not his
own. Certainly if he showed favor to the Muses the
debt has been most amply repaid.[2]

Frank and open as were the statesmen of that age in
their conversation with their·friends, they were, and
with good reason, reserved and cautious in their correspondence while their adversaries were in power. This
arose from the ill practice, continued to a much later
period, of opening letters at the post. In the reign of
Queen Anne we may observe frequent complaints on
that score. Thus, when in the autumn of 1710 Craggs
was returning home from his post at Barcelona, we
find him address Stanhope as follows from the Hague:
"I writ you the 9th instant I would go straight to England. But having considered better, I am resolved to

---

[1] Journal to Stella, January 31, 1713. In a letter from Swift to Pope
dated January 10, 1721, we further find: "I can never forget the answer he
(the Earl of Oxford) gave to the late Lord Halifax who, upon the first change
of the Ministry, interceded with him to spare Mr. Congreve; it was by repeating these two lines of Virgil,

Non obtusa adeo gestamus pectora Pœni:
Nec tam aversus equos Tyriâ Sol jungit ab urbe."

[2] I allude especially to the noble lines which were addressed to him in
Pope's Epistle to accompany the gift of Parnell's poems. They commence

A soul supreme in each hard instance tried.

go to my Lord Duke first (at his camp in Flanders), for I believe he will be glad to give me several commissions which he dares not trust in writing, because they break open his letters in England; and the new ones say they have already found several material things in letters betwixt him and my Lord Treasurer. I will write to you very plainly from the army, but I am afraid I shall not be able from England."[3]

Political writings in this reign acquired for the first time perhaps an immediate influence on political events. Nor is the reason hard to trace. There were as yet no regular reports however meagre of the principal debates. There had already arisen in the country a desire to learn the motives and the main-springs of affairs. Thus when St. John had spoken in the House of Commons, or Cowper in the House of Peers, it was known that the best orator among the Tories, or the best orator among the Whigs, had set forth, with every grace of eloquence and every power of argument, the tenets of his party. But no one could be stirred by that eloquence or won over by those arguments beyond the members of either House, and the handful of strangers in the gallery. It became necessary therefore for a party chief, desiring to have influence with the public, either himself to take up the pen, as was sometimes the case with St. John and others, or else to seek writers of ability who could do in pamphlets what he had done in speeches.

In the last administration of Queen Anne, this war of pamphlets was waged with especial acrimony and no less ability. On the Tory side the most conspicuous writer was Swift; on the Whig side Addison. Swift

3 Letter dated Sept. 12, 1710 (MS.).

directed for some months a weekly paper, "the Examiner," in which his adversaries were most fiercely assailed. Addison contributed some essays to the Opposition print "the Whig Examiner," which was doomed to a speedy extinction, but which was succeeded by another of the same class, "the Medley." Of Swift and Addison—those early friends, those ever eminent adversaries—it may however be said that they were equal rather than alike. For graceful style, for polished satire, for delicate delineation of character, Addison has never been surpassed; but, on the stage of active politics, he was scarce a match for the passionate ardour, the withering irony, of Swift.

It was not merely in periodical publications that these and others were at this period contending. There also came forth from time to time separate pamphlets of great popular effect. Thus in the autumn of 1711, Walpole published "The Debts of the Nation stated and considered" and "The Thirty-five Millions accounted for"—these giving in a small compass an answer to the charges against the late administration. [4] Thus again, in the spring of 1712 there was sent out by Swift "The Conduct of the Allies;" his object being to show that our confederates had grossly failed in their engagements both as to money and to troops, and that, as Dr. Johnson puts it, "we had been bribing our neighbours to fight their own battles." [5]

Two other men who wielded their pens with powerful effect were Steele on the Whig and Prior on the Tory side. At the heels of each came a numerous tribe of writers, all full of party zeal, but most of them, such

---

4 Coxe's Memoirs of Sir Robert Walpole, vol. I. p. 35.
5 Life of Swift (Johnson's Works, vol. XI. p. 14, ed. 1810).

for instance as Oldmixon, little distinguished by ability, and not at all by truth.

Far, very far, above these last in genius and power of writing stood Defoe, though not raised beyond their level in points of party rancour. Of this a strong instance occurred during the prosecution of Sacheverell. That prosecution, however we may deem it ill-considered and unwise, was at least clear and straightforward. It was aimed at a public discourse—it was pressed upon national grounds. But it was not the fault of Defoe that it did not degenerate into a prying and inquisitorial process of the lowest kind. For thus did he address General Stanhope in a letter which is preserved at Chevening: "Sir, as it is my misfortune not to have the honor to be known to you, so at this time it may be some loss to the public interest in the affair of Sacheverell which you are managing—pardon me the word—with so much applause... Nothing, Sir, has withheld me from blackening and exposing this insolent priest but a nicety of honor, that I thought it dishonourable to strike him when he was down, or to fall on him when he had other enemies to engage. But since, Sir, his defence is made up of false suggestions as to his being for the Revolution; and his character is part of his applause among the rabble; and particularly since you find it necessary to represent him right to those who are his judges, I chose rather to be impertinent than that you should not be let a little way into his character, to the truth of which I will at any time appear and produce sufficient testimony; at the same time running the venture of the indignation both of the Doctor and his rabble, with which I am severely and openly threatened. First, Sir, as to his morals. I do not say there are members in your House who have been drunk with him a hundred times and can say enough of that to you, because I know it would be said to press gentlemen to betray conversation; but if you please to converse with Mr. Duckett, a member of your House, or with Colonel Oughton, of the Guards, they will (especially the first) furnish you abundantly on that head; or, at least, they can. Then, Sir, as to his favouring the Revolution, that he has drunk King James's health upon his knees—that he has spoken so scandalously of the Government that some strangers have asked him if he had taken the oaths to the Queen, and being answered by him that he had, have expostulated with him how it was possible either that talking in that manner he could take the oaths, or that taking the oaths he could talk in that manner. And lastly (as to the Revolution also) I shall name you two persons, viz. Samuel Eborall of Birmingham and the Minister of Birmingham—I think his name is Smith, but can come to a certain knowledge of the name. These can make proof even to conviction, that in their hearing he said with an oath in the late King William's reign, he (Sacheverell) believed that he (the King) would come to be De Witted, and that he hoped to live to see it. .. If I had the honor to know you, Sir, I might give you fuller accounts, and if you should think it for your service I shall do it whenever you please." [6] It is only just to General Stanhope to observe, that he took no heed of these ignominious counsels, and invited no further communication from Defoe.

It is worthy of note that at this period all or nearly all the writers connected with the monied interest took

[6] Letter dated March 8, 1710 (MS.).

part with the Whigs. Nor is this surprising when CHAP. XVI.
we find that interest so much undervalued and dis-
trusted on the other side. What, for instance, would be THE AGE OF ANNE.
deemed in the present day of such a doctrine as the
following? "I ever abominated that scheme of politics,
now about thirty years old"—this was written in 1721
—"of setting up a monied interest in opposition to the
landed. For I conceived there could not be a truer
maxim in our government than this, that the possessors
of the soil are the best judges of what is for the advantage of the kingdom."—Yet this was no hasty opinion
expressed in party heat. It was written deliberately
and in retirement from politics. Nor was it the judgment of any obscure or inferior writer; for these are
the words of Swift. [7]

In nearly all the cases of party pamphlets in this
reign the author's name was not given, and great pains
were taken to withhold all official proof of it. And
that with very good reason. The prevailing party,
whichever it might be at the time, was equally prone,
either through the Queen in Council or through one or
other House of Parliament, to take the most rigorous
measures against any publication which displeased them,
and if the author were not declared or not discovered,
they would fine and imprison the printer.

A striking instance may be given how in that age
even a rhyming parody or jesting pasquinade was
deemed sufficient to call forth the strong arm of the
law. Swift, upon a hint from Lord Oxford, had composed an imitation in verse of Lord Nottingham's
famous speech against the peace. It was produced at
a meeting of the newly-formed Society or Club of the

[7] Letter to Pope, January 10, 1721.

choice spirits among the Tory party. Swift has noted in his diary how at the close of dinner "the printer came before we parted and brought the ballad, which made them laugh very heartily a dozen times."[8] On the public it seems to have had a like effect. It begins: "An orator dismal of Nottinghamshire;" Dismal having been his former nickname; and it certainly contains many most severe and spiteful touches, but as certainly it would be passed by in the present day as a matter of no concern, unworthy the attention of Parliament. In the reign of Queen Anne it was not so regarded. Nottingham himself brought it forward as a subject of complaint in the House of Lords, and on the 15th of December, 1711, a Committee was appointed "to inquire who is the author, 'printer,' and 'publisher of the said paper.'" On the 22nd the Duke of Devonshire reported from the Committee "that their Lordships find the said paper to be false and scandalous and printed by a sham name; and that by the oath of Sarah Vickers it appears to have been printed by Andrew Hind, living in Peterborough Court, near Fleet Street." The Committee recommended and the House ordered that Hind should be taken into the custody of the Black Rod; and in custody he remained until the 19th of January, when upon petitioning their Lordships he was discharged.

From this and from other indications, it seems clear that the sting of satires and libels was much more keenly felt in that age than it is in ours. This is most striking in the case of a man so serene, so self-possessed, so far raised, it might be thought, above such puny attacks as Marlborough. We find him in his confidential letters to

---

[8] Journal to Stella, December 6, 1711.

the Duchess from abroad declare that he is in the power of the Ministers, "especially" he adds "by the villanous way of printing which stabs me to the heart."[9] So disquieted was he that he applied to Secretary St. John on the subject in a manner by no means consistent with his dignity. He referred to some recent articles in the Examiner, and entreated that the writers in that paper might have directions to spare him for the future. St. John thus loftily replied: "Your Grace may be assured of my services in every instance, and I shall be glad to see you—which it is in your power to be—the subject of universal panegyric. .. I have taken care to have the proper hint given to the Examiner."[1]

The Duchess was much less sensitive to libels than her husband. Many of those on her own side of the question were composed under her influence, and sent to press through her trusty agent Mr. Maynwaring. It was also probably at her instigation that the Duke's Chaplain, Dr. Hare, preached a political sermon, of which the Ministers complained, reflecting severely on the terms of peace. In return the Duchess became the object of many and most virulent attacks, not only in ballads or pamphlets but also in novels and romances. Of these last, one of the most curious now lies before me. It is a small volume in French with the titlepage as follows: "Histoire secrète de la Reine Zarah et des Zaraziens; ou la Duchesse de Marlborough démasquée. A Oxford, 1711. Avec approbation de la Nation Brittannique."—To name Oxford however as the place of printing seems to me only a blind, and I have

---

[9] Letter dated April 6, 1711. Coxe's Marlborough, vol. VI. p. 9.

[1] Bolingbroke's Correspondence, vol. I. p. 60 and 71.

 no doubt at all that the volume came from a foreign press.

In this volume the imputations are for the most part political; they refer in the main to Court and State cabals. But what shall we say of the New Atalantis? There the affairs of the nation are reduced to the second rank. There the great ladies then in Opposition, and as chief among them the Duchess of Marlborough, fill the principal place. They are described as engaging in amours that had no foundation at all in fact, and that are given with such glowing minuteness of detail as only the favoured lover could supply. [2] Never yet has party rancour assumed a more unjustifiable, a more malignant form. Such being the character of the book, and such also the dangerous fascination of its style, we may wonder to find it allowed as reading to young ladies of that day. We find the beautiful Lady Mary Pierrepont, afterwards so well known as Wortley Montagu, eagerly expecting the second part by the Nottingham carrier, and promising to lend it to her friend Miss Hewet. She adds, "But do you know what has happened to the unfortunate authoress? People are offended at the liberty she uses in her Memoirs and she is taken into custody. Miserable is the fate of writers; if they are agreeable they are offensive, and if dull they starve." [3]

That authoress was by name Mrs. Manley. Considering her loose book and still looser life it is greatly to the discredit of Swift that he was in communication

---

[2] For the Duchess of Marlborough's love-adventure (wholly fictitious) with Godolphin, see vol. II. p. 134-140, in the later edition of 1736. In that edition the names are given in the notes; but in the former there was a separate "key."

[3] Works of Lady M. W. Montagu, vol. III. p. 211 and 213. Lord Wharncliffe's edition.

with her on her writings, and endeavoured to promote
her interests.   Thus he writes to Stella, July 3, 1711:
"Lord Peterborough desired to see me this morning at
nine. I met Mrs. Manley there, who was soliciting him
to get some pension or reward for her service to the
cause by writing her Atalantis, and her prosecution
upon it. I seconded her, and hope they will do something for the poor woman."

Besides the numerous pieces in verse which in this
age served as the vehicle of party attacks, there were
others that better deserved the title of national.   Such
were those on the battle of Blenheim, which certainly
produced almost as much bad poetry as it did good
fighting.   A large collection might be formed of the
pompous effusions in epic or high heroic style—some of
them printed in folio size—which appeared on this great
event.   It has often been related how Godolphin, much
displeased with these poor performances, asked Halifax
to name to him some poet worthy the occasion—how
Halifax named Addison, then lodging up three pair
of stairs over a shop in the Haymarket—how Godolphin sent Henry Boyle, his Chancellor of the Exchequer, with a message to that garret chamber—and
how Addison undertook the task thus honourably tendered to him.   The poem which he produced in consequence, called "the Campaign," was hailed at the time
with admiration; and even now, when its immediate
interest has passed, it may still be read with pleasure.
It laid, as it deserved, the foundation of his subsequent
fortunes.

Some seven years later it fell to the lot of Addison,
by another composition of high merit, to promote the
cause if not of his country at least of his friends. The

first four acts of his tragedy of Cato had lain unfinished in his desk ever since his foreign travel. But in the spring of 1712 a fifth act being added, the Whig chiefs considered that it might be turned to political account. At that crisis, when they were charging on their opponents a tendency to arbitrary principles and despotic rule, the noble lines of this tragedy if declaimed with spirit might produce a powerful effect. Cæsar and his followers might be held to represent the Tories, and Sempronius those Whigs who had been drawn in to support them, while the lofty bursts of patriotism which Cato utters, would point to another as unswerving opposition, and indicate the party of Halifax and Somers.

Addison, a man as is well known of most modest and sensitive temper, would greatly have preferred to print his play without exposing it to the hazards of the stage. But the importunity of his leaders in public life at length prevailed with him, and he gave the tragedy to the managers of Drury Lane. Every effort was made to ensure its triumphant success. Booth, the first tragedian of his time, undertook the part of Cato. Steele, incited both by party zeal and by personal friendship, promised to pack the House. The first representation had been fixed in Easter week, on Friday the tenth of April, and on that night, in eager expectation, the boxes were thronged with rank and beauty, chiefly though by no means wholly from the Whig side. Into the pit there was poured, as Steele devised it, a band of friendly and intelligent listeners from the Inns of Court. Another such band came from Will's Coffee-house, which was then to men of letters what the Athenæum is now. These together made up the class of persons called, in the quaint language of their day, "men of wit and honor about town." It is to them that Pope referred some time afterwards. Full of spleen and jealousy at the success of his early friend, he declared that, whenever Addison held forth, "wits and Templars every sentence raise."

Nor were allies from the City wanting. Sir Gilbert Heathcote, at this time Governor of the Bank and well known for his zeal in Opposition, sent down a whole array of clerks and accountants; men eager to show their true Whig principles, but, as was noticed at the time, requiring considerable guidance as to what passages they ought properly to cheer, and exposed to some ridicule on that account. But several even of the Whig chiefs and leaders, men perfectly skilled in criticism, might perhaps have been the better that night for something of check and control. The callousness to shame of one of them has been with great force condemned by Lord Macaulay. "Wharton" he says "who had the incredible effrontery to applaud the lines about flying from prosperous vice and from the power of impious men to a private station, did not escape the sarcasms of those who justly thought that he could fly from nothing more vicious or impious than himself." [4]

With such precautions and such appliances the tragedy, independent of its merits, could scarcely fail to succeed. But there was one circumstance which had not been foreseen, and which, while it enhanced the triumph of the author, dimmed that of his political friends. The Tories saw no reason why they should

[4] Essay on Addison, first published in the Edinburgh Review, July 1843, vol. v. p 133. (Tauchnitz Ed.).

take to themselves the passages reflecting on arbitrary power. Therefore, admiring as they did the fine lines, they began to cheer them quite as loudly as the Whigs. It was reserved for Bolingbroke however, by a most ready retort, to parry in the completest manner the party thrust that his enemies intended. Having summoned Booth to his box, in the interval between two acts, he publicly presented him with a purse of fifty guineas, and thanked him for having defended the cause of liberty so well, against a perpetual Dictator. This was clearly understood as referring to the attempt which had been made by Marlborough, and which I have elsewhere related, to extort from the Queen a patent creating him Captain-General for life. The Whigs, says Pope, design a second present when they can accompany it with as good a sentence.

The literary works of the Queen Anne period, both prose and verse, show a considerable approximation to the style of France. Thus the very performance which I have just now been discussing, is formed much more upon the model of the great French writers in the reigns of Louis the Thirteenth and Fourteenth than upon our own in the reign of James the First. If we compare the Cato of Addison with the Cinna of Corneille and the Julius Cæsar of Shakespeare—all three plays relating to the same people at nearly the same period—this divergence from the last-named writer becomes especially apparent. The same tendency went on increasing to the next age. As examples it may be noted that the diction of David Hume or Horace Walpole is far more French than that of Bolingbroke, although of the three Bolingbroke had resided much the longest time in France, had married

a French wife, and even at almost the outset of his
career had made himself, as his French despatches
prove, a thorough master of that foreign idiom. In
writing French he would even sign himself St. Jean
instead of St. John. But he had kept pure and un-
defiled in his mind the well-springs of his native
language; and his style in his political writings is perhaps the very highest perfection of English prose.

The men of letters of Queen Anne's reign—those
above all of the Whig party—derive especial lustre
from the collections of periodical essays which in their
various merits have never yet been equalled in any
other country, or in any other age. Of these periodical
papers Steele was the founder, but Addison was the
prop and mainstay. Steele had been appointed, by
the favor of Lord Sunderland, to the post of Gazetteer.
As such, besides receiving a salary—very acceptable to
a man of his spendthrift habits—he had early access
to foreign intelligence; and it occurred to him that a
paper would be certain of success, which should communicate that intelligence at once to rural readers.
According then to the plan of Steele, the new paper
was to appear on the days, on which in that age, the
post left London for the country, namely on Tuesdays,
Thursdays, and Saturdays; and besides the news from
abroad, the paper was to contain some articles on the
current topics of the day, however various in kind, as
criticism, accounts both of popular sermons and of
popular plays. To give unity to the whole by the
name of an Editor, Steele announced that the paper
would be published by "Isaac Bickerstaff, Esquire,
Astrologer," a fictitious person, already the occasion of
much banter among the wits of that age. Such was

the origin of "the Tatler," of which the first number appeared on the 12th of April, 1709.

Addison was then in Ireland as Secretary, with Wharton as Lord Lieutenant—most truly an ill-assorted pair. He had not been consulted on this scheme, but no sooner was it started than he gave it his active support. Mainly through him, it was raised far above the ephemeral character which had been at first designed; and there came to be inserted, a succession of essays which, afterwards collected into volumes, have taken a permanent place in the literature of this country.

Of the essays which appeared in the Tatler, two hundred and seventy-one in number, not less than fifty were contributed by Addison. In merit these were greatly superior to the rest. It is probably no exaggeration of Lord Macaulay to declare, that any five of his writing are more valuable than all the two hundred numbers in which he had no share.

The change of Ministers from Whig to Tory, which affected so many other things, affected the Tatler also. Steele lost his place as Gazetteer. By the intercession of his personal friends, he was suffered to retain another small office that he held as Commissioner of Stamps, but this was on a pledge, implied if not expressed, that he should take no active part against the new administration. Thus the Tatler ceased to retail foreign intelligence. It ceased also to discuss home affairs. Its whole character was changed. Better far, thought Steele, bring it to a close, and start another series of papers on a more consistent plan. This was done accordingly. The last number of the Tatler appeared on the second of January, 1711, and the Preface of "the Spectator" on the first of March

ensuing. Unlike its predecessor this new series was
to be published daily, Sundays however excepted.

The character of the Spectator was drawn by
Addison—certainly not without some reference to his
own. The Spectator is described as a gentleman of
middle age and studious habits, with a cultivated mind
improved by foreign travel, but afflicted with an in-
vincible shyness, so that although he makes many
observations on men and manners, he is almost always
a mute in society, and at his ease only with a small
club of familiar friends.

In the members of this small Club, besides the
Spectator himself, it was intended to delineate some
of the principal classes and professions. There was
Sir Roger de Coverley, the Tory baronet of Worcestershire, and Sir Andrew Freeport, the Whig merchant
of London; there was Will Honeycomb, a gray-haired
man of pleasure about town, conversant in all the
fashionable follies of the time; there was Captain Sentry
the soldier; there was also, though only in dim outline,
the lawyer and the clergyman.

The first sketch of this Club, as the first design of
the Tatler, was due to Steele. But Addison took at
once into his hands the characters of Sir Roger de
Coverley and Will Honeycomb, and moulded them
with a degree of genius and skill to which Steele
could make no claim. The portraiture of Sir Roger
above all, and the several essays which unfold it, have
taken rank among the classics of the language. So
delicately is it poised that the goodnatured ridicule in
many passages is never inconsistent with sincere
respect, nor yet the respect with ridicule. While we
smile at the stubborn prejudices of the good old

Knight, we are touched by his overflowing kindliness and genial warmth of heart.

There are many things that may be gleaned from those vivid pages, in regard to the manners and feelings of the time, both when the Spectator goes to visit his friend in the country, and when Sir Roger appears in town. At Coverley Hall the Spectator surveys the ancient mansion and the patriarchal household—"the domestics all in years and grown old with their master. You trace his goodness even in the old house-dog, and in the grey pad that is kept in the stable, with great care and tenderness, in regard to his past services, though he has been useless for several years." The Spectator is put under the special charge of the butler, "a very prudent man," and he consorts chiefly with the Chaplain, who has been in the house thirty years—no deep Divine perhaps in School Theology but unbounded in his kindness to the parish poor. "Wishing to put him under an obligation" said Sir Roger "I intend to leave them thirty marks in my Will." The Chaplain has moreover all the requisites that Sir Roger in selecting him desired, namely "plain sense, a good aspect, a clear voice, and a sociable temper, and if possible to know a little of backgammon." The Spectator attends the Sunday service at the Church, where Sir Roger has presented to each of the parishioners, all of them his tenants, a Prayer Book and a hassock—he observes the stable doors "patched with noses that belonged to foxes of the Knight's own hunting down"—he rides with his friend to the Assizes, and sees Sir Roger rise and make a speech of two or three sentences, "with a look of much business and great intrepidity"—all the gentlemen of Worcestershire afterwards gathering about him and striving who should compliment him most, and all the common people gazing with awe at the great man who was not afraid to speak to the Judge.— On the other hand we find the Knight come up to London for the purpose of seeing Prince Eugene, or as he always calls him Prince Eugenio, during the few weeks that great chief was in England. He walks among the monuments in Westminster Abbey and listens open-mouthed to the recitals of the guide, "particularly to the account he gave us of the Lord who had cut off the King of Morocco's head." He is rowed upon the Thames, which he declares to be the noblest river in Europe, but is moved to grief at observing so few steeples on this side Temple Bar. "A most heathenish sight!" he cries. "But the fifty new churches will very much mend the prospect." He has fears lest he should be assailed by the Mohocks, and does not wish to venture forth in the evenings, but he is comforted by Captain Sentry, who assures him that he, the Captain, has put on the same sword that he made use of at the battle of Steenkirk. Under such auspices, and flanked also by the old butler with an oaken cudgel, Sir Roger takes heart and consents to go out and see the new tragedy by Ambrose Philips, at Drury Lane.

It is much to be regretted that at this juncture Steele, without the consent of Addison, thrust in his coarser hand. The good old Knight was represented in another London scene wholly alien to the dignity and delicacy of his character. Addison, as was natural, took fire; and resolved, at any sacrifice, to guard from farther blemish the favourite creation of his brain. "I will kill Sir Roger" he said "that nobody else may murder him."[5] There came forth accordingly a final essay from his pen. The old butler writes to the Spectator from the country, and announces in homely but pathetic terms of grief, the demise after a short illness of his honoured master. "It was a most moving sight to see him take leave of his poor servants, commending us all for our fidelity, whilst we were not able to speak a word for weeping."

But if even Steele had forborne his untoward interference, it is probable that the Spectator would soon have been brought to a conclusion, since it was beginning to be felt that the rich mine of humor, yielded by the members of the Club, was nearly worked out. And there was yet another reason. During the Session of 1712, there had been many complaints of the licentiousness of the press as tending to "false and scandalous libels." It had been one topic both in a Message of the Queen to Parliament and in the Address of the House of Commons in reply. A victim was sought and was not long to find. In the course of April, Samuel Buckley of the Dolphin, Little Britain, printer of the first daily newspaper the "Daily Courant" and printer also as it chanced of the Spectator, was brought in custody to the bar of the House of Commons. He was charged with having inserted in his paper a Memorial of the States General severely reflecting on the conduct of the English Government in relation to the terms of peace. For this offence—no more in fact than reproducing a foreign state-paper as an article of news—the poor man

5 The Bee, p. 26, as cited in Mr. Wills's notes to the Coverley Papers. Addison may, in part at least, have derived this saying from the play of *L'Avocat Patelin*, where the shepherd *Agnelet* declares: "Quand mes moutons ont la clavelée, je les tue pour les empêcher de mourir!"

was sent to prison. But the incensed majority in the House of Commons was intent on a more general measure that should serve for prevention as well as punishment. With this view, after passing some strong Resolutions against the licentiousness of the press, they proceeded to impose a halfpenny stamp Duty on all periodical papers. Under the weight of this Tax many of the journals succumbed—probably the very thing that the framers of the Tax desired. But the Spectator, though compelled to double its price, maintained its ground. By that time its daily distribution of copies had grown to almost four thousand, so that there was margin for the considerable falling off which ensued. It might however afford another motive to put a close to the paper in good time before its popularity had waned or its decline become apparent.

Under such circumstances Number 555 appearing on the 6th of December, 1712, was the last in this series of Spectators. The essays hitherto single were collected and published together, making seven volumes, to which an eighth was subsequently added by Addison, its first number appearing in June 1714. The sale of these collected essays was wholly without precedent in that age. It was said, probably with some exaggeration, that full ten thousand copies of each successive volume were disposed of in the first issue.

Steele, ever fertile in schemes, was already planning a new paper, to be called "the Guardian" and to comprise a different set of characters; Nestor Ironside especially and the whole of the Lizard family. The first number was published on the 12th of March, 1713. Addison at the outset withheld his aid. It was not till the sixty-seventh number that there came any contribution from his pen. The main cause was no doubt, as Lord Macaulay states it, that he was at that time busy in bringing Cato on the stage; but it may be also that he had not quite forgiven Steele for poaching in the Coverley preserves.

The Guardian had but scant success. Its characters were ill drawn and feebly supported, and the decline of the publication was decided, ere Addison's help arrived.[6] Only by party aid, and by a larger infusion of party spirit, did it carry into the autumn months its lingering existence. It was seen that the Spectator could not be rivalled—not even by the writers of the Spectator themselves. Still less was it rivalled in the ensuing age, even although the great genius of Dr. Johnson produced "the Rambler," and a whole cluster of wits combined to illustrate "the World."

But the Spectator has yet another claim of merit. In the very short but light and graceful stories, or the vivid sketches of character which it comprises, lies perhaps the germ of the modern novel. There was scarce any work deserving of that name in its higher sense, when Queen Anne commenced her reign. There was scarce any thing beyond licentious tales like those of Mrs. Behn, or interminable romances, describing in fact the manners of Versailles, though in name the manners of Persia and Babylon, as above all in the Grand Cyrus translated from the French of Mademoiselle de Scudery. It was reserved for Addison especially to show the English people how prose-fictions may be made most interesting without any admixture of loose scenes, or

---

6 "Did I tell you that Steele has begun a new daily paper called the Guardian?—they say good for nothing. I have not seen it." Journal to Stella, April 1, 1713.

being drawn out in all the pomp of Eastern story. Not that the existing defects were at once removed. We find them still subsist, though greatly mitigated, in the next ensuing age. We find ample traces of the former English grossness in Roderick Random and Tom Jones. We find as ample traces of the former French LONGUEURS in the six volumes of Sir Charles Grandison, and the seven of Clarissa Harlowe. But passing by these instances and looking to the English novel-writers of the present century, we may perhaps acknowledge that Addison and others in Queen Anne's reign laid the slight foundation, on which so vast a superstructure has been raised. Looking to the novels of this century, that is to the best of them, and to their writers—some of whom have also in other spheres of eminence imprinted their spirit on the age, and shone forth as master-minds in poetry or politics— it must be felt on all sides how great is the variety of interest which they have afforded, and how high the pitch of excellence which they have attained. Few writers have ever comprised so much of wit and wisdom in so agreeable a form; none have ever addressed themselves to a wider circle of readers. Novels are read by women, even by those who read nothing else; and novels are read by men, even by those who read every thing else.

The excellent example set by Queen Anne in her private conduct, as also the observance of virtue which she maintained in her Court and household, have been acknowledged even by those who did not entirely approve it, and were inclined to a laxer rule of life. As an unwilling, or it might be said unconscious, witness to her merit on this point we may cite Lord Chesterfield.

In a memoir which he prepared with care, but with good
discretion left unpublished, he observes, "Queen Anne
had always been devout, chaste, and formal; in short, a
prude. She discouraged, as much as she could, the usual
and even the most pardonable vices of Courts. Her
Drawing Rooms were more respectable than agreeable,
and had more the air of solemn places of worship than the
gaiety of a Court... Public and crowded assemblies,
where every man was sure of meeting every woman,
were not known in those days. But every woman of
fashion kept what was called 'a Day,' which was a
formal circle of her acquaintances of both sexes, un-
broken by any card-tables, tea-tables, or other amuse-
ments. There the fine women and fine men met perhaps for an hour; and if they had anything particular
to say to one another, it could be only conveyed by the
language of the eyes. The other public diversion was
merely for the eyes, for it was going round and round
the ring in Hyde Park and bowing to one another
slightly, respectfully, or tenderly, as occasion required.
No woman of fashion could receive any man at her morning toilet without alarming the husband and his friends.
If a fine man and fine woman were well enough disposed to wish for a private meeting, the execution of
their good intentions was difficult and dangerous. The
preliminaries could only be settled by the hazardous
expedient of letters; and the only places almost for the
conclusion and ratification of the definitive treaty were
the Indian houses in the City, where the good woman
of the house from good-nature, and perhaps some little
motive of interest, let out her back-rooms for momentary
lodgings to distressed lovers. But all these difficulties
and dangers were in a great measure removed, by the

arrival of the present Royal Family. King George the
First loved pleasures, and was not delicate in the choice
of them."[7]

There can scarcely be named any point in knowledge
and science, or in their practical application, which
has not received great improvement since the reign of
Queen Anne. Manufactures and trade, the Fine Arts,
public teaching in all its branches, the repeal of barbarous penalties, the order and rule of prisons, the
speed and security of travelling, the comforts and appliances of daily life—all these have immensely advanced; and there are new discoveries which in former
days even the wildest flights of fancy could never have
surmised. But perhaps the same amount of research,
which serves to bring forward these results in full
detail, may convince the mind of the inquirer, as it
has my own, that the people of Queen Anne enjoyed
much the larger measure of happiness.

It is to be observed in the first place, how far more
widely spread, was in those days the spirit of contentment. Men were willing to make the best of the present, without a feverish anxiety for the past or for the
future—without constantly longing that yesterday might
come back, or that to-morrow might come on. The
laws were not so good, but the people were better satisfied with them. The Church was less efficient, but was
more cheerfully maintained.

My meaning may be further illustrated. The tendency of the people in Queen Anne's reign was I think,
according to the figure of speech which we find in the

---

7 "On the Mistresses of Kings George I. and II." (MS.). Some other
extracts from this Memoir were inserted by me under two different headings in
my edition of Lord Chesterfield's Works, vol. II. p. 439-442. But much the
greater part remains unpublished.

First Book of Kings, "to dwell safely, every man under his vine and under his fig-tree." The tendency of the present age, unless I much mistake it, would be rather to contend by ingenious arguments that the vine and fig are not the best of all possible fruit-trees—that we ought immediately to root them up, and to plant in their stead some saplings of another kind. It may not be wholly prejudice that views this disposition with regret. Is there any real happiness in such constant yearning and striving for something other than exists? Is it good to live in an age when everything is being improved away off the face of the earth?

But let us view the question in more detail. If we look to the country districts, we shall judge perhaps that in Queen Anne's time, the harsh features of the feudal system had passed away while some of the milder ones remained. In other words, there was no trace of serfdom or compulsory service, but there lingered the feeling of protection, due by the lord of the soil to his retainers in sickness or old age. Labour was then no mere contract of work done for value received. Service was still in some degree requited, even when it ceased to be performed. As between landlord and tenant also, a more cordial spirit, a more intimate relation, appears to have prevailed. There was wholly absent, that main cause of alienation whenever at present alienation does occur—the excessive preserving of game. We find it laid down in the Spectator as an admitted truth, that "the sport is the more agreeable where the game is the harder to come at."[8] In those days and in days much later, the return of the shooting season was hailed with pleasure not by the landlord only but

---

[8] No. 131, July 31, 1711. This paper is by Addison.

by the farmer also. The young squire would cheerily CHAP.
step into the homestead for his midday meal; and sit XVI.
down with a well-earned appetite to a dish of eggs and THE
AGE OF
bacon, with a glass—or it might be two—of the honest ANNE.
home-brewed, instead of the luxurious luncheon-baskets
which according to the present fashion would be spread
before him. He would point with some pride to "the
birds" which his morning's walk had gained him, and
descant at some length on the sagacity and skill of his
dogs; for at that time—before the time of "driving"—
these were deemed no small part of the enjoyment of
the day. In return he would be most warmly greeted
and made welcome, undisturbed by any little questions
which would be reserved for another time, as of the
mouldering floor in the barn, or the leaky roof in the
"beast-houses;" and when he again stepped forth he
would see his tenant at his side taking interest in his
sport, and eager to point out to him the haunts of the
nearest coveys. All was cheerfulness and sunshine between the two classes when they met not for business
alone.—Surely that was a more manly system—a nobler
incentive to country life in the autumn months—than
the one which at present in some counties at least too
often prevails; when the entire object seems to be
ostentatious display—to produce a bulletin of the greatest
possible number of killed in the smallest possible number of hours—to station each distinguished guest at the
corner of a wood and bid him there stand still, while
pheasants and rabbits by the score are made to pass
before him.

It may be said indeed, that at the present day those
persons, who for political objects are striving by speech
or print to sow dissension between the owners and the

occupiers of the soil, find no argument so ready to their hand or so persuasive as this excessive increase, and effeminate pursuit, of game. It may be said that, in several of our English shires, the rabbit is now the best ally of the Radical. But it was not so under Queen Anne, nor even under George the Third.

Passing to the towns, and pursuing the comparison of the two periods, we may deem that under Queen Anne, there was much less of wealth but much less also of abject poverty. The contrasts were not so sharp, nor stood as it were so closely face to face with each other. Nevertheless, in that day also, trade was not a little lucrative. As is stated by Budgell in the Spectator: "I have observed greater estates got about 'Change than at Whitehall or St. James's."[9]   And we must not forget that he wrote thus, at a period when the salaries and emoluments of public service were by many degrees more considerable than at present.

It would seem, so far as negative evidence can show it, as if under Queen Anne the handi-craftsman and the labourer had no difficulty in obtaining employment without dispute as to the hours of work or the rate of wages. Most grievous is the change in that respect, which has since ensued. Let another pen instead of mine relate the again and again recurring tale—how often in this century we have beheld the over-speculation of one period result ere long in the discharge of workmen and the collapse of trade. Let another pen, I say, describe "the old sad story of masters reducing their establishments, men turned off and wandering about, hungry and wan in body, and fierce in soul, from the thought of wives and children starving at home, and the last sticks of furniture going

9 Spectator, No. 283, January 24, 1712.

to the pawnshop. Children taken from school, and lounging about the dirty streets and courts, too listless almost to play, and squalid in rags and misery. And then the fearful struggle between employers and men; lowering of wages, Strikes, and the long course of oft-repeated crime, ending every now and then with a riot, a fire, and the County Yeomanry."[1]

Such are the words of an accomplished living writer, not liable certainly to the suspicion of any aristocratical leaning. I am not now concerned in tracing out the causes or seeking to foretell the consequences of those most deplorable scenes—either of that dire, and not at the time to be repelled, distress which results from want of employment, or of that artificial and, as I may call it, voluntary and self-inflicted misery produced by the system of Strikes. I only desire at this place to record the fact that none of this suffering, none of this crime, can be traced in the reign of Anne. Can it be doubted to which side the scale of greater happiness inclines?

In Queen Anne's reign the anxiety of the merchants and tradesmen was of quite another kind. It was remembered that, under the late King, the adherents of the exiled Prince had most warmly opposed the system of public loans; and it was thought that, if that Prince should come to be restored, one of his first measures would be to wipe off the National Debt. For this reason we find that in a popular allegory of that period, the Pretender is represented as a young man with a sponge in his left hand.[2] But this alarm was so prospective and contingent that it cannot have affected in

CHAP.
XVI.
<hr>THE
AGE OF
ANNE.

---

[1] Tom Brown's Schooldays, p. 263. ed. 1858.

[2] Spectator, No. 3, March 3, 1711. This paper is by Addison.

any serious manner the present comfort of those who entertained it.

As regards the liberal professions and the employments in the Civil Service it may be deemed, from the absence at least of any indications to the contrary, that under Queen Anne there was more of equality between the supply and the demand. The number of men of good character and good education who desired to enter any career was not disproportioned to the number of openings which that career presented. It followed that any person endowed with fair aptitude and common application, and engaging in any recognized walk of life, was in due time certain or nearly certain of a livelihood. Riches and distinction were of course, as in every state of society, the portion of the few, but there was competence for the many. How greatly the times have changed! At present there are few things more distressing to any one who desires to see general prosperity and content prevail than to find start up, whenever any opening in any career is made known, not one or two but ten or twenty candidates. Every one of these twenty may be in many cases perfectly well qualified to fill the place that he seeks, yet only one can be chosen. What then is to become of the nineteen?

Of this superabundance however, increasing from year to year, the cause is twofold and easy to assign. The general spread of first class education has on this point perhaps been no unmixed advantage. It has sent forth a crowd of persons of both sexes well qualified by their position for any liberal profession or place of intellectual labour; and it has in the same measure disinclined them, for other posts less literate, or of less rank in the social scale, which in former days would have contented them. Thus it happens that while the number of claimants has immensely increased, the number of places to which they aspire has, at least in some departments, grown less.

It is certainly a great practical hardship, such as we do not trace under Queen Anne or under the first Georges, that a young man entering life with a good character and careful education should see every profession overcrowded, every avenue of advancement hemmed in, that he should be unable in so many cases to earn his bread, and be cast back for subsistence on his family. There is something very grievous both to himself and others in this not his wilful but his compulsory idleness.

I remember that the present state of things in this respect was once ingeniously illustrated in conversation by Lord Macaulay. He pointed out to me, that the ancient device of the Templars had been two Knights upon one horse, to indicate the original poverty of their Order; and he observed that the same device might be as aptly applied to the modern members of the Temple—two barristers at least to one cause!

If however for the grounds alleged, and for some others that might be added, we come to the conclusion, that in spite of the modern discoveries and improvements individual happiness so far from advancing has receded since the reign of Anne, it by no means follows that this unfavourable change can be imputed as blame to any person or any party. It has perhaps arisen less from any positive legislation than from the natural growth and development in some respects of an aspiring and highly gifted race. But dismissing that branch of the subject there is another in which, not by accident, not by good fortune, nor yet by wisely framed institutions, but by their own lofty spirit, the people of England in the reign of Anne have set us a bright example. I refer to the constancy with which they encountered the ambition of Louis the Fourteenth, and bore without repining, until that ambition was humbled, the burthen and toil of the war in which they had engaged. At the outset they had no special call to arms. There was no immediate or imminent danger to themselves. Whatever danger to themselves might arise from their too powerful neighbour could be guarded against or be turned aside by a strictly maritime system, such as Nottingham and Jersey desired. But the people of England at that time felt the duty that they owed as a member of the great European family. It was not enough for them to stand free in their insular security, if the yoke of France were to weigh on Holland and Germany, on Italy and Spain. Therefore they courageously braved the risk and peril, the cost of money and the cost of men, which a continental war implied; and while the Dutch and the Germans especially shrunk in many cases from their just contingents, England in truth sustained the main brunt of the conflict that ensued. It was this spirit that nerved the arm of Marlborough and gave effect to the statesmanship of Somers. It was this spirit which, a century later, was manifested by the same nation under almost the same circumstances; arrayed no longer against Louis but the first Napoleon, and guided instead of Somers and Marlborough by Pitt and Wellington. It was this spirit which, in spite of the turbulence of parties and the misconduct of statesmen, has made the reign of Queen Anne a scene of glory and renown, which any Englishman may feel it a pleasure to contemplate and an honor to portray.

THE END.